THE ART OF
BUDDHISM

BY

DIETRICH SECKEL

GREYSTONE PRESS/NEW YORK · TORONTO · LONDON

Translated by Ann E. Keep

Title-page: STŪPA I, SĀNCHI, INDIA. View from
north-west. Massive brick building encased in sandstone; railings and gateways in yellowish-grey sandstone, originally polished and painted red. Height of
stūpa 16.50 m., of gateways 10.36 m., of lowest railing
3.23 m.; diameter at ground level 31 m. The core of
the stūpa originates from the time of the emperor
Ashoka, approx. mid-3rd cent. B.C.; enlarged during
first cent. B.C.; sculptured decoration of gateways
completed during first cent. A.D. Restored by Archaeological Survey of India under the direction of John
Marshall from 1912 onwards. Behind the lowest railing
there is a processional path, and there is a second one
on the base behind the railing. The gateways (*torana*)
face the four points of the compass. Around this largest
and richest stūpa are grouped several more stūpas and
ruins of other monuments.

REVISED EDITION 1968
TRANSLATION © 1964 HOLLE VERLAG G.M.B.H., BADEN-BADEN, GERMANY
LIBRARY OF CONGRESS CATALOGUE CARD NUMBER: 64-23800
MANUFACTURED IN THE UNITED STATES OF AMERICA

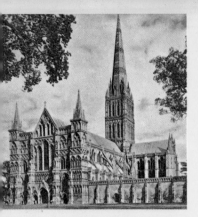

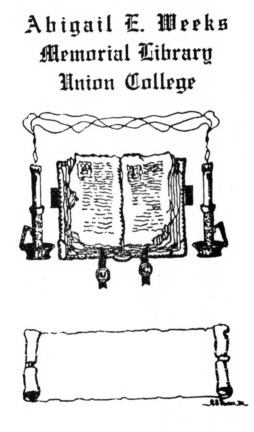

CONTENTS

List of plates (4) . List of figures (5) and maps (8) .

FOREWORD 11

INTRODUCTION Oecumenical unity of Buddhist art 15

PART I The spread of Buddhist art through Asia 23

    I. India 25

    II. Ceylon 45

    III. Indonesia 47

    IV. Indochina 51

    V. Central Asia 63

    VI. China 81

    VII. Korea 93

    VIII. Japan 102

    IX. Retrospect 108

PART II Types and forms 111

    I. From the stūpa to the pagoda 113

    II. Monasteries and temples 136

    III. The Buddha image 162

    IV. The hierarchy of sacred figures 223

    V. Narrative works 261

    VI. Symbolism and ornamentation 277

APPENDICES 289

    Appendix of plates 299

    Maps 66, 109, 153, 301, 310-312

    Chronological table 302

    Bibliography 313

    Index 319

LIST OF PLATES

Stūpa I, Sānchī, India   Title-page

Reliquary from a stūpa at Bīmarān. British
Museum   35

Borobudur, Java: the three uppermost terraces with the central stūpa   36

Towers featuring Lokeshvara faces. Bayon,
Angkor   37

Cave-temple at Tun-huang (No. 243), western Kansu   38

Representation of a stūpa. Nāgārjunakonda
Museum   55

Votive stūpa from Nālandā. National Museum of India, New Delhi   56

Pagoda of T'ien-ning-sse, Peking   57

Kumsan-sa pagoda, built of stone. Korea   58

Five-storeyed pagoda at Murōji near Nara,
Japan   75

Rāhula before his father, the Buddha.
Archaeological Museum, Amarāvatī   76

Buddha seated on a throne. From Mathurā.
Museum für Völkerkunde, Munich   77

Preaching Buddha. From Loriyan Tangai.
Indian Museum, Calcutta   78

Standing Buddha from Ceylon (?). Museum
van Aziatische Kunst, Amsterdam   95

Torso of a standing Buddha from Mathurā.
Archaeological Museum, Mathurā   96

Standing Buddha with two monks. Wall-
painting in Cave X at Ajantā   97

Preaching Buddha. Relief from Sārnāth.
Archaeological Museum, Sārnāth   98

Borobudur: Amitābha figure   139

Head of a Buddha with a crown. Thailand.
Museum für Völkerkunde, Munich   140

Standing Buddha in princely attire. Stöcker
Collection, Amsterdam   141

Colossal statue of Buddha. Bāmiyān,
Afghanistan   142

Seated Buddha. From the cave of Kirin at
Shorchuk. Museum für Völkerkunde, Berlin   143

Standing Buddha. Bronze figure dating
from 536. China. University Museum,
Philadelphia   144

Amitābha Buddha preaching. Cave 45,
Tun-huang   145

Vairocana Buddha. From Pulkuk-sa near
Kyongju, Korea   146

Shākyamuni Buddha. Detail from a scroll.
Jingoji, Kyōto   163

Amitābha. The colossal Buddha of
Kamakura   164

Shākyamuni under a blossoming tree. Scroll.
After Wei-ch'ih I-sêng (?). Museum of Fine
Arts, Boston   165

Amitābha Buddha preaching, surrounded
by Bodhisattvas and monks. Scroll from
Tun-huang. British Museum   166

The three preaching assemblies of Maitreya
Buddha. From a scroll. Chinese National
Palace Museum, Taichung, Formosa   169

The Buddha preaching to Bodhisattvas and
monks. Frontispiece of a sūtra scroll, Japan.
Museum für ostasiatische Kunst, Cologne   170

Amitābha appearing from behind the
mountains. Scroll. Zenrin-ji, Kyōto   179

Bodhisattva Padmapāni. Wall-painting in
Cave I at Ajantā   180

Bodhisattva Padmapāni. Relief. Archaeological Museum, Sārnāth   182

Head of Lokeshvara. Museum van Aziatische Kunst, Amsterdam   191

Maitreya or Shākyamuni as Bodhisattva.
Duksoo Palace Museum, Seoul   192

Torso of a Bodhisattva from Tien-lung
Shan. Rietberg Museum, Zurich   193

Bodhisattva in the Golden Hall of the
Hōryūji near Nara   194

Avalokiteshvara as a guide of souls. Hanging
scroll from Tun-huang. British Museum   195

Kuanyin (Avalokiteshvara). Museum van
Aziatische Kunst, Amsterdam   196

Cintāmani-Cakra Avalokiteshvara. Kanshin-
ji near Osaka   197

Vajrasattva from Nālanda. National
Museum of India, New Delhi   198

Prajnāpāramitā. Eastern Java. Rijksmuseum
voor Volkenkunde, Leyden   207, 208

4

The Bodhisattva Kshitigarbha. Hanging
scroll. Dan Collection, Tokyo   209

Horse-headed Avalokiteshvara. Hanging
scroll. Japan. Museum of Fine Arts, Boston   210

Acala Vidyārāja (Fudō Myōō). Hanging
scroll. Japan. Myōō-in, Kōya-san   211

Dvārapāla (Guardian of the Gateway) from
Tun-huang. British Museum   212

Bust of a worshipping deity from Shorchuk.
Museum für Völkerkunde, Berlin   213

Arhat (Lohan). From a hand-scroll. Chinese
National Palace Museum, Taichung,
Formosa   214

Arhat (Lohan). Hanging scroll. Japan.
National Museum, Tokyo   231

The Patriarch Shubhākarasimha. Hanging

scroll. Japan. Ichijō-ji, Kyōto   232

Myōe-Shōnin. Detail from a hanging scroll.
Japan. Kōzanji, Kyōto   234

Bodhidharma (Daruma). Hanging scroll.
Japan. Ehemals Staatliche Museen, Berlin   251

Buddha bathing before his first sermon.
Relief. Borobudur, Java   252

Prince Mahāsattva sacrificing himself to a
ravenous tigress. Detail from a wall-painting
in Cave 428, Tun-huang   254

The first bath and first steps of Shākyamuni.
Detail of a hanging scroll from Tun-huang.
British Museum   271

Shākyamuni's entrance into Perfect
Nirvāna. Hanging scroll. Japan. Museum
für ostasiatische Kunst, Cologne   272

Ceiling ornament in Cave 320. Tun-huang   274

LIST OF FIGURES

1 — Frontispiece of a sūtra scroll from Tun-huang. Facsimile wood-cut by Jung Pao-chi, approx.
1960. After J. Tschichold, Der älteste erhaltene Bilddruck   79

2 — Ground-plan and elevation of the stūpa at Ghantashālā: reconstruction. Bulletin de l'École
Française d'Extrême-Orient, Vol. 32, 1932, p. 388   116

3 — Ground-plan of Mahācetiya stūpa. P. R. Ramachandra Rao, The Art of Nāgārjunikonda,
Madras, 1956, p. 36   116

4 — Votive stūpa from Gandhāra. G. Combaz, L'évolution du stūpa en Asie, Vol. 2, Fig. 6 . . .   116

5 — Stūpa in a cave-temple. Ibid., Fig. 9   117

5a — Reconstruction of Top-i-Rustam stūpa. Bukkyō Geijutsu (Ars Buddhica), Issue 15, Tokyo,
1952   118

6 — Ground-plan of the Wata-da-ge. B. Rowland, The Art and Architecture of India, Fig. 36 . .   119

7 — Elevation of the Thūpārāma. Ibid., Fig. 32   119

8 — Stūpa at Ayuthia. Combaz, op cit., Vol. 2, Fig. 33   120

9 — Types of Lamaist stūpa in China. Ch. Itō, Architectural Decoration in China, Vol. 2, Tokyo,
1941, Pl. 37   120

10 — Evolution of Indian stūpa into Far Eastern pagoda. D. Seckel, Buddhistische Kunst Ostasiens,
Stuttgart, 1957, Fig. 9   122

11 — Evolution of Chinese pagoda from Indian stūpa. W. Willetts, Chinese Art, Vol. 2, Fig. 104 .   122

12 — Stūpa crowning a pagoda. Combaz, op. cit., Vol. 2, Fig. 46   123

13 — Tower on a torana relief, Mathurā. Ibid., Vol. 3, Fig. 13   123

14 — Mahābodhi Temple. Ibid., Vol. 2, Fig. 12   124

15 — Stūpa on top of Mahābodhi Temple. Ibid., Vol. 2, Fig. 13   124

16 — Meru at Mandalay. Ibid., Vol. 4, Fig. 6   125

17* — Ground-plan, section and elevation of pagoda at Ling-yen-sse. E. Boerschmann, Pagoden,
Pl. 142   126

18 — Elevation and section of pagoda at Hōryūji. F. Baltzer, Die Architektur der Kultbauten
Japans, Pl. 288, 289   128

19 — Tahōtō. Drawing from a Japanese mandala. D. Seckel, op. cit., Fig. 14   129

20 — Elevation and section of the Tahōtō, Ishiya-ma-dera. F. Baltzer, op. cit., Pl. 313   129

21 — Reliquary in basement of pagoda at Hōryūji. Hōryūji Gojū-no-tō Hihō no Chōsa (Study
of the secret treasures of the 5-storeyed Pagoda at Hōryūji), Kyōto, 1954, Pl. 3   130

22 — Gorintō. D. Seckel, op. cit., Fig. 33 (drawing by Dr. P. A. Riedl)   130

23 — Japanese sepulchral monuments, etc. Tōba no Kenkyū (Pagoda Studies), ed. K. Saeki, Nara,
1943, p. 121   131

24 — Ground-plan of the Borobudur. Bernet Kempers, Ancient Indonesian Art, Fig. 1   134

25 — Section of the Borobudur. Ibid., Fig. 2   135

26 — Monastery at Taxila. Combaz, op. cit., Vol. 3, Fig. 12   136

27 — Monastery at Jamālgarhī. Combaz, op. cit., Vol. 3, Fig. 12   136

28 — Ground-plan of rock-cut monastery (vihāra) and section of caitya hall at Bhājā. Kl. Fischer,
Schöpfungen indischer Kunst, p. 122   137

29 — Ground-plan of Cave I, Ajantā. H. Rau, Die Kunst Indiens, p. 50   138

30 — Caitya hall at Kārlī. Drawing by H. Prüstel after H. Rau, op. cit., Pl. 19   147

31 — Caitya hall at Elūrā. Drawing by H. Prüstel. Ibid., Pl. 57   148

32 — Ground-plan of so-called 'university' at Nāgārjunikonda. R. Rao, op. cit., p. 150   149

33 — Ground-plan of Tjandi Sewu. Henri Marchal, L'architecture comparée dans l'Inde et
l'Extrême-Orient, Paris, 1944, Fig. 147   150

34 — Ground-plan of rock-hewn chapels at Bāmiyān, near the 53 metre-high figure of the Buddha.
J. Hackin, Nouvelles recherches archéologiques à Bāmiyān, Paris, 1933, Fig. 3   151

35 — Ground-plan of a chapel built against the rock face at Bezeklik, Turfan area. A. von Le Coq,
Chotscho, p. 14   152

36 — Ground-plan of Caves V-XIII, Yünkang. S. Mizuno, Unkō (= Yünkang) Sekibutsu-gun,
Tokyo, 1944, Fig. 3   152

37 — Ground-plan and section of the Sokkul-am, near Kyongju. A. Eckardt, Geschichte der
koreanischen Kunst, Pl. 79 and 240   154

38 — Ground-plan of the Hsien-t'ung-sse on the Wu-t'ai-shan. E. Boerschmann, Chinesische
Architektur, Vol. 1   155

39 — Elevation and ground-plan of the main hall of the Hsien-t'ung-sse. Ibid., Vol. 1   155

40 — Golden Hall of the Tōshōdaiji, Nara. W. Speiser, China (ART OF THE WORLD), 1960, p. 135 . .   156

41 — Section and elevation of main hall of Fo-kuang-sse, Wu-t'ai-shan. L. Sickman and A. Soper, The Art and Architecture of China, Fig. 19   157

42 — Original layout of the Hōryūji. A. C. Soper, The Evolution of Buddhist Architecture in Japan, Fig. 10   157

43 — Development of the temple compound in Japan. Drawing by the author   158

44 — Types of Siamese temples. K. Döhring, Buddhistische Tempelanlagen in Siam, Berlin, 1920, Figs. 19, 87, 94-8, 103-5   159

45 — Types of Siamese temples. Cf. Fig. 44   159

46 — Ground-plan of temple hall in the Vat Thepsirin, Bangkok. Cf. Fig. 44   159

47 — Ground-plan of the Vat Mongkut Krasat, Bangkok. Cf. Fig. 44   161

48 — Yaksha figure from Patna and Buddha from Mathurā. W. Willetts, op. cit., Vol. 1, Fig. 49 .   176

49 — Seal from Mohenjo-daro. H. G. Rawlinson, India: A Short Cultural History, 5th ed., London, 1954, Fig. 3   177

50 — Seal from Mohenjo-daro H. Zimmer, The Art of Indian Asia, Vol. 2, Fig. 1b   177

51 — Gold coin of the Kushān king Kanishka. L. Adam, Buddhastatuen, Stuttgart, 1925, p. 21 . .   178

52 — Development of the Buddha's head-dress. W. Willetts, op. cit., Vol. 1, Fig. 50   185

53 — Symbolic gestures. D. Seckel, op. cit., Plate 1 in text (after Sh. Mochizuki, Bukkyō Daijiten, Vol. 1)   186

54 — Development of the Buddha figure. W. Willetts, op. cit., Vol. 1, Fig. 52   187

55 — Buddha relief at Ma·hao. S. Mizuno, Bronze and Stone Sculpture of China, Fig. 35   215

56 — Buddhist figures on Chinese bronze mirrors. Ibid., Figs. 40-2   215

57 — Development of seated Buddha figure. W. Speiser, op. cit., pp. 120-1 (after S. Mizuno) . . .   217

58 — Central section of the Garbhadhātu mandala. R. Tajima, Les deux grands Mandalas, folded plate   224

59 — Diagram of a wall-painting in the Golden Hall of the Hōryūji. T. Naitō, The Wall-Paintings of Hōryūji, Pl. 11   227

60 — Wood-cut representing the so-called Taima mandara. Bukkyō Geijutsu (Ars Buddhica), Issue 45, Tokyo, 1960, p. 65   228

61 — Torsos of Bodhisattva from India and China. W. Willetts, op. cit., Vol. 1, Fig. 61   236

62 — Form of Buddha Vairocana. Japanese Art in the Seattle Art Museum, Seattle, 1960, Pl. 61 . .   244

63 — Rāgarāja, one of the 'kings of wisdom'. E. D. Saunders, Mudrā, Fig. 72   246

64 — Scenes from the life of Shākyamuni. Detail of wall-painting from Kyzyl. H. Härtel, Indische und zentralasiatische Wandmalerei, Pl. 26   265

65 — Self-sacrifice to a tiger. Detail of wall-painting from Kyzyl. A. von Le Coq, Die buddhistische Spätantike, Pt. 6, Fig. 59 266

66 — Wheel of the Doctrine. Saunders, op. cit., Fig. 104 278

67 — Frieze with leaves of pipal-tree. Drawing by H. Prüstel after H. Ingholt, Gandhāran Art in Pakistan, Pl. 463 278

68 — Five-pointed vajra. Butsuzō Zukan (Buddhist Iconography), ed. R. Gonda, Tokyo, 1931 Vol. 4, Fig. 230 279

69 — Vajra bell. Saunders, op. cit., Fig. 69 279

70 — Symbolic character (siddham). Sh. Mochizuki, Bukkyō Daijiten (Large Buddhist Encyclopedia), Vol. 1, Tokyo - Kyōto, 1944, p. 24 280

71a-d — Vine-scroll ornaments Drawings by H. Prüstel after H. Seyrig, Ornamenta Palmyrena Antiquiora, in Syria, 21, 1940, Pl. 29; H. Ingholt, op. cit., Pl. 461; S. Mizuno, Unkō Sekibutsugun, Fig. 13; Catalogue of Art Treasures of Ten Great Temples of Nara, Vol. 13, Tokyo, 1933, Pl. 12 282

72 — Diffusion of ornamental motifs across Asia. Compiled by the author after Ch. Itō, Nippon Kenchiku no Kenkyū (Studies on Japanese Architecture), Tokyo, 1942, Vol. 2, pp. 390 ff . . 283

73 — Diffusion of ornamental motifs. Table to Fig. 72. Ibid., p. 453, modified by the author . . . 284

LIST OF MAPS

Routes Taken by Chinese Pilgrims 66

Spread of Buddhism 109

Buddhist Cave-Temples in China 153

India 301

Indochina 310

Indonesia 310

Central Asia 311

China 311

Korea and Japan 312

ACKNOWLEDGEMENTS

The coloured plates on the following pages were kindly supplied by:

D'Arbois, Paris   254   R. Braunmüller, Munich   77, 140

W. Bruggmann, Winterthur 55, 56, 76, 78, 196, 98, 182, 193, 198	**J. A. Lavaud, Paris** 163, 179, 192, 209, 234
Dr. K. H. Buschmann, Hamburg 1	**R. L. Mellema, Amsterdam** 95, 191, 196, 207, 208
R. Goldberg, Philadelphia 144	**Dr. P. Reimann, New York** 58, 146
F. Distelbarth, Rittelhof 38, 145, 274	**Prof. A. Schüller, Heidelberg** 57
Prof. B. Ph. Groslier, Paris 36, 37, 252	**W. Shostal, New York** 164
Dr. G. Knauss, Heidelberg 142	**J. S. Skeel, Ashford, Kent** 35, 166, 195, 271
	W. Steikopf, Berlin 143, 213, 251

FOREWORD

The author of this volume finds himself faced with a problem very different from those confronting his colleagues who have contributed the other volumes to the 'Art of the World' series. He is not attempting to give a more or less comprehensive outline of the art of a single area, but rather to trace one particular kind of art — that inspired by Buddhist religious beliefs — through all the cultures which it has influenced. His task is not limited to a certain region or regions clearly defined by their historical development or geographical circumstances. It is to provide a comprehensive historical survey that will do justice to Buddhism as a world religion. The same problem confronts only one other contributor to this series: the author of the volume on Islamic art — and for similar reasons. Whereas he treats the religious art of Asia west of the Indus, in its world-historical context, we shall deal with Asia east of that river. The Indus forms a fairly clear dividing line between the 'Near East' and the 'Far East', although there is naturally a certain overlap between the two regions. The Near East is very closely linked with the Western world, with its Graeco-Roman and Judaeo-Christian traditions. The Far East is fundamentally different in character, being the spiritual counterpart of Europe and western Asia. Each of these vast cultural zones comprises several quite distinct areas. But this does not detract from the undeniable fact that the peoples of each civilization to a large extent share a common outlook, and that their historical destinies have been closely intertwined.

Any attempt to cover comprehensively the thought and art of such a vast area demands some knowledge of the cultures of the individual regions that comprise it. To avoid repetition, we shall confine ourselves in this account of Buddhist art in Asia to a survey of the works and styles peculiar to each country, concentrating primarily on those that are of more than mere regional significance. We shall examine the course of historical development, the routes by which Buddhist art became diffused, the links that existed between various countries, the influences which they exerted upon one another, and which radiated from the major centres, as well as the role played as intermediaries by points situated along the way. We shall also consider the basic concepts, the subjects treated, the iconographic types and the forms of expression. All these remained by and large unchanged despite all the various regional peculiarities that existed and the historical metamorphoses that they underwent. It is this continuity which gives Buddhist art as we know it its inner homogeneity.

In other words, we shall apply three interconnected methodological approaches, which can only in theory be distinguished from one another: the geographical and regional approach, the chronological and historical approach, and the systematic and typological approach. Thus, for example, one of our most important tasks will be to study the type of Buddha figure: to learn how, where and when it developed, the specific form it acquired among the various Asian peoples, the changes it underwent in the course of time, as well as the features that remained unchanged, since they were indispensable to a being not limited by space or time — features inseparable from the very concept of the Buddha. We shall also have occasion to trace the most characteristic type of Buddhist religious architecture, the stūpa, in its various modifications, which led to the pagoda of eastern Asia and other forms besides. We shall see that, in spite of what appear to be great differences in external form, we are dealing basically with one and the same religious concept, expressed architecturally. In the course of its journey across the whole of Asia it underwent a consistent process of formal evolution. The homogeneity and inner constancy of Buddhist art, transcending all local differentiations and metamorphoses, can also be seen distinctly in such religious symbols as the lotus; even at places situated far apart from one another these symbols bear an astonishing similarity. Yet it is not enough to draw attention to these constant factors. Special consideration must also be given to the different ways in which religious ideas were represented in the art of different nations at different times. Each specific style of each cultural region must be given its due.

All this could equally well be said, *mutatis mutandis,* of Islamic and Christian art. Imagine what an immense undertaking, what a hazardous venture, it would be to try to represent the whole Christian art of the Western world — its origins, diffusion and development — within the limited scope available to us here. I must therefore invoke the reader's indulgence for the fact that in this survey I shall confine myself to the most important issues, and shall make a rigorous selection from the vast mass of material relevant to the subject. This volume is not designed as a handbook or a work of reference. In conformity with the intentions of the publishers, it is not addressed to the specialist but to the interested layman in many lands. It seeks to provide reliable information about the most important aspects of the subject, taking into account the results of the latest research. We shall, however, have to presume some knowledge of Buddhist thought on the reader's part. He is recommended to refer for background information to the other volumes in this series which deal with the art of the Asian countries: India, Indonesia, Indochina, China, Korea and Japan. It is impossible to treat this background in a relatively short work such as this. Inevitably, this must be an outline sketch or essay, not a complete account. Some areas, such as Burma or Tibet, will not be dealt with at all, since I cannot claim sufficient familiarity with them. Their exclusion can perhaps be justified on the grounds that the two contributions in this series dealing with these two countries will be concerned almost exclusively with their Buddhist art. I myself have treated the Buddhist art of China and Japan in systematic fashion in my *Buddhistische Kunst Ostasiens* (Stuttgart: Kohlhammer Verlag, 1957). In this book the material has been arranged topically, with sections devoted to architecture, sculpture, painting, etc., as well as to general questions such as the religious functions of a work of Buddhist art. I have drawn on this book here, but have treated the subject-matter within a wider framework.

Two thousand years of development, in such a large number of countries where the human spirit has manifested such a high degree of creativity, have led to the production of countless Buddhist artistic treasures. Our illustrations are no more than a choice selection of these works, which I fear may not satisfy all my readers. I share their misgivings; for it is hardly possible to give an adequate idea of these riches in about one hundred illustrations. The most characteristic aspects of the subject are nevertheless shown, and the selection also includes some less well-known works. Reference is also made to the additional plates included in other volumes of this series. I am particularly grateful to the publisher, Herr G. Holle, for his kind understanding in meeting my desire for an appendix of illustrations, which should help to fill some of the inevitable gaps in the coloured plates that accompany the text. A general historical survey such as this requires more than a random selection of typical examples: the illustrations should show various comparable types, and the most essential stages in the process of historical development.

It would have been impossible to produce such a comprehensive survey of the subject had it not been for the work of the large number of scholars who have investigated the field of Buddhism and Buddhist art in Asia over the last fifty years. For reasons of space, footnotes have had to be dispensed with. I should therefore like to take this opportunity to express my profound gratitude to all the writers listed in the bibliography.

University of Heidelberg, April 1962   Dietrich Seckel

INTRODUCTION
OECUMENICAL UNITY OF BUDDHIST ART

Buddhism was the first world religion known to history. Gautama Shākyamuni, the Buddha, lived several centuries before Christ (probably 563–483 B.C.). His doctrine did not at first display any notable tendency to become diffused or claim to possess universal validity. But already the Emperor Ashoka (?273–232 B.C.) regarded it as a suitable spiritual and moral basis for his great empire, which he ruled in accordance with humane principles. He sent out missionaries, some of whom are said to have travelled as far as the Hellenistic world. Buddhist missionaries cannot at any time be accused of having carried out their functions in a fanatical, energetic or obtrusive manner. Still less did they put their faith at the service of a militant political power. On the contrary, in some way that cannot readily be explained, the Buddhist spirit prevailed peacefully by the gentle force of conviction. From its main centre of origin, in north-eastern India, it spread across vast areas of Asia, radiating outwards in all directions — except towards the west — bringing its universal doctrine of salvation for all men and living creatures, its philosophy and ethics, its learning and art. It bridged all the differences that existed and still exist between the uniquely rich and creative cultures of India, Indochina, Indonesia, China and Japan. In the course of the 1st millennium A.D. Buddhism led to the rise of a great spiritual and cultural community which may justly be called 'the Buddhist *oikoumene*'. In spite of the marked differences that existed between the various regions into which it penetrated, and the many metamorphoses which it underwent, Buddhism created a profound and far-ranging inner unity of spiritual consciousness, manifested in remarkable similarities in patterns of life and thought, and not least in art. We shall trace this unifying oecumenical continuity that runs through Buddhist art, which went hand in hand with a vital many-sidedness that enabled it to avoid rigidity and ossification.
It was possible for Buddhism to develop into one of the world's great religions because it was not restricted in its appeal to certain peoples, states, or social groups, as was the case with the Vedic religion and later with Hinduism in India, or with the characteristically Chinese concept of 'universalism', the basis of both Taoism and Confucianism, or again the specifically Japanese cult of Shintō. Indeed, this fact was frequently held against Buddhists by Brahmins, Confucianists and Shintoists. Instead, Buddhism burst the bounds imposed by the social structures of these peoples, their codes of behaviour and mythologies, and introduced them to new realms of thought, which in turn made possible a new sense of freedom and raised their culture to an unprecedentedly high level. Buddhism helped many

Asian peoples or tribes that were still 'under-developed' by comparison with the advanced societies of India and China to attain a higher level of civilization. Thanks to Buddhism they became aware for the first time of the fact that they belonged to a larger cultural area and had a role to play within it. This applies not only to the peoples of South-eastern Asia, Korea, or Japan, but also to the nomadic peoples of Central Asia. The latter were to play a particularly important part as intermediaries in the spread of Buddhist culture. They adopted Buddhism so readily and whole-heartedly because, having penetrated into areas that were under the influence of more advanced civilizations, they were not permitted to become integrated into the well-established social and religious systems they encountered, and thus were not fettered by them. Typical was the decisive role played by the Kushān Empire, in the northern part of India, in Buddhist religion and art. It was this empire that was responsible for the model Buddha image found in Gandhāra and Mathurā. Or, to take another example, the Wei Dynasty in North China, which was founded by the (probably Turkic) T'o-pa Tartars, played a major role in introducing Buddhist art into China itself, and also into areas as far distant as Korea and Japan.

Other reasons also contributed to the success of Buddhism as a unifying force in Asia. It did not have a closed, established, centrally organized ecclesiastical hierarchy, headed by a sacrosanct authority. Nor did it have a consistent orthodox doctrine absolutely binding on all believers. On the contrary, the Buddhist community crystallized into a variety of schools (it is misleading to use the term 'sects', since this implies the existence of some ecclesiastical authority representing orthodoxy), whose tenets and modes of religious life often showed wide divergences. Each of these had its authoritative sacred literature, its prominent teachers, and its influential centres of worship and learning. Naturally, each of these schools regarded its own teachings and traditions as the best and surest road to salvation. But generally speaking they were loath to condemn and persecute those who followed other roads. It was believed that each spiritual way had its own advantages: that not all the faithful were able to comprehend easily the purest and highest truths, or to adhere to the strictest code of ethics; even the Buddha himself, it was asserted, revealed his doctrine only gradually, according to the ability of his disciples to grasp it. One of the most fundamental Buddhist convictions was that it is not possible to express in words what is most real, sublime and ultimate; for it is in the nature of such concepts that they radically transcend all empirical means of perception and communication. For this reason even the finest, most lucid and consistent doctrine was regarded merely as provisional and non-real, as obscuring the ultimate truth instead of revealing it; at the very best as a limited aid to understanding.

It will be appreciated that this was not the foundation upon which one could establish an obligatory dogma, an insistence on unconditional belief, or a claim to exclusiveness. Unlimited tolerance is an essential principle of Buddhism, and not simply a concession to human nature under certain circumstances. Hence Buddhism could easily adapt itself to alien ways of thinking, doctrines, and cultural conditions, without sacrificing its basic concepts. This of course meant that it had to renounce the idea — if, indeed, it had ever entertained it — of dominating completely the lives and thoughts of the peoples under its sway, as Christianity and Islam had endeavoured to do, and had occasionally succeeded in doing. It was presumably this modesty in its claims that enabled it to spread peacefully into such vast areas, where the cultural pattern was so different. Wherever Buddhism penetrated it succeeded in adapting itself to traditional native beliefs, so that there frequently appeared a form of syncretism, upon which it left a relatively strong imprint. For example, in China Buddhism absorbed Taoist elements; in Japan it adjusted itself to the Shintō myth; and in South-east Asia it fitted into the cult of the ruler. On the other hand, in India, its native habitat, the process was in the reverse direction: Buddhism became absorbed into Hinduism until it almost disappeared completely. It was probably due to the very fact of its adaptability and capacity for symbiosis that Buddhism spread over such vast areas, exercised an influence of such intensity, and survived for so long among peoples so different from one another — of which at least one (the Chinese) could boast of an extremely vigorous advanced culture, self-reliant and rich in tradition. Buddhism did not merely adapt itself to other spiritual influences; it also transformed them, and presented a challenge which brought out their latent potentialities and led them to make a creative response. This capacity of Buddhism for fertilizing other traditions and promoting their development is particularly evident from the part it played in stimulating artistic production among the peoples of Asia.

Buddhist doctrine and culture spread mostly by way of the trade-routes. In Southeast Asia commercial settlements were the first centres of Indian influence, and Buddhist communities soon sprang up in them. Buddhist cultural influences penetrated northwards and eastwards along the 'silk roads' which ran from northwestern India across the Pamirs and Central Asia. The oases along these routes were not only centres of commerce and administration, military strongholds, but above all religious centres. They contained huge Buddhist monasteries which transmitted India's religious and artistic heritage to the peoples of Central Asia and the Far East. These trade-routes were at the same time well-frequented routes for pilgrims. In particular, Chinese monks journeyed in large numbers to the sacred land of the Buddha. Their aims were to pay homage at the places where he had lived and worked; to study at its source, in the tradition-drenched monasteries of India, the true doctrine and the true monastic life; to perfect their knowledge of

Sanskrit; and to take back home a large number of sacred texts and images. There was traffic in the reverse direction as well. Monks from India and Central Asia, some of whom were of Iranian origin, travelled to China as missionaries, and especially in order to help in translating Buddhist texts. The difficulties they encountered were tremendous, and could only be mastered slowly. For the translations were made from Sanskrit, an Indo-European language rich in grammatical forms and highly developed as a medium for logical and philosophical thought. Chinese, however, is a completely different kind of language. It is monosyllabic and uninflected, with an ideographic script based on an ancient independent tradition, at that time not suited for expressing abstract thought.

This transmission of Buddhist Sanskrit literature of the Mahāyāna (for it was this, and not the Pāli Canon of Buddhism known in the south, that became of fundamental importance for eastern Asia) through pilgrims, missionaries and textual commentators proved to be one of the most effective means for blending Indian culture with that of Central and eastern Asia. Still more important for the historian of Buddhist art in Asia was the fact that these monks brought with them works of art as well as texts. They included copies of standard cult images and buildings in the form of small plastic figures, models, etc. In addition they also brought iconographic drawings, with accompanying explanations, as well as instructions for the ritually correct representation of sacred figures. In this way the religious content of the images was transmitted over great distances, as were certain styles that became sanctified through the models on which they were based. This tradition played an important part in establishing the oecumenical unity of Buddhist art throughout Asia. But the northern route along the silk roads of Central Asia, with their numerous monasteries, was not the only one whereby Buddhist influences made themselves felt. The southern maritime route also played a vital part in establishing links between India and eastern Asia. This route was an extension along the coast of those routes mentioned above whereby Indian commerce and culture made their way into South-east Asia.

These contacts within the Buddhist *oikoumene* were facilitated by the rise of important kingdoms such as the Kushān or Gupta Empire in India, the kingdom of the Shailendras in Indonesia, or the T'ang Empire in China; these exercised a strong attraction upon their neighbours, whether close at hand or far distant. At the same time these kingdoms also acted as centres of cultural diffusion, sometimes linked with political expansion. Those that upheld and promoted Buddhist culture were of the greatest consequence in spreading particular Buddhist doctrines and artistic styles. This point will be illustrated in detail in Part I of this volume. These contacts were particularly effective and fruitful where these kingdoms were situated at a major point of intersection on well-frequented transit routes, or in certain border areas where different cultures impinged upon one another and cross-fertilization took place. This is true of the Kushān Empire (including Gandhāra), and especially of the whole of Central Asia, with its various political units and routes of communication. This area can be considered as a single vast zone of cultural contact and exchange. Up to the 8th century, at least, when it was broken up by the Uighur Empire and Islam, it was, so to speak, the backbone of the Buddhist *oikoumene* on the continent of Asia.

These various factors were not the only ones that produced and promoted the spread of Buddhism as a universal religion. The real driving force lay in the Buddhist philosophy and concept of life, which must have held a unique fascination for the various Asian peoples. All these political, economic and cultural developments redounded to its advantage. Despite the vast differences between them, these peoples certainly found the Buddhist world-view congenial; they felt that it enriched their own cultures, which were at first restricted to the particular ethnic group concerned. Buddhism served to raise their spiritual life to a new level — the highest that existed anywhere in the Asian world at that time. It opened up new dimensions of thought, which even the most advanced native philosophies and creeds (Brahmanism in India, Taoism and Confucianism in China) had not been able to reach. At the same time this decisive step towards a spiritual life that transcended regional limitations was only made possible through the far-ranging contacts and exchanges which Buddhism facilitated — on a more extensive scale than was the case with any other cultural movement.

This applies to the art of the Asian peoples as well. In many instances it was only with the coming of Buddhism, only through the stimulus it provided and the aspirations it awakened, that art could develop fully and reach standards acceptable in all parts of Asia. Thanks to Buddhism the various art traditions, which until then had been largely regional in scope and self-sufficient, were enabled to establish contact with one another on an ever-growing scale, to exchange ideas, and to fertilize each other. Buddhism succeeded in solving one of the major problems of Asian art: the problem of rendering the sacred in a human form of universal validity and appeal.

Yet this was not the only theme that Buddhism required artists to treat, even if it was the most important one. We shall see below the large number of problems that had to be solved in order to express in imagery the great variety of religious concepts which Buddhism brought into being. One point of great significance for the development of art was that there was no such thing as a single system of Buddhist ideas and artistic themes laid down by orthodox doctrine, with their limits clearly defined. Instead, primarily because all obligatory dogmas were lacking from the very beginning, and because a continuous dialogue took place with other philosophies, 'primitive Buddhism' (which is admittedly hard for us to envisage with any degree of certainty) began to divide already at an early date into a large number of different 'schools', representative of almost every type of religious thought and practice. The difference between Hīnayāna and Mahāyāna is in itself significant. Both 'vehicles' or 'careers' that were open to the Buddhist believer were divided into numerous movements (sects), sometimes very divergent from one another. They catered for a wide variety of religious needs, some of them diametrically opposed to one another. The same was true of their underlying motivations, the salvation they held out, and the means which they prescribed for attaining it. They also manifested considerable differences in their spiritual level, ranging from simple magic, often used for very secular purposes, to the most sublime heights of philosophical speculation and mystical insight. Each of these forms of religious thought and experience provided manifold opportunities for symbosis or even synthesis with non-Buddhist regional and ethnic ideas and practices.

A parallel process occurred in art: all these manifold tendencies and types of Buddhist thought and belief have left their imprint upon certain visual images, many of which had been put into poetic form already in the sacred scriptures, and lent themselves to artistic representation. This produced an iconographic repertoire that is tremendously rich, if one takes account of all the various Buddhist schools in all the Buddhist countries of Asia. This variety becomes more complex as a result of the fact that in art, as in religion and culture generally, a process of assimilation took place: in the course of the long history of Buddhist art (its period of development and full flowering extends from approx. 200 B.C. to 1500 A.D.) each people and epoch contributed, from its own rich tradition, all manner of concepts, images, and forms of representation.

Although Buddhist art was strongly influenced and greatly stimulated by the creative genius of the many peoples with whom it came into contact, and this led to great complexity and diversity, it nevertheless possesses an underlying unity. This unity is illustrated by the fact that the problems it seeks to solve, and the forms it develops, have a certain constancy. Among these problems are: building religious edifices for ritual purposes and for monastic life; creating valid images to convey the idea of the Buddha, Bodhisattvas, monks, and other sacred personages; representing 'sacred history', the treasury of stories and legends, with their abundance of narrative motifs; setting up a vocabulary of symbols to convey the main religious ideas; and, last but not least, devising convincing visual images of the world's metaphysical structure, and especially the structure of the spheres lying beyond the limits of the empirical terrestrial world. The form-types that were devised and made universally acceptable include the following: artistic treatment of the human body in such a way that it conveys certain religious ideas — e.g. that of the Buddha; certain principles of arrangement and construction in architecture, and also in pictorial compositions, capable of representing the Buddhist view of the terrestrial and supernatural worlds; or creating a certain language of lines and colour schemes that could symbolize adequately the content of the representation, and at the same time give it a spiritual quality.

All these points will be dealt with later in detail. It stands to reason that each of the Asian peoples evolved its own individual forms of expression, which varied in each creative epoch of its history. For this reason these artistic problems have been solved in a great many different ways. But underlying all these iconographic and stylistic modifications, the product of conditions in particular regions or epochs, there are two factors that make for unity and universality. In the first place, there are certain ideas common to Buddhists everywhere, which are not affected by circumstances of time or place, and which remain essentially unchanging, making identical demands upon all artists. In the second place, there are certain types of representation, first evolved in Indian art to formulate the basic themes, which then became protoypes followed throughout the Buddhist world in later ages. This process can be demonstrated with particular clarity by tracing the history of the image of the Buddha himself. These protoypes set a high standard which artists in each Asian country had to attain, and reformulate in their own way, without making a breach in historical tradition, or arbitrary deviations from it, that would cause the figure of the Buddha to lose its quality of timelessness. It would be unseemly for the Buddha figure to acquire characteristics too strongly marked by the period or locality when or where it was produced. The fact that such a tradition should have existed, that each country became acquainted with these models, and continually modified them — all this was in turn made possible by the network of links that spanned the entire continent of Asia. All the peoples that came under the sway of Buddhism were brought together as members of a single spiritual community, which left each of them free to retain its independence. The result was that the peculiarities of each region and period of history came to be imbued with supra-historical and universal characteristics. The general influenced the particular, and *vice versa,* in an exchange that was to the benefit of both.

PART I

THE SPREAD OF BUDDHIST ART THROUGH ASIA

I. INDIA

We do not know whether Buddhist art existed in any form during the first two centuries after the Enlightened One had entered Perfect Nirvāna — i.e., after his death, probably in the year 483 B.C. No traces of such art have survived, and its existence is unlikely. The rather exclusive and very frugal body of monks who constituted the Buddhist community of that time did not need temples or monasteries, since they did not worship images, and it was only during the rainy season that these mendicant friars sought temporary shelter. When, at a later date, simple buildings were erected for ritual purposes, perishable materials were used of which no trace has remained. Nor was there any need for images, which would have been wholly out of harmony with the original teaching of the Buddha. It is more probably that memorial places existed for deceased members of the community, and especially for those who had accumulated great spiritual merit, in the first place the Buddha himself. These monuments were presumably in the form of a stūpa, or hemispherical burial mound — the type of monument that was to have such a great future throughout Asia. It was the custom to walk round the stūpa in reverence and piety, from left to right, following the course of the sun, in the same way as is still done at the present day.[1]

The earliest Buddhist monuments to have survived were erected by Ashoka, the great ruler of the Maurya Dynasty (approx. 324—187 B.C.), which rose to power after the troops of Alexander the Great had left India. Ashoka became converted to Buddhism and caused his subjects to be guided in their daily lives by its tolerant, humane and ethical teaching. The huge stone columns[2] which he erected in many places throughout his great empire, which extended over almost the whole of India, proclaim these principles in their inscriptions. Some of them feature monumental figures of animals — bulls, lions, elephants and horses — and stylized lotus ornaments, as well as a huge 'Wheel of the Doctrine', the wheel which the Buddha began to turn when he first preached in the Deer Park at Benares, and which symbolizes the preaching of the Truth. It was also symbolic of the sun, the cycle of birth and re-birth, and of sovereignty. In their appearance, and indeed also in their function as official monuments, belonging to imperial and courtly art, these columns were based upon an Achaemenid model. Ashoka copied this model in many other ways, especially in the layout of his capital of Pātaliputra (Patna) on

[1] B. P. Groslier, *Indochina* (London, 1962), p. 214.
[2] H. Goetz, *India* (London, 1959), p. 46.

the Ganges, and in the design of the palace that he built there. These columns are the easternmost offshoots of the iconographic and stylistic tradition that radiated outwards from the ancient Near East. There is also a Hellenistic influence visible in the life-like modelling of the animals' bodies.

It may be assumed that Ashoka, who was a generous and tolerant benefactor of many religious groups, built accommodation for Buddhist monks, although these buildings have not survived, since they were constructed of perishable material. He no doubt also erected stūpas, since by this time it had become a common practice to worship the relics of holy men, above all those of Shākyamuni. These relics consisted of the mortal remains of the deceased, after his cremation (bones and ashes, and later crystal beads, etc., as well), which were deemed to contain the essential substance of the person concerned. It is said of Ashoka that he divided up the relics of the Buddha and sent them to many different places, so that his entire empire might enjoy their blessing; at these places stūpas were then erected over the relics. These were not only funerary and reliquary monuments, but also served to commemorate important personages and in particular — here the Enlightened One was said to have given his consent — places which had acquired a sacred character on account of the part they had played at decisive moments in the life of the Buddha: his birth-place in Lumbinī Grove (at Kapilavastu); the place where he attained Enlightenment (Bodh Gayā, south of Patna on the Ganges, the most sacred place of pilgrimage for Buddhists all over Asia); the place where he first preached (at Sārnāth near Benares); and the place where he died, i.e. where he attained the state of salvation in the great perfection of nirvāna (at Kushinagara). This in itself indicates that a certain shift had occurred in the direction of a cult linked with sacred objects and places. This was later to become a decisive factor in bringing about the flourishing of Buddhist art. At the same time the erection of stūpas throughout his empire served Ashoka as a means for propagating Buddhism as the officially sanctioned religion. Ashoka was also responsible for the original structure, the nucleus of the well-known Stūpa I at Sānchī, which we can see today in the form it was given after it was enlarged during the 1st century B.C. and embellished with sculptured gates in the 1st century A.D.

It is only in this period, some two to three centuries after the reign of Ashoka, that we find the earliest important monuments of Buddhist art: the stūpas of Bhārhut and Sānchi, which are surrounded by an imitation in stone of a post-and-rail fence and gateways *(toranas)* featuring sculptures in relief; and monasteries hewn into cliff-faces containing monumental halls used for ritual purposes, whose liturgical centre again has the shape of a stūpa. These sanctuaries, which served as basic prototypes for Buddhist architecture throughout Asia, will be considered in greater detail in Part II. It was here that the ancient ascetic and monastic spirit of Hīnayāna Buddhism was expressed in monumental form for the first time. It was here, too, that the Buddhist's unquenchable desire for visual representation of religious themes found satisfaction for the first time. Not that the Buddha himself, of course, was as yet depicted: he appears only in a later phase of Buddhist doctrine and art. (We shall deal with the creation and transformation of the Buddha image in a subsequent chapter.) The early phase, however, remains aniconic — i.e. it forgoes pictorial representation of the Buddha as a human person and suggests his presence by symbols alone. This was quite consistent with the original doctrine, since it was thought impossible to represent him once he had passed into nirvāna, a state of being inconceivable in human and this-worldly terms.

PLATE
P. 76

The reliefs in stone featured on the railings and beams of the stūpas at Bhārhut (early 1st cent. B.C.) and Sānchī (1st cent. A.D.), particularly the latter,[3] are teeming with life. This makes the sacred legend vivid but fails to convey any impression of asceticism, of renunciation of this world. These narrative compositions are inspired by a popular delight in spectacular and lively imagery, typically Indian. It gives the impression of an illusionary, transient kaleidoscope. The compositions deal mainly with subjects taken from the life of Shākyamuni and the Jātakas. The latter are edifying legends, taken from his earlier incarnations, often based on typical motifs from tales. In these incarnations he acquired such great religious merit by his piety, wisdom and boundless self-sacrifice that during his last re-birth he was able to prepare for Buddhahood, to reach perfection in nirvāna, and to proclaim it to the world. The panels of these reliefs are entirely filled with innumerable figures and a background of landscape and architecture. In their midst the Buddha is represented only by symbols. Moments of crucial importance in his life are suggested by the tree under which he attained Enlightenment, by the Wheel of his Doctrine, and by the stūpa, as a sign of his passing, and so on.

The gateways and railings at Bhārhut and Sānchī also feature many figures taken from popular mythology, particularly tutelary and fertility genii in the shape of male *yakshas* and female *yakshīs*,[4] as well as luck-bringing loving couples *(mithuna)*. All these figures are shown surrounding and blessing the sanctuary dedicated to the Buddha, which symbolizes the doctrine of liberation from the suffering brought about by karma and the delusion that fills man's existence. But they have to remain on the outside, as protectors and servants; the innermost part is devoid of any decoration, and expresses with simple grandeur the great void of nirvāna, which overcomes the world, transcends all existence, and for this reason cannot be represented. At Sānchī this basic concept of ancient Buddhism is expressed in a particularly convincing manner in the contrast between the simple archetype of the hemispherical stūpa and the wealth of pictorial relief featured on the gateways.

[3] H. Goetz, *India* (London, 1959), p. 54.
[4] H. Goetz, *India* (London, 1959), p. 50.

Whereas the Bhārhut reliefs are rigid, austere, sparse and monumental, Stūpa I at Sānchī represents a style that, although still archaic, is much more lavish and realistic. There is an abundance of narrative material in the compositions of many figures, modelled with a lively plasticity, which to some extent give the impression of the third dimension. The gods, human beings and animals that cover the pillars and horizontal beams have powerful swelling volumes, yet at the same time are restrained by the strict treatment of form. This also applies to the rich ornamental decoration.

The early phase of Buddhist art manifests an opposition between impersonal symbols on one hand, and on the other hand narrative legends that abound in figures and are full of vitality. The Buddha figure did not develop until the next phase — probably in the 1st century A.D., after the Mahāyāna doctrine, following upon earlier tendencies, had brought about a new concept of the Buddha. He was now seen as the embodiment of an absolute world principle, a personification of the highest truth, wisdom and goodness. In connection with this outlook there developed a desire to behold and revere his sacred person, and to show pious devotion *(bhakti)* to him as the merciful redeemer. This step, which was of decisive importance for the whole subsequent development of Buddhist art in all parts of Asia, was taken more or less simultaneously in two places: in Mathurā (situated on the river Jumna, a little south of Delhi) and in Gandhāra, in the north-western-most part of India (now belonging partly to Pakistan and partly to Afghanistan). This was during the first half of the 2nd century A.D., at a time when some of the most important *sūtras* of Mahāyāna appeared, on which the subsequent history of Buddhism was based and in which the new concept of the Buddha was already fully developed. Whether Mathurā or Gandhāra came first is a question that scholars have debated for many years. Today it seems as though Mathurā was ahead by a few decades, but the issue has lost much of its significance in view of the small difference in time involved. Of greater importance than the actual chronological sequence is the fact that the Buddhist art of Mathurā developed on ancient Indian foundations, whereas Gandhāran art was almost exclusively in-spired by foreign models, especially those of Late Antiquity.

Since the style of the Buddha image and its development in the various Asian countries will be considered in greater detail in Part II of this volume, we need only mention here the most essential points about these early schools of Buddhist art. Both areas were important political and economic centres in the great empire of the Kushān in northern India. The Kushān were originally a nomadic people from Central Asia, who inhabited Kansu on the western border of China. In the 1st century A.D. they penetrated to the Indus, where they founded (from approx. 50 A.D.) a great empire. Its borders extended to the north-west far into what is now Afghanistan, and to the north-east as far as Khotan in eastern Turkestan.

Most of this empire was destroyed by the Sassanids, in or about the year 240, but for some two centuries it survived in the north, in the area around Kabul, until the White Huns (Ephthalites) invaded the country and brutally destroyed the whole of Gandhāra. The Kushān Empire was situated at the point where several cultures met. Important international trade-routes ran through it, linking the Roman Empire, Mesopotamia, and Persia in the west with vast areas between India and China in the east. From this trade the Kushān derived great profit. On the other hand, they could not boast of a firmly established creative tradition of their own. This explains why their culture, religion and art were from the start cosmopolitan, particularly in the north-western border areas. Their indiscriminate religious syncretism is clearly reflected in their coinage, with its extensive repertoire of gods. Among them one may already find the Buddha (according to the Greek inscription, BO△△O).[5] By contrast Mathurā, the other great centre in the Kushān Empire, was situated closer to the centre of the Indian cultural sphere, and was firmly rooted in Indian traditions.

FIG. 51

The most important centre of Gandhāran art was the town of Taxila (Takshasilā). In close proximity to this town, and in its vicinity, a great number of monasteries were built. They owed a great deal to the patronage extended by Kanishka, and probably also to donations by wealthy merchants. These monasteries were usually built around a large central stūpa. The great multi-storied tower constructed by Kanishka at Peshāwar, which played a vital part (although one that is as yet not fully studied) in the development of the Indian stūpa into the Far Eastern pagoda, was for a long time regarded as one of the wonders of the world, and attracted the admiration of countless pilgrims. With most of these monuments only the foundations or basements are in a reasonably good state of preservation. The decoration on the walls frequently bears motifs of arcades typical of Late Antique art, with classical capitals on the pilasters, but with an Indian ogee type of arch, such as may also be seen on the Bīmarān reliquary. In the midst of the acanthus leaves that decorate many of these quasi-Corinthian capitals are small enthroned Buddhas or Bodhisattvas. All these monuments were lavishly embellished with sculptures executed in the local schist, in clay coated with stucco, or in terracotta. The Gandhāran figures or reliefs were thus always connected with buildings. There were no free-standing figures, but only figures worked in high relief, often almost completely round, in the niches along the external walls of the buildings, or in chapels. Their original appearance must have been very different from that which they present to us today. We have to imagine them covered with a layer of stucco, painted in many rich colours and gilded. The buildings, too, and especially the stūpas, once gleamed brightly, with their white coating, gaily-coloured decoration,

FIGS. 26, 27

PLATE
P. 35

PLATE
P. 78

[5] H. Goetz, *India* (London, 1959), p. 67.

and rich gilding. The brittle bluish-grey schist that we now see is thus only the basic material, which was not intended to appeal to the eye. This fact is not always sufficiently appreciated when these works are judged from an aesthetic point of view.

APPX. PL. 16, 21 Among the relief figures that are virtually free-standing the most important are the Buddhas and Bodhisattvas: we shall have more to say about them later. The illustrative reliefs of which so many have been preserved usually represent scenes taken either from the legendary life of the Buddha, who in this case appears *in persona,* and no longer merely as a symbol, or from the Jātakas. They carry on the very popular art of pictorial narrative we already came across at Sānchī, but the manner of presentation and the formal idiom are based on models taken from Antiquity — for example, from mythological friezes, or from reliefs on sarcophagi and triumphal arches, dating from the Late Antique period. The changes that took place in the latter style are reflected here step by step. The decisive influence on Gandhāran art was that of the Roman Empire — to be precise, of the provincial variants of Roman style found in Syria (Palmyra), which blended with Parthian elements. For this reason it is now customary to speak of 'Romano-Buddhist' art, in preference to the old term 'Graeco-Buddhist' art. It used to be thought that Gandhāran art was derived from Hellenistic models, particularly in the post-Alexandrian empires, such as Bactria. But this view overlooked the point that the Bactrians apparently never produced any monuments of classical style, and that their main artistic achievements were their coins — which were very fine indeed. Another point is that too long an interval of time separates Hellenism proper, which lasted from the 3rd to the 1st century B.C., from Gandhāran art, which was probably not fully developed before the second quarter of the 2nd century A.D., for the latter to have been influenced by the former. The supporters of this old theory thought that Gandhāran art dated from much earlier, even from the pre-Christian era. A new dating became necessary when consideration was given to the general cultural and historical situation, and to the important role played by trade with the Imperium Romanum, when a comparison was drawn between the evolution of Gandhāran art and that of Rome, and when more became known about Kushān chronology.

The current view is that Gandhāran art flourished during the period from approx. 130—150 A.D. to 430—450 A.D. This does not necessarily exclude the possibility that it began to develop as early as the end of the 1st century A.D. The pace of development was relatively rapid, for already in the year 300 or thereabouts we find recently discovered works of early Buddhist art in China. Their Indian models, which belonged to a comparatively late stylistic phase, must have been produced about the years 250—270 A.D. Recent research has thus continually narrowed down the chronological limits of Gandhāran art; but for various reasons it is difficult to give a precise dating. There are hardly any fragments surviving to which a date may be ascribed with any certainty, and where exact dates are given (which is not infrequently the case), they relate to different chronological systems, the starting-points of which are either unknown or debatable. This is in particular true of the chief figure in the Kushān Empire, King Kanishka, whose accession is variously dated to the years 78, 128 and 144 A.D. The two latter dates are now fairly generally accepted as probable, some of the strongest evidence in their favour being drawn from a comparison between stylistic developments in Gandhāran and Roman art.

Such a comparison shows that, from the reign of Hadrian right up to the era of Late Antique art, during the 4th and early 5th centuries, all phases of Roman sculpture, and particularly Roman provincial sculpture, left traces upon Gandhāran art. The stylistic development that took place there was strikingly similar to that of early Christian art. This is not surprising, for in both areas a change of world-wide import took place: a change from an art serving a humanistic myth, which set out to render natural forms realistically, or intensify them ideal-istically, and which, especially during its late phase, was closely linked to the political power — from this to a completely different kind of art, which turned away from myth, and neither copied nor idealized reality, but spiritualized it, and made it serve a transmundane kingdom. Thus the stylistic parallels between late Roman and early Christian art on one hand, and early Buddhist art on the other, which extend even to the manner of representing drapery and other details, are by no means based only upon the direct influence exerted by Late Antique models. Instead, they may be attributed to the underlying spiritual transformation that occurred at this time. Indeed, without such a change it would not have been possible for these direct influences to have had any effect. In studying the development of Gandhāran art, we can trace a gradual withdrawal from sensuality towards spiritualization and formal abstraction. The result is problematical. The prototype itself was already a late hybrid phenomenon, a blend of many different elements: Greek, Hellenistic, classical Roman, provincial Roman and Near Eastern (princi-pally Mesopotamian and Iranian). It followed that the orientalization of this style, once it had become imbued with Indian and Buddhist thought, could only occasionally bring forth really great works of art. As we shall see below, this process was influenced to a considerable degree by the native Indian style of the Mathurā school, from the 3rd century onwards, and later still by Gupta art. Gandhāran figures show only too obviously that they are derived from a prototype that was itself derivative, in which a large number of historical influences overlaid one another.

It is therefore not surprising that Gandhāran art should wear many varied aspects during the several centuries that it existed. For it does not always follow provincial Roman models, with their tendency towards rigidity and schematization of form.

During the late period (4th—5th cents.) in particular, and especially in the case of the stucco heads from Hadda, near Kabul,[6] and sometimes also earlier (Taxila, 2nd cent.), Gandhāran artists produced works of a distinctly Hellenistic style. They were characterized by gentle modelling, often verging on luxuriant sensuality, by supple flowing bodily forms, and by a rich variety of expression, ranging from delicate sensibility to a tragic pathos, suggestive of Praxiteles, Scopas and their school. Other sculptured heads call to mind portraits of young men from the early Imperial period, with their air of melancholy classicism. All this was transmitted by way of Late Roman art, which itself bore traces of all these elements, which went through classicistic and archaistic phases of its own, and whose neo-Atticism is, for example, clearly reflected in some Gandhāran works. Some Hellenistic elements may, however, have reached Gandhāra by way of the Parthians. The latter not only formed a link between India, China and the Imperium Romanum (notably by the trade which they carried on), but were very definitely philhellenes — as the Taxila finds show clearly. There are also some threads that lead to Alexandria, which maintained active commercial relations with the Orient through Syria (Palmyra) and Mesopotamia (Seleucia, and Charax at the confluence of the Tigris and Euphrates). This explains the presence at Begram (near Kabul) of amazing finds dating approximately from the 2nd and early 3rd centuries B.C. with Hellenistic, Egyptian and Syrian features. And this link may possibly also explain the technique and style used in Gandhāran stucco sculpture. For Alexandria was a centre of this technique, since it had plentiful supplies of gypsum but was short of stone, and from Alexandria knowledge of it spread to other parts of the world. But it is also possible that the stucco technique used for decoration in Gandhāran architecture may have been adopted — possibly at the same time — from Iran, where there was a long tradition of such work. In any case this area must have exerted considerable influence upon Gandhāran art generally, especially after the Sassanid conquest of Taxila (241). All these questions need further study.

In Gandhāran sculpture we can therefore distinguish several parallel traditions, derived from various areas; different techniques also exerted an influence upon style, and thus we find several styles co-existing at the same time, each corresponding to an individual type of figure, thereby performing a particular function. The majestic detached type of the Buddha and Bodhisattva becomes more austere, idealistic and abstract. On the other hand, other types such as monks, devotees and deities (as well as atlantes, centaurs, erotes, etc., of Hellenistic origin) are depicted in a freer and more gentle style, occasionally picturesque and frequently quite realistic. This development occurs not only because certain foreign models were available for the artists to draw upon, but in particular because these types were

[6] H. Goetz, *India* (London, 1959), pp. 75, 76, 83.

felt to be closer to empirically-perceived reality, in terms of Buddhist doctrine, because they were linked to the idea of *samsāra* — the transmigration through successive incarnations — and have not yet attained the state of nirvāna. It may even have been the case that models suited for representing particular religious figures were sought and found now in one place and now in another. For it is surely not a coincidence that, to represent the majestic figure of the Buddha, the model was found in the Antique statues of rhetors or emperors, with their characteristic pathos and ideal canonical form. It would thus be wrong to draw conclusions as to the time when a Gandhāran work was produced on the basis of differences in technique and style, and to deduce from this a consistent line of development — perhaps too consistent, and for this very reason incorrect. Very careful analysis is necessary in attempting to work out an accurate chronology of Gandhāran art. This task is rendered particularly difficult by the fact that there are almost no works that are dated, or to which a definite date can be ascribed. But scholars have made a good deal of progress in this field over the past fifteen years.

It is probably not being unfair to Gandhāran artists to say that they did not produce any really great masterpieces, even though they did succeed in creating many fine, noble and expressive works of a high standard of technical competence. Their importance lies not in the absolute artistic merit of their achievements, but rather in their historical situation. Seen in relation to what went before, they absorbed influences drawn from the whole of the Mediterranean and Near Eastern world in the age of Antiquity, and then created a synthetic product, which existed, as it were, side by side with an autochthonous Indian art. They created an art that was under the influence of native Indian religious thought (Buddhism, with all the tasks that this implied for the artist), but did not draw upon specifically Indian artistic traditions to a decisive extent. Seen in relation to what came later, their achievement was of even greater significance, for the future generally and for other geographical areas: the types of figure produced in Gandhāran art and their specific styles exerted a tremendous influence upon Central Asia, and through this area reached China and other countries of eastern Asia, such as Korea and Japan, which were under Chinese influence.

In earlier days there was a classical Europo-centric theory (still not entirely extinct) according to which the whole of Buddhist art in eastern Asia was seen as originating ultimately in Greece. But even Gandhāran art contains elements that are quite different from those found in the classical world, and is inconceivable without its specifically Indian spiritual content. There is another reason besides this why this theory is wrong. It overlooks the very strong cultural, and in particular artistic, forces that made it possible for China and the other Far Eastern countries to react to the stimuli received from Gandhāra, and to produce independent creative works of their own. It may be true that, if one analyses the question closely enough, many

Far Eastern Buddha or Bodhisattva figures are inconceivable without the influence of Gandhāra. But they could not have developed on the basis of these models alone, i.e. by mere copying, with the addition of a few variations. Yet another reason why we cannot speak of direct imitation is because there are several strata of tradition and influence between a characteristically Chinese figure from, say, the T'ang period (7th—10th cents.) and one in the Gandhāran style. Among these strata, as we shall see, there are again some that are specifically Indian and not Antique in character.

Thus we are by no means dealing with a case of Asiatic art forms becoming imbued with the Antique, but precisely the reverse: certain stimuli exerted by Antique art acted as catalysts or ferments, while they themselves became increasingly subject to Asian influences and blended with them; but these stimuli were not in themselves the essential elements that brought about this flowering of spiritual life and art. Gandhāran art was derivative and synthetic; and the fact that it could have the effect it did indicates that is possessed the power to set up valid models on which others could build. With the aid of Antique art, by skilfully utilizing its repertoire of types and forms, it succeeded in solving one of the most important and difficult problems in Buddhist art: creating an acceptable image of the Buddha and Bodhisattva that could serve artists from large parts of Asia as a basis on which to develop their own characteristic works. This achievement will indisputably always remain the glory of Gandhāran art.

Of course Gandhāra was not the only centre of early Buddhist art in India. For this reason we shall not go on here to follow the northern route, which ran from India across the whole continent to eastern Asia; instead we shall first turn to consider the situation in the central part of northern India, and then in the southeast. For it was here that, from the 2nd century A.D. onwards, simultaneously with Gandhāra, there existed two other centres that were of the utmost significance both artistically and historically: Mathurā and Amarāvatī. Both of them were much more firmly rooted in Indian tradition than was the case with Gandhāra, which was at first at a lower cultural level than the central part of India. Owing to its prominent role as a centre of transit trade, Gandhāra tended to absorb spiritual influences of all kinds; for this reason its art patterned itself all too readily on foreign models.

Mathurā (now Muttra) was an important political, economic and religious centre already before the Kushān Empire came into being, and it continued to maintain its position later as well — i.e. during the Gupta period. Its golden age, which was of such consequence for Buddhist art, dates from the reign of Kanishka and his successors, between 150 and 250 A.D. Of the numerous Buddhist monasteries that were built then hardly anything has survived — far less than at Gandhāra. This is due to the fact that the Muslim invaders took good care to destroy them. It is only

from descriptions by Chinese pilgrims who visited Mathurā between the 5th and 7th centuries that we can gain an idea of its rich Buddhist art and culture. The type of Buddha figure that developed there during the Kushān period will be discussed later. Like all Mathurā art, it derives from Indian tradition, and only subsequently absorbed certain influences from Gandhāra. At the same time Mathurā also exerted an influence upon Gandhāra. This is a quite natural histori-cal phenomenon, since both regions were the most important cultural centres in the Kushān Empire, and maintained contact with one another throughout. The routes linking them were used by pilgrims as well as traders. Whatever else has survived of Mathurā Buddhist sculpture is directly derived from the art of Sānchī, and especially of Bhārhut. But by comparison with the earlier archaic style a certain change can be noted, in that the figures of *yakshas* and *yakshīs* on the stone pillars of the *stūpa* railings are full-bodied and at times almost athletic; they have greater flexibility; and they are modelled more delicately and expansively, although with considerable vigour and tension. Almost the same stylistic tendency is evident in the sculptured figures that embellish the rock-cut sanctuary at Kārlī. What is lacking in Mathurā art, however, is the sense of rich joyous vitality conveyed by the carved narrative friezes at Sānchī and Gandhāra. In treating these themes Mathurā art is more reticent. It simplifies the story, concentrating upon the central figure of the Buddha, in the company of a few attendants. The fact that the Buddha should appear at all here in person, in an anthropomorphic form, is of course mainly due to the new concept of the Buddha found in Mahāyāna. The icono-graphic and stylistic treatment in particular bear traces of Gandhāran influence, which led to a gradual modification in the Mathurā type of the Buddha figure. The latter, however, was probably an independent creation of Mathurā artists.

PLATE
P. 77

FIG. 54

The third main centre of early Buddhist art, Amarāvatī, takes us for the first time to the south of India. In this area there existed, in part contemporaneous with the Kushān Empire in the north, the Late Āndhra Empire (25 B.C.—320 A.D.), which was ruled by the Shātavāhana Dynasty. It stretched right across India from the

PLATE 4 — CAVE-TEMPLE AT TUN-HUANG (No. 243), western Kansu, China. View of the cave by natural light; the floor is modern. Since the soft stone does not lend itself to fine carving the cave-temples, the niches in them containing figures, and their ceilings are hewn out of the rock in the form of a simple cube. The statues are of clay — frequently over a crude stone core — and are offset against a lavishly coloured background. The paintings are executed on a coat of plaster in tempera. In the cult niche are a seated Buddha and two standing Bodhisattvas, flanked by kneeling Bodhisattvas in the corners. Behind them are wall-paintings of huge Bodhisattva figures under canopies (a corresponding figure to the left). On the wall on the right, as on that on the left: a huge group of figures around a central Buddha in his 'Pure Land' Sukhāvatī. Above, on the sloping part of the ceiling, smaller groups borne aloft on clouds. The square panel in the centre of the ceiling has the shape of a canopy, with the drapery hanging down in festoons and a lotus in the centre. This is a symbol of heaven (cf. p. 274). The style of the figures and ornamentation is that of the T'ang period (approx. 7th—8th cents.).

39

east coast to the west, and its ports carried on an active trade with the Romans. Buddhism had spread fairly quickly over the greater part of India, and had already penetrated the area of Amarāvatī by the 3rd century B.C. Missionaries travelled to and fro between the Āndhra and Kushān empires. Indeed, from this time onwards the influence of Buddhist teaching and art already began to radiate outwards from India. Its impact was particularly strong in Ceylon, but a little later also extended as far afield as Indonesia and Indochina. It is of significance — and this is a phenomenon which we shall encounter again in South-east Asia — that the members of the dynasty, although they adhered to Hinduism, nevertheless promoted Buddhism by making generous donations. (This was particularly true of the women of the court.)

In the latter half of the 1st century and in the 2nd century A.D. Buddhism experienced a hitherto unparalleled growth in several widely separated areas of India: at Gandhāra, in the central part of northern India (Mathurā, etc.), at Amarāvatī in the south-east, and also in the north-western Deccan (where important rock-cut temples were built, such as that at Kārlī). One powerful centre exercising a wide attraction was Nāgārjunakonda. This was a place with huge monasteries, and even a kind of university, situated on the river Krishna (now Kistna), near Amarāvatī. It was the home of Nāgārjuna, one of the 'Church Fathers' of Mahāyāna Buddhism, the creator of the 'Middle Doctrine' (Mādhyamaka-darshanam). This doctrine is of the greatest philosophical significance and forms the basis of the beliefs held by a great majority of Asian Buddhists. Its main concept is that of 'Void' *(shūnyatā)*. This denotes the ultimate reality and truth, which in principle cannot be defined, since it lies beyond all the diversities and antitheses of this world, and thus also beyond the antithesis of *samsāra* and *nirvāna* that results merely from our relativistic way of thinking. In the world in which we live all things — even the Buddha and his doctrine — have only a limited validity, although from the standpoint of supreme absolute truth they are also 'Void', i.e. they can neither be termed real nor non-real, since even this alternative is but a category of thinking bound by the limits of our empirical world, with its relativities and dualities. Thus the world of physical phenomena possesses at the same time validity and non-validity, although on different planes of insight. On the highest plane this difference, like all others, is overcome: truth and salvation (which comes from recognition of truth) lie in the 'Void' — in the middle which as a matter of principle transcends all categories of thought and all alternatives. This doctrine and others related to it provided a new basis for Buddhist art. It now became possible to render without hesitation the things of this world, and even the Buddha; but this had to be done in such a way that it did not set out to be a valid definition of a true reality, but only something temporary and makeshift, a mere reflection of ultimately valid truth — in other words, of the undefinable, invisible and unrepresentable 'Void', which at the same time means both 'yes' and 'no', 'neither' and 'nor', and whose apparently negative character actually implied the supreme positive. This development of Mahāyāna philosophy — one of the most important foundations for Buddhist art in general — was thus accomplished already as early as the 2nd century A.D., in a fruitful period of rapid growth which was to determine the whole course of future development.

The first effects of this doctrine may be observed in Amarāvatī and Nāgārjunakonda art, which flourished during the 2nd and 3rd centuries A.D. Vestiges of·the old Hīnayāna concept are still discernible, as in the fondness for portraying the Buddha by means of symbols; but at the same time he is also represented as a person — partly under the influence of Gandhāran art. In other respects this art offers little that is basically new: as elsewhere, its function was to embellish stūpas and simple monastery buildings. The decoration of the stūpas, however, now became much more lavish, for reliefs are featured not only on the bases, as before, but also on the drums and hemispherical domes. For some of this work stone was used, but for the spherical surfaces stucco was preferred. These reliefs on stūpas frequently represent other stūpas, so that we can obtain a fairly accurate idea of their structure, iconography and decoration. The architectonic and symbolic features will be considered later; but one characteristic point worthy of note here is the habit of erecting, within each of the four approaches to the stūpa, five slender votive pillars (āyaka-stambha) topped by symbols of the Buddha and his doctrine. The pillar- or column-shaped monument is a popular ancient type, found already during the reign of Ashoka, when it was doubtless introduced from Persia.

The style of Amarāvatī and Nāgārjunakonda sculpture may be derived in part from Mathurā and in part from Sānchī, but it has clearly marked individual features.[7] The vigorous modelling and the healthy warm quality of the figures are reminiscent of Mathurā, while there is a link with Sānchī sculpture in the rich profusion of figures, which are depicted in a great variety of movements, recalling groups of dramatic actors between stage-settings. This is the more impressive as deep undercuttings and overlappings result in a lively, almost painterly, play of light and shade. Quite unique to this art is an element that apparently derives from southern India: a fondness for slender and supple figures, shown either in movement, in a dance posture, or standing in a graceful and nonchalant attitude. In these works the accomplished treatment of the body and its functions, the wealth of compositional arrangements, and the sensitive modelling are indicative of a greater degree of artistic freedom and maturity. By comparison with Sānchī and Mathurā a considerable step forward has been taken towards the high classic age of Indian Buddhist art. Amarāvatī art exerted a strong influence upon southern

PLATES
PP. 55, 76

PLATE
P. 55

PLATE
P. 76

7 H. Goetz, *India* (London, 1959), p. 58.

Asia, thereby effectively fulfilling a historical function with far-reaching consequences. Evidence of this may be seen in Ceylon, Sumatra, Borneo, Java, Celebes,
PLATE
P. 95
Thailand and Annam, particularly in the type of the Buddha figure. But once this
task had been accomplished, no further worth-while progress was made in the
area from which it sprang, where already after the end of the Āndhra period
(320 A.D.) Buddhism began to weaken and give way to Hinduism.

The classical age came during the Gupta period (320—approx. 650, in art until
approx. 750 A.D.), particularly in the Ganges valley, where a mighty new empire
arose. It boasted an advanced culture centred upon the court and the larger towns.
Literature, music and the visual arts all flourished. The latter reached what was
by Indian standards a level of perfection: all the developments initiated up to that
time now reached their climax, and began to exert their influence as classical
models over vast expanses of Asia. Under a government that was for the most part
tolerant, various religions were able to co-exist peacefully. Within Buddhism
followers of Hīnayāna lived side by side with followers of Mahāyāna. The latter,
it is true, began to take on the character of a theistic religion, with a large pantheon
and a predilection for complex magical ritual, resulting in a process of Hinduiza-
tion — evident above all in the adoption of elements of Shivaism. Therefore it was
not long before Buddhism became extinct in northern India as well. This process
began in the 8th century and continued until approx. 1200, when Buddhism
finally yielded to Islam. But at first, during the Gupta period, it reached another
great climax. For example, Nālandā, situated not far from Pātaliputra (now Patna),
was the best known 'scholastic' university of Mahāyāna. It was visited by travellers
from all over Asia and must have worn a truly cosmopolitan aspect. A lively
description of this place was given by the Chinese pilgrim and 'Church Father'
Hsüan-tsang, who came to Nālandā in or about the year 640, during the reign of
Harsha (606—647), one of the most important rulers in Indian history. Among the
great art centres in existence at this time was Mathurā, which retained its earlier
importance; another was Sārnāth, near Benares — the place where the Buddha
had delivered his First Sermon; and even in the south-west there appeared imposing
and significant monuments, built in the mature and Late Gupta style. Among them
are the rock-cut monasteries at Elūrā (especially II, X, XII, approx. 600 and 8th
cent.), which contain monumental Buddha statues and a magnificent sacred hall
PLATES
PP. 97,
180
with a stūpa; and the related sanctuaries at Ajantā, which house the most lavish
and best preserved Buddhist wall-paintings from the 6th and 7th centuries.

Further important progress was made in the architecture of the cave-temple and
the stūpa, as we shall see in a later chapter. More will also be said below about the
development of the Buddha image, which now reaches its final stage so far as
PLATE
P. 96
Indian art is concerned. The earlier Mathurā type, which influenced and was
influenced by the Gandhāran type, is now taken a stage further and reaches

maturity. At Sārnāth, on the other hand, we find another type that is entirely free from all Gandhāran elements. Some of the great masterpieces of classical Buddhist art — indeed, of world art generally — originate from this flowering period, in the 5th and early 6th centuries. The wall-paintings and rock carvings at Ajantā, and the innumerable reliefs that decorate the walls of the stūpas and monasteries, as in earlier times, have a tendency towards rounded bodily forms, a gentle suppleness and noble elegance such as one found in Āndhra art — although it is now that they reach full maturity. Everything that formerly was rough and stiff — in a sense 'archaic', everything indistinct and inconsistent in the earlier style, now disappears; and also the lively exuberance of the Amarāvatī reliefs, for instance, gives way to a spirit of calm concentration. Thus there developed works which are self-sufficient, full of truly classical harmony; they have an air of inner calm, a high degree of humanity, a vital sensuality, a delicate emotional quality, and yet a beauty inspired by a sublime spirituality. This is the case even where they depict typically Buddhist subjects such as world-renunciation and self-sacrifice. But Mahāyāna doctrine affords the artist a wide scope for rendering all the alternatives that exist between, on one hand, a relative truth that acknowledges empirical reality, human life and activity, and, on the other hand, an absolute truth that transcends all this, but which can only be envisaged in pictures and similes. Gupta art, which is based on the non-dualistic Mahāyāna doctrine, moves smoothly, without dualistic caesuras, between the vitality and warmth of the *samsāra* kaleidoscope and the nirvāna state of the lofty, detached, spiritualized Buddha or Bodhisattva figure. Its classical beauty is symbolic of its matchless spiritual perfection and detachment; it leads the viewer by its very beauty to the verge of the Absolute, and enables him more easily to transcend the bounds of worldly phenomena.

On a less philosophical plane, however, the Buddhism of this period is becoming permeated by an essentially alien spirit. The view that reality is sublime and can only be grasped by deep meditation is replaced by one that attaches importance to a large number of ritual acts and magical practices — by popular forms of religion which undermine its basic content to such an extent that Buddhism comes ever closer to Hinduism. Viewed in this perspective, Gupta art must also be considered as an intermediary stage in this process of decline, although in its initial period at least it did succeed in avoiding the ultimate consequences of this process. This decline was embodied from the 6th century onwards in the Vajrayāna, the esoteric and magical 'Diamond Vehicle'. It led in particular to the Lamaism of Tibet; to various tendencies found in the Buddhism of southern and eastern Asia; to the absorption of an increasing number of non-Buddhist elements, such as Shaktism; and to a readiness to adapt Buddhism to native forms of belief and cult — often to such a degree that it lost its original identity. On the other hand, the free play which this decline gave to iconographic imagination was of great significance for

Appx.
PL. 7

the development of art.

We shall encounter later in a more or less modified form the effects which the Gupta style, with its supreme perfection of form and mature spiritual content, had upon several widely separated areas of Asia, such as Ceylon, Java, Thailand, Central Asia, China and Japan. It had found a successful solution to the fundamental problems of representation, in particular by the establishment of a perfect norm of universal validity — i.e. a perfect balance between sensuality and spirituality, which in addition possessed a charm and beauty at once both human and more than human. It was for these reasons able to serve as a standard and a solid basis for independent creation — especially among peoples who stood in need of such an authoritative model because they found it difficult or impossible to create a classical art of their own. It stimulated them to bring their creative abilities into play and, by producing splendid works of art, to interpret anew the great and timeless themes of Buddhist imagery. Even in India itself classical Gupta art formed the basis for further progress, although its influence was of only limited benefit to Buddhist art, due to the continuing tendency towards Hinduism in religious life.

PLATES
PP. 98,
182
Among those who succeeded the Gupta in north-eastern India, the Pālas in Bengal and Bihar (approx. 750—approx. 1100—1150 A.D.), we find a sculpture that is typically post-classical in style. It manifests great perfection in form and technique, but also possesses a certain glibness, or languidness, and is lacking in warmth. One also misses the originality found in earlier sculpture. This is the work of epigones — but it is of importance for the history of Buddhist art for two reasons. First, because from the 8th and 9th centuries onwards Vajrayāna art spread from north-eastern India to Nepal and Tibet; secondly, because it exerted an influence upon Indonesian Buddhist art (especially from Nālandā, the most important spiritual centre). The chief medium of this influence were the easily transportable bronze statuettes, which were exported to the whole of South-east Asia. As more or less accurate replicas of well-known Gupta cult images, they were designed to transmit the salutary qualities of the latter to the countries whither they were brought. But at the same time the styles of these works were introduced to those areas. Many artistic influences were also exerted upon Indonesia and Indochina by the Pallava Empire, on the south-eastern coast of India, which was at that time one of the foremost maritime powers in the region.

Bengal and Bihar were the only areas in India where Buddhism was still professed — until here, too, it succumbed to a Hindu reaction under the Sena Dynasty, which in turn was finally expelled by the Mohammedans in 1194. A most impressive, and indeed tragic, testimony of this process is the fate of the well-kown monumental sanctuary at Bodh Gayā. This was probably erected under the Kushān rulers, at the place of Shākyamuni's Enlightenment under the Bodhi Tree; it was then

44

enlarged by the Guptas to form a splendid tower-like temple;[8] during the Pāla FIG. 14 period (approx. 810—850) it was restored; and finally it was transformed into a temple dedicated to Vishnu and Shiva, with Buddha relegated to a place among the ten manifestations *(avatāras)* of Vishnu. Thus Buddhist art in India, the land of its origin, after a vigorous life lasting for more than a thousand years, came to an end in a period of gradual decline — just as in nature a plant withers away once its allotted time is past, and returns to the soil from which it sprang, yet its seeds are carried hither and thither, to strike root in alien soil, in a different spiritual climate, where they produce blossoms and fruits of a characteristic kind.

II. CEYLON

Buddhism is said to have been introduced to the 'Lion Island' (Simhala-dvīpa) by the son or younger brother of Ashoka. In any case there is no doubt that it was the dominant religion there from the 2nd century onwards — in its Hīnayāna form, or more precisely Theravāda, the 'Doctrine of the Elders'. This doctrine is still a living force in Ceylon today. It was from this island that it spread outwards at various times to other regions. From the 8th and 9th centuries, however, there is sporadic evidence of Mahāyāna, and even of Vajrayāna trends.

The earliest capital was Anurādhapura. A sprig from the Tree of Enlightenment at Bodh Gayā is said to have been transplanted there. During the 8th century the residence was moved to Polonnāruwa to escape attacks by Tamils from southern India. But for several centuries Anurādhapura remained a religious centre and place of pilgrimage. Finally it fell victim to the encroaching tropical jungle, until the ruins of its stūpas, monasteries and palaces were brought to light again by archaeological excavation. From the 11th century onwards, and especially from the 12th, Buddhist culture in the Hīnayāna form experienced a revival under the rule of a native dynasty. It left behind it some outstanding monuments, above all at Polonnāruwa.

Ceylonese sacred monuments and monasteries are distinguished from those in India by certain features which they have in common with those of Indochina, but there are few entirely new types of building. Buddhist plastic art in Ceylon drew inspiration mainly from Late Āndhra art at Amarāvatī. This is clearly apparent from the earliest Buddha figures, which date from the 2nd and 3rd centuries A.D.

[8] H. Goetz, *India* (London, 1959), p. 91.

This type re-occurs at many places in South-east Asia. It spread widely in this area, partly on account of the extensive commerce carried on there by traders from the Āndhra Empire, and partly because this form was considered by Buddhists to be a convincing representation of the Buddha, and to have great artistic significance. The combination of refinement and humanity with sublime spirituality, of delicate modelling with austere monumentality, gave it a wide appeal. Some other works of Ceylonese monumental sculpture have a primordial grandeur: for example, the scene showing the death of the Buddha, carved in the rock at Polonnāruwa during the 12th century. The recumbent figure of the Buddha entering the state of nirvāna measures 14 metres in length; his disciple Ānanda is depicted standing beside him in mourning, wearing an expression of dignified composure. From a formal point of view this style may be explained as a development of the Amarāvatī style in the direction of monumentality and abstraction, while from a spiritual point of view it may be explained by the sober severity of Theravāda Buddhism. A certain influence of Pallava sculpture, which contained Gupta elements, made itself felt in the art of the Polonnāruwa period from the 7th century onwards.

Of a very different nature are some of the small Ceylonese bronze statues, dating from the 8th century or thereabouts, the iconography of which shows that they belong to the Mahāyāna school. The soft graceful style is akin to that found in Late Gupta art. After the conquest of Polonnāruwa by the Tamils soon after 1290 no works of significance were produced. However, even up to the present day these ancient monuments, and especially the stūpas, have been reverently renovated — although not always in the best of taste. Some of them were built only a few centuries ago. In the monasteries, in contrast to the mainland, the monks still keep up their ancient traditions, which were never subjected to the threat of Islam. But the impact of these Buddhist traditions did not reach the masses of the population to the same extent as it did in Burma, Thailand or Cambodia, although a certain revival has taken place in recent decades.

III. INDONESIA

The impact of Indian art upon Indonesia — by which we mean in the first instance Java, and then Sumatra — took effect in several successive phases, as such processes generally do. First of all (until approx. 500–600 A.D.) foreign works were imported *in corpore* and then copied; but soon afterwards (from the 7th century onwards) an independent tradition developed, which sprang from a sure command of the basic spiritual and technical principles contained in the model, which had been fully assimilated. Finally (from the 8th to the 13th centuries) this resulted in a mature classic style that rested upon indigenous premisses and has an unmistakable character of its own. We shall have the opportunity to observe a similar process in Indochina, China and Japan.

Buddhism was introduced into Indonesia between the 2nd and 6th centuries A.D. This was partly due to the influence of settlements founded by Indian merchants from the Āndhra Empire. These merchants carried on trade by sea with Burma, Indochina and China itself, and brought the population of Indonesia their own more highly developed social structure, political organization, culture and religion. But is was also partly due to the influx of minor Indian dynasties, forced to emigrate by the rise of vast empires such as that of the Gupta. The Hīnayāna doctrine was the first to be introduced, but from the first quarter of the 7th century onwards it was followed by Mahāyāna, which soon came to hold a paramount position.

At the close of the 7th century the Chinese pilgrim I-ching found flourishing monasteries in the Shrīvijaya area. The Vajrayāna variant of Mahāyāna was also quite widespread. Since this late form of Indian Buddhism contained many Hindu elements, it is not surprising that a pronounced syncretism should have evolved between it and Hinduism, as well as primitive native beliefs. Also of Indian origin were the rulers of the Shailendra Dynasty, whose political power helped to maintain this Buddhist-Hindu culture in being. They ruled over Java from 778 to 864, and then in the 9th century extended their power to the Shrīvijaya realm in Sumatra and southern Malaya. At times they succeeded in bringing territories as far away as Cambodia under their sway. They controlled the main east-west trade-route through the Straits of Malacca, and thus their state became one of the leading powers in Asia.

The area in India whence the Shailendra Dynasty originated was situated not far from Amarāvatī, which was the most important of the places from which these merchants set forth. It was this area that exercised a decisive impact upon Indonesian art in the early period. At a somewhat later date these influences were supplemented by others from the Gupta Empire, particularly from centres in the west such as Ajantā and Elūrā. Later still, from the 8th century onwards, a very strong influence was also exerted by the Pāla art of north-eastern India. The sacred places associated with the Buddha during his earthly life were frequently visited by pilgrims. The monastic university at Nālandā welcomed Indonesian students, for whose benefit one of the Shrīvijaya kings had a separate monastery built there. It was from Nālandā that Vajrayāna elements found their way into Javanese Buddhist culture and art. At the same time they were passed on from the Pāla kingdom northwards to Nepal and Tibet: this explains why there is often such a remarkable affinity between Javanese and Nepalese-Tibetan bronze statuettes or implements used in Vajrayānist rites — such as the Bodhisattva with many arms, or the multi-pronged *vajra* symbols; this similarity extends even to corresponding works of the same school in Japan (Shingon).

As elsewhere in the Buddhist world where such models were transmitted from one area to another (for example, from India to China by way of Central Asia), this contact assumed various characteristic forms: foreign workers (in this case Indian ones) were given commissions by native patrons and instructed native craftsmen; visitors saw Indian originals at first hand and copied them directly (although this was relatively rare); statuettes of bronze, clay, wood or ivory, or paintings were brought back by pilgrims and students; manuscripts containing descriptions and liturgical instructions were illustrated by iconographic drawings; and fairly often descriptions of monuments were probably passed on by word of mouth. As one can see, there was a whole range of possibilities, varying from direct personal perception or creation of original works to indirect transmission, often of copies that were poorly executed or failed to convey the meaning of the original. All these methods of contact may well have been used in furthering close links between Indonesia and the Āndhra, Gupta and Pāla empires.

Pāla influences, it is true, did not come into their own until some time after the real flowering period, which in Java occurred under the Shailendra Dynasty during the 8th century. It obtained a powerful stimulus from advanced Gupta art. In this case, however, it is impossible to speak any longer of copying: classical Javanese art, as exemplified by the Borobudur sculptures (750—800: we shall deal with them in greater detail below) is unmistakably a unique variant of Gupta style. The great Buddhist monuments in Java are for the most part imbued with Vajrayāna ideas, and combine the ancient type of the stūpa with that of the mandala. The principal monument of this type, the Borobudur,[9] as well as Tjandi Mendut (circa 800) or Tjandi Plaosan (mid-9th cent.) also have very important works of architectural sculpture, in the form of figures in niches and mural reliefs. Tjandi

PLATE
P. 139
APPX.
PL. 9
FIGS.
24, 25

[9] F. A. Wagner, *Indonesia* (London, 1959), p. 90.

Sewu (9th cent.) contained, in the niches of its numerous individual chapels, an abundance of bronze statues, and it is particularly regrettable that these have not survived. This so-called central Javanese art[10] reflects Gupta style, but gives it a note of sonorous exuberance and animated beauty which never fails to arrest and enchant the beholder. While Gupta sculptures have an austere courtly elegance that sometimes seems lacking in warmth, these works have an engaging and congenial humanity about them. In the reliefs, which continue the ancient Indian narrative tradition, with its fondness for spinning out a tale in the form of pictorial images, this humanity manifests itself, not only in the psychologically convincing and delightful exposition of the story, but also in the supple animated modelling of the bodies, as well as in the perfection with which movement and expression are depicted. Works such as the three seated cult figures in the central chapel of Tjandi Mendut — Buddha the Teacher, flanked by the Bodhisattvas Vajrapāni and Lokeshvara — are of a monumental grandeur, that makes them comparable with the Late Gupta sculptures, some of which are only slightly more recent in date, such as those at Elūrā and Ajantā. The Indonesian works, however, surpass them in delicacy of expression and form. Even relatively late post-classical specimens, such as the well-known figure of Prajnāpāramitā, now in Leyden, have a humanity about them that is generous, true to life, and yet austere, noble and majestic, although the details are treated with a certain dryness. Thus works of great charm appeared even after the flowering period, in the so-called eastern Javanese period, and occasionally up to 1300 or thereabouts. After that date Buddhist and Hindu syncretism, blended with native ancestor worship and animism, gained the upper hand during the later Javanese dynasties, which were mainly Shivaist. By that time a specifically Buddhist art scarcely existed any longer: in so far as it had appeared at all in Indonesia in pure form — as at Borobudur — it was essentially the work of the ruling upper class, and was thus superimposed upon an indigenous tradition that was completely different in character. Even during the golden age, between the 7th and 9th centuries, there always existed, alongside the Buddhist art promoted by the ruling dynasty, a Hindu art that found its most impressive statement in the purely Shivaist and Vishnuist temples on the Dieng plateau in the western part of central Java. It is to be noted that Buddhist art also had to serve a cult which, although it had first developed in India during the Gupta period, was particularly characteristic of Indonesia and Indochina — the cult of the deified ruler, who was identified with one of the great gods and regarded as his incarnation. This ideology was indeed Shivaist — for in addition to his many other functions, Shiva was protector of the state — and contained a strong element of ancient fertility cult, as is shown by the veneration

FIG. 33

APPX. PL. 8

PLATES PP. 207, 208

[10] F. A. Wagner, *Indochina* (London, 1959), p. 111.

accorded to the sacrosanct *lingam* (phallus), as its most important symbol. On the other hand, there also appeared sacred representations of other Hindu deities or Buddhist beings, which were given the name of a ruler or dignitary and were regarded as their 'portraits'; these could also be used in the native ancestor worship. Consequently it was possible for the consort of the ruler to appear in the guise of

PLATES PP. 207, 208

Shakti, as a female form of divine energy and force, as well as a personification of the loftiest Buddhist concept, Prajnāpāramitā ('Sophia'). The very fact that the latter assumed a female form shows to what extent Buddhist ideas were re-interpreted in a Hindu sense. This cult of the ruler brought Indonesia into affinity with Indochina. Many Javanese temples, of which some are basically sepulchral temples of deified kings, bear greater resemblance to those at Angkor than to those in India itself. This is no chance phenomenon, for the Shrivijaya kingdom was a great power with extensive maritime connections, and exerted a powerful influence upon Indochinese (particularly Khmer) culture over a lengthy period of time. In this way much of the Buddhist and Hindu culture of Indonesia was passed on to Indochina in good time, before it succumbed to the Moslems (in the 13th and 14th centuries). The only part of Indonesia where this culture survived was the island of Bali. But we have to look back in time and examine the early Buddhist art of Indochina.

IV. INDOCHINA

The cultural and religious history of the various regions of Indochina is so complex that we can only touch on those points that are of immediate relevance to our theme. To obtain a general view — although at the price of considerable over-simplification — it will be convenient to divide the history of Indochinese art into five phases, to mention the most important events and works in each, and to indicate their relationship to one another and to other art regions. But at the very start it must be pointed out that one of the principal cultural and religious border-lines in Asia runs from north to south through the eastern part of Indochina. To the west lies the area fertilized by Indian culture; to the east, i.e. above all in Annam (now North Vietnam), lies an area that was under Chinese influence.

If we consider the development of Buddhist art and culture in general, there is, on one hand, a movement from north-eastern and south-eastern India towards south and south-east Asia, which makes a slight turn to the north-east and so reaches the border-line we have mentioned; here in Indochina it encounters another branch coming from the north, by way of Burma. On the other hand, from the northern and north-western part of India there is a great migration right across Central Asia as far as China, where it divides: one line continues eastwards to Japan via Korea; another turns southwards until it reaches the Indian sphere of influence along the Annamese-Cambodian border. Thus the two jaws of a giant pincer movement meet in this area. MAP P.109

Curiously enough, this encounter — especially the contact established between Champa, the outpost of the Indian cultural movement, and Annam, the Chinese one — was of no particular artistic consequence. This was partly due to the fact that the geographical and ethnographical dividing-line was fairly sharp, and partly to the fact that neither the Annamites nor the Cham possessed great creative powers in the sphere of culture. The furthest point to which Indian artistic influences penetrated, as a consequence of their extensive religious and commercial connections, is marked by a Buddha figure in bronze found at Dong-duong (half-way down the east coast of Indochina). It was produced in or about the year 300 and exhibits distinctly the features characteristic of Amarāvatī style during the 2nd and 3rd centuries. This dividing-line did not, however, prevent Indian influences of every kind extending further afield from Indochina, to southern China. Some of them infiltrated directly, but for the most part they avoided this obstacle by way of the much-frequented maritime trade-route between India, Indonesia, Funan and Tongking.

1. During the first phase, which lasted from the first centuries A.D. until approx.

650, we find two main cultural centres in Indochina. One is situated in the north-east, in the Chinese province of Tongking. It was from here that the whole of Annam gradually became sinicized, as a result of conquest. During the 2nd and 3rd centuries in particular Tongking boasted a notable Buddhist culture. Later it was able to serve as an important way-station for Chinese pilgrims travelling to India, either by sea, following the coast, or overland via Burma. In the southern-most part of Indochina there was a kingdom which the Chinese called Funan. It was founded during the 1st century A.D. by colonists and missionaries from India. It maintained trading links with Rome and Persia (evidenced by finds made at Oc-eo which date from the 2nd century) as well as with China, and also played a vital role as an intermediary between Indian and Chinese culture, between western and eastern Asia. Brahmanism prevailed, but in the 4th and 5th centuries Buddhism flourished alongside it. This mighty empire was at that time repeatedly under Indian influence, as may be seen from its Buddha figures, in bronze as well as in wood or stone, all of which bear features of Gupta or post-Gupta style. From approx. 550 onwards Funan went into a decline. It had two successor-states that were destined to become most important kingdoms: Cambodia, the kingdom of the Khmer, in the south and centre of Indochina, and Dvāravatī in the north, in the area that was later to be known as Thailand.

2. (Approx. 650–800). A large part of Funan was now incorporated into the Cambodian state of Chen-la. During the early part of the 7th century it produced the first style in Khmer art, which carried on the cultural tendencies prevalent in Funan; both were based on early Indian influences. Thus here, too, Buddhist art — now a specific Mahāyāna art — does not undergo any break in the continuity of its development. During the 7th and 8th centuries it bursts forth into flower for the first time. In this early period it bears the distinct imprint of the specific sense of form possessed by the Khmer. At first, during the 6th and 7th centuries, it kept close to models from India, Ceylon and Dvāravatī, but then it became increasingly independent. Its original models were of a very heterogeneous character, as can be seen, for example, from the Buddha figures that date from the so-called pre-Angkor period. (An analogous development took place simultaneously in Champa.) But it should not be overlooked that Buddhism did not by any means have exclusive rights: the religion professed by members of the dynasty was Shivaism (in conjunc-tion with Vishnuism), and the ideology of the deified ruler that was founded upon this. Their temples represented the world mountain, as the centre of the universe and the abode of the god. This was also the period of Shrīvijaya hegemony under the Shailendra Dynasty, which extended its power to the Khmer kingdom and promoted the amalgamation of the cult of the ruler and Mahāyāna Buddhism which we have already encountered in Indonesia. Only at a much later stage did Buddhism become the leading religion in this part of Indochina.

In the north-west, in what is today Burma and Siam, there existed from the 6th century onwards, if not earlier, colonies in which Hīnayāna was professed. These bore the stamp of Amarāvatī and Ceylonese culture and artistic styles, as was the case with the early settlements in Indonesia. But in the 7th century a distinctly individual art developed in Dvāravatī, one of the successor-states of Funan. It was the product of the spirit and sense of form innate in the Mon people. Yet it would never have come about without the far-ranging stimulus exercised by classical and post-classical Gupta art, or the monumental rock-carvings at Ajantā, Elūrā, and elsewhere, the fertilizing influence of which was felt in Indonesian art as well. The type of Buddha figure produced in Dvāravatī became a prototype followed in one way or another throughout Indochina. More will be said about this later. Together with Hīnayāna Buddhism, it had a great impact on south-eastern Indochina at a later stage. At first its influence made itself felt upon Khmer art, and later upon Thai art. Of the works that have survived most are executed in stone and bronze, and date from the Dvāravatī period (between the 6th–7th and the 12th–13th centuries). But plastic works in stucco and terracotta are also found, which served to embellish stūpas, as they did at Gandhāra and elsewhere. The surviving fragments of these works — mostly heads — are of such charm that one must regret bitterly the fact that so many of them have been lost.

Appx. pl. 10, 11

Only a few remains bear witness to Dvāravatī architecture. These ruins include the five-storeyed stepped tower of Wat Kukut at Lamphūn (old name: Haripunjaya),[11] which was erected in 1218 to take the place of its predecessor, which dated from the 12th century and had been destroyed. It had 60 niches with huge standing figures of the Buddha in terracotta. In the north-west it was possible for Dvāravatī art to survive for longer than it could in the central area, on the Menam, which was absorbed into the Khmer Empire as early as 1020. It was from this area that Mahāyāna reached Dvāravatī, but since the ruler adopted a tolerant attitude Hīnayāna was able to survive as well. Another reason for this was that direct connections could be maintained with Burma, and thus with Ceylon. Powerful influences on Dvāravatī style were exerted by Khmer art, particularly in the Lopburi area during the 11th and 12th centuries. More important than this was the fact that Dvāravatī was the source of the iconographic and formal repertoire of all Hīnayāna art in Indochina, which subsequently, from the 13th century onwards, had a decisive influence upon the culture and art of Thailand. Thus there is another major dividing-line running through Indochina: that between Hīnayāna and Mahāyāna. The former, in the relatively pure form of Theravāda, stemmed from Ceylon. It described a great arc through Burma until it reached the heart of Indochina from the north. The latter stemmed from eastern India, and reached

[11] B. P. Groslier, op. cit., p. 209.

Indochina from the south, mainly by way of Indonesia. It was closely associated with Hinduism. This was due in part to the close historical and geographical links that bound it to Hindu southern India, and in part to a gradual approximation to Hinduism in matters of doctrine and ritual. This border-line is, however, none too clearly marked. It fluctuates considerably from one period to another, with a steady shift in favour of Hīnayāna.

3. (Approx. 800—1200). In discussing these events, and in particular the extremely important effects of Dvāravatī art, we have run far ahead of our story. The third phase of development in Indochina sees the foundation and flowering of the great Khmer Empire of the Angkor period, from the 9th cent. to 1177, when it was temporarily brought to a close by the Cham. The official national art fostered by the rulers of this period, represented especially by such well-known monuments as Bakong, Bakheng and Angkor Vat, is predominantly Hindu in character — even the superb friezes in relief at Angkor, and the other sculptural decoration there, are not Buddhist. The kings regarded themselves as incarnations of the supreme god, and were for the most part strict Shivaists. But Buddhist monasteries and statuary were built and produced as well, thanks to the tolerant attitude of the court. Under Yashovarman (889—900), for example, and particularly under Sūryavarman I (1011—1050), there came into being a new phase of Khmer Buddhist art, as a result of contact with Dvāravatī. It is to the close of this epoch that we owe the charming classical Buddha and Bodhisattva heads, which admittedly

PLATE
P. 191
become rigid in the course of time, owing to constant repetition. These heads may perhaps have done even more than the monumental buildings to give Khmer art its world renown. If one compares them with non-Buddhist Khmer works, one sees that the latter, for all their majestic beauty, cannot rival them in spirituality and animation. It seems as though a specifically Buddhist attitude of piety were responsible for the expression they wear — a smile suggestive of mystical meditation and blissful withdrawal from worldly cares.

PLATE 5 — REPRESENTATION OF A STŪPA. Tablet in relief from the stone railing (vedikā) of a stūpa at Nāgārjunakonda, Āndhra province, India. Light greenish-grey limestone. 2nd or 3rd cent. A.D. Height 153 cm. Nāgārjunakonda Museum.
On the structure of stūpas, cf. Ch. I. A relief of this kind provides a fairly accurate idea of the appearance of such monuments in situ. The stūpas at Amarāvatī and Nāgārjunakonda are distinguished by having four platforms added, facing the four points of the compass (cf. ground-plan, p. 116), each with five tall octagonal votive pillars (āyaka-stambhas). These frequently bear votive inscriptions and symbolize the five main events in the life of the Buddha (his birth, renunciation of the world, Enlightenment, First Sermon, entrance into nirvāna). Often they are topped by equivalent symbols. This plate shows a stūpa on the central pillar symbolizing nirvāna. We see the front of the platform with pillars, flanked by pairs of lions; the platforms on the sides are represented more cursorily in profile on the borders of the tablet, as may be distinctly seen from the lion figures. Below is the Buddha descending from the Tushita heaven to assume his final incarnation on earth; he is, however, already represented in his supra-temporal state,

as *Buddha aeternus*. Next to him is his protective attendant Vajrapāni, carrying a thunderbolt; below are worshippers. Right on top figures of deities can be seen hovering: inhabitants of the Tushita heaven venerating the Buddha made manifest in the stūpa. On the dome of the stūpa are reliefs showing scenes from the Buddha legend.

PLATE 6 – VOTIVE STŪPA in bronze. From Nālandā, Bihar province, India. Pāla period, approx. 9th–10th cents. Height 19 cm. *National Museum of India, New Delhi.*
On the stepped base, which faces the four directions of heaven, are niches containing Bodhisattva figures. Above this is a rectangular substructure supporting a hemispherical dome resting on a lotus; over this is a cubic *harmikā,* crowned by three slabs, which in turn supports a mast with eight discs and a finial. This is a well-proportioned model of a relatively ancient form of stūpa. The figures on the eight sides of the substructure depict eight principal events in the life of the Buddha: on the right we see his birth, on the left his victory over Māra, the enemy of Enlightenment (seated Buddha in *bhūmisparsha-mudrā*).

PLATE 7 – PAGODA OF T'IEN-NING-SSE, PEKING. Octagonal building of thirteen storeys, with a sanctuary on the first floor. The upper storeys are not accessible. Brick, decorated with stucco and terracotta. Roof-tiles glazed yellow and green. Approx. 1100, but restored on several subsequent occasions. Height 58 m.

By the dummy gateways of the main storey are two Dvārapālas (guardians of the gate), with *apsaras* hovering above them. On the intervening walls are Bodhisattvas, topped by Mañjushrī on his lion. On the tiers of the base, which also represent the lotus-throne motif, are numerous figures of Buddhas, *yakshas*, demonic animals, etc., all executed in high relief.

57

PLATE 8 – KUMSAN-SA PAGODA, south-western Korea. Stone. Height approx. 10 m. In the background a stūpa (height approx. 2.20 m.) on a terrace used for initiation ceremonies. Approx. early 12th cent. A.D. The pagoda stands on a broad base and has five (or according to a different method of calculation, six) cubic storeys, each of them with a broad projecting roof. This simplified variant of the Chinese multistoreyed pagoda is especially popular in Korea. On top is a hemispherical structure reminiscent of the original dome of the stūpa; above it is a pinnacle divided into several tiers. The monument on the left shows more clearly the ancient basic form of the stūpa.

The religious situation in Champa was similar. The cult of the monarch dominated, but Mahāyāna Buddhism was able to develop unhindered as well. The only difference is that these monuments and statues testify to a pronounced Chinese influence, probably transmitted either by Chinese pilgrims travelling to India by sea, who visited Champa ports, or through the medium of the Sino-Annamite art of the adjoining area. The centre of Buddhism here was the monastery of Dong-duong, built in 875. It was founded by the ruler, and characteristically enough was dedicated to Lakshmīndralokeshvara. This name consists of two Hindu elements (Lakshmī and Indra) and one Buddhist element (Lokeshvara), and shows very clearly that syncretism was prevalent in this area, as it was in the Khmer Empire and Indonesia as well. During the 11th and 12th centuries Champa fell more and more under the political and cultural influence of Annam. Chinese elements came to dominate in its Buddhist art. The only modification made was to incorporate certain Cham elements, above all in the ornamentation of buildings.

4. (Approx. 1200–1450). The building of Angkor Vat (under Sūryavarman II, 1113–1150) marked the apogee, and simultaneously the end, of the national art that flourished in the Khmer Empire. It was mainly Hindu, although the smaller buildings exhibit an ever-increasing concern with Buddhist themes. Dhāranīndravarman II (1150– ?) was the first Buddhist ruler at Angkor. The catastrophe of 1177, which ensued shortly afterwards, brought the extinction of the Hindu cultural tradition. Jayavarman VII (1181–1220?), who once again built up a large empire, was a deeply devout man who gave strong encouragement to Buddhism. It is true that the Hindu cult of the deified ruler was by no means abandoned, and that the Bayon (erected soon after the year 1200) was still regarded as a temple-mountain in the centre of the cosmos and of the kingdom. But it clearly bears the stamp of Buddhism. This is evident from the gigantic faces of the Bodhisattva Lokeshvara ('the Lord of the World'), which look outwards in all directions from the 54 towers of this temple. These are at the same time 'portraits' of the king, depicted as an incarnation of the supreme god.[12] Prior to this Jayavarman VII had erected monuments — one in honour of his mother, at Ta Prohm monastery, in the image of Prajnāpāramitā, and one in honour of his father at Preah Khan monastery, in the image of Lokeshvara — which manifest a distinct shift in favour of Buddhism within the traditional syncretism. The Bayon is by no means a purely Buddhist monument, although its focal point is a Buddha statue that it at the same time a representation of the king. In spite of this the Bayon plays an important part in the history of Buddhist art — if only because it demonstrates clearly how adaptable Mahāyāna Buddhism was.

It must be borne in mind that the ideas of representing the universe in architecture,

PLATE
P. 37

12 B. P. Groslier, op. cit., p. 176.

and of the stepped building as the world mountain, are also to be found in other monuments — in stūpas or pagodas, for example, or at Borobudur, which are universally considered to be purely Buddhist. Within the ample scope furnished by certain basic Buddhist ideas and certain types of works, which may even include non-Buddhist elements, in each case it is a matter of emphasizing one element or another, rather than of keeping within clearly defined dividing-lines. And it is largely this factor which gives Buddhist religion and art their oecumenical unity, and also accounts for the variety of ideas they contain, and for the differences that exist between individual regions.

With the death of Jayavarman VII, however, this national art comes to an end. The old cult of the ruler, associated with hinduized Mahāyāna, and the social structure that supported it, gradually sink into decline, and the Khmer people become converted to Hīnayāna (Theravāda) Buddhism, as professed in Ceylon. This provides further confirmation of the old rule that Buddhism helped men to free themselves from traditional hierarchic social structures, or afforded them solace when these collapsed. It seems symbolic that later, in the 16th century, even Angkor Vat should have become a widely known Theravāda monastery. In the centuries that followed this religion penetrated ever more deeply into the lives of the people. It expressed itself on a grandiose scale in sculpture, which developed greatly during the 13th century.[13] It carried on the earlier Khmer styles, but also took up the Hīnayānist tradition of Dvāravatī, as is particularly evident in the Buddha types. Thus one can observe a continuity in the process of transition from Mahāyāna to Hīnayāna art. Overlappings also take place — as, for example, where a type of Buddha that is Mahāyānist in concept, the 'Buddha in royal attire' (Buddha paré), gains in popularity, as it did both in this area and in Thailand (which influenced Khmer).

PLATES
PP. 77,78

The other great event of the 13th and 14th centuries that is of significance for Buddhist art was the advance of the Thai — initially a Mahāyānist people, who were driven out of southern China and migrated southwards. At first they established contact with the Mon culture of Burma and Dvāravatī — to be precise, with the kingdom of Haripunjaya (Lamphūn), which had not been completely assimilated by Khmer culture. They then soon became converted to Hīnayāna and spread their power over extensive areas in the western part of Indochina, wedging themselves between Burma and the Khmer Empire. The first Thai kingdom was Sukhothai, whose chief ruler was Rāma Kamheng (not later than 1281—approx. 1315). The second was Chiengmai, further to the north, which developed a specifically Siamese type of Buddha figure. But in 1349 the ruler of the Thai kingdom of Ayuthia, to the south, annexed Sukhothai and in 1353 conquered Angkor. From

[13] B. P. Groslier, op. cit., pp. 169, 188.

then until 1767 Ayuthia remained the capital of Siam. With the final collapse oɪ Angkor (1431), which was encircled by Siam and Annam, the Thai people completed their southward expansion. Thus Hīnayāna culture, which had prevailed in Cambodia from as early as the 12th—13th centuries, had now firmly established itself in Indochina. This meant that from approx. 1450—1500 onwards Mahāyāna Buddhism became extinct throughout India and southern Asia. It had already been forced to give way to Hinduism and Islam in Indonesia, from about 1300 onwards, and in India itself this had happened much earlier still. But Ceylon, Burma and Indochina, under Thai hegemony, have retained their Hīnayāna Buddhist culture and art up to the present day.

Seen as a whole, Buddhist art in Indochina is far less plentifully supplied with iconographic types and themes than other areas are. Inevitably, therefore, it manifests a tendency towards monotonous repetition and variation, particularly in representing the Buddha and Lokeshvara. Quite frequently, however, these few types are developed to such a pitch of concentration and refinement that they exhibit a unique spiritual intensity and formal perfection. Two reasons may be adduced for the limited rein given here to the creative imagination. In the first place, Mahāyāna art in the Khmer Empire was so closely associated with the ideology of the god-king that it could not develop freely, and so produced only a few different types; the narrative reliefs on the monuments at Angkor are also based on Hindu iconography. Secondly, so far as the Hīnayānist countries are concerned, particularly Siam, the doctrine itself prevented the development of a pantheon with a wealth of figures. Only in the sphere of pictorial narrative for illustrative purposes were artists somewhat freer to use their imagination. The results may be seen in Siamese stucco reliefs featuring legends of the Buddha and other such themes.

5. (From the 15th century onwards). In its initial stages, in the Sukhothai period, Thai sculpture developed out of a fusion of the Dvāravatī tradition with the Buddhist art of Cambodia produced after the Bayon period in the 13th century. Possibly some elements imported by the Thai from southern China were involved as well. Buddhist architecture is also a combination of several different styles: effective use is made, however, of the ancient native type of roof, with multiple pointed and curved gables, which frequently gives these buildings a particular charm.[14] The specifically Siamese Buddha figure is also unmistakably unique, in spite of the fact that it took over elements from India, Dvāravatī and Khmer.[15] It probably matured in Sukhothai during the 14th century, and later, as it spread outwards from Ayuthia, became the standard type for the whole of Siam. It was

[14] B. P. Groslier, op. cit., p. 205.
[15] B. P. Groslier, op. cit., p. 207.

a fusion of various regional types. Of the latter special mention must be made of that from Lannā: some very important bronze statues in this style were produced in the area of Chiengmai. Of particular interest to art historians are those with inscriptions, the dates of which range from 1470 to 1565. Another important regional type is that of U-Thong, in the south, which was subject to Khmer influence. Works of this type were produced in the area of Ayuthia and elsewhere, in particular during the 14th and 15th centuries. It will be seen that Indochinese art is characterized by a continuous process of interaction, fusion and synthesis between elements of varying origin, which makes its history exceedingly complex and difficult to describe in a brief outline. In Siamese art, too, the Buddha depicted in royal attire becomes more and more popular from the 16th century onwards, but as a consequence of mass production it also becomes increasingly schematized. After 1782, when the capital was moved to Bangkok, Buddhist art in Thailand lost almost all its creative drive — despite the fact that Buddhism became the state religion and many magnificent monuments and statues were erected, seemingly testifying to a flowering of this art.

APPX. PL. 12, 13

PLATES PP. 140, 141

Laos maintained close cultural links with Siam from the 14th century onwards, and absorbed artistic influences from Ayuthia as well as from Khmer.[16] On the other hand, Vietnam, which held sway over the entire eastern part of Indochina from approx. 1500 to the 18th century, belonged wholly to the Chinese cultural sphere. It combined Mahāyāna Buddhism with elements of Taoism, Confucianism and ancestor worship. It has not, however, produced any really outstanding works of Buddhist art. Thus these two small countries face in different directions: one towards India and the west, and the other towards China and the east. The two great cultural zones in which Buddhism developed to such effect meet here, as it were, back to back.

[16] B. P. Groslier, op. cit., p. 218.

V. CENTRAL ASIA

Apart from a few special instances, no productive links of any consequence were established between Indochina and eastern Asia, despite the opportunities that existed for such contact. Buddhist religion and art reached China by a different route — the northern one. We must therefore now return to Gandhāra, which we left because it exerted scarcely any influence upon the development of Buddhist art in southern Asia. We have seen that Gandhāra was situated at a cross-roads of world history, where cultural movements from various points of the compass met. Whereas it exerted its influence on artistic development in India proper by way of Mathurā, the second centre of the Kushān Empire, it radiated a much stronger direct influence upon the north and north-east. For this art, lacking in originality and derived from all manner of sources, was unable to prevail against the powerful and independent art of India, and gave rise only to a few stylistic variants. But the inhabitants of the countries situated in the region around the Pamirs, and those living in the adjoining Central Asian territories to the east, were at a lower level of civilization. For them Gandhāran art could serve as a model.

These peoples were, moreover, not compact nations with states and cultural patterns of their own. They were in a constant state of flux on account of the large number of migrations that were always taking place, as a result of tribes conquering one another, fusing with one another, or superimposing themselves upon one another. In a cosmopolitan social and spiritual climate such as this, so open to influences from all directions, Buddhism could play the role of an intermediary force. In this it was not alone, for in this melting-pot of peoples, cultures and religions an important part was also played by Manichaeism, as well as by Nestorian Christianity, both of which came from Iran. The path taken by Buddhism naturally led eastwards, since the routes to the west were blocked. The commerce that flourished between China and the Roman Empire as late as the 2nd century ceased almost completely. The powerful Sassanid Empire (226–651), with its Iranian nationalism, afforded no opportunity for religious or cultural proselytization, and later any spiritual movement extending across the whole of Asia was entirely blocked by Islam. Thus from the middle of the 1st millennium onwards there came about that fateful division between East and West, the after-effects of which are still felt today. The cultures of western Asia established a much closer contact with the West than they did with those of southern, central or eastern Asia. The only major attempt to overcome this dichotomy — the campaigns of the Mongols — had a predominantly destructive effect. The general picture was little affected by partial overlappings, such as the conversion of Indonesia to Islam, or its establishment in large parts of India. Between Gandhāra and eastern Asia, however, the routes remained open until the Arabs won their decisive victory over the Chinese army of the T'ang Empire on the Talas (751), and another breach was made in eastern Turkestan by the consolidation of the Uighur Empire. Between 755 and 840 this was the most important power in Central Asia. The western part of this area gradually became Islamic between the 8th and 10th centuries. In the eastern part Manichaeism was the main religion of the upper classes until this area was overpowered by the Mongols in the 12th century. The broad mass of the population, however, still clung to their Buddhist beliefs — hence the existence side by side of Buddhist and Manichaean finds at Turfan and Tun-huang. (No mention will be made in this survey of the third Buddhist movement, besides those to southern and South-eastern, and to Central and eastern Asia — namely, the spread of Tantric Vajrayāna from the 7th–8th centuries onwards from north-eastern India to Tibet by way of Nepal, where it developed into Lamaism; it exerted an influence upon the Mongols from the 13th, and especially from the 16th, century onwards. Tibetan art developed out of Indian, Nepalese and Chinese elements.)

The first important way-station on the route taken by Buddhist culture from Gandhāra to Central and eastern Asia — and the last stop for pilgrims coming to Gandhāra from this direction — was Bāmiyān. It was situated 200 km. from what is now Kabul, i.e. in the far north-west. This location can be explained by the fact that the most-frequented route passed through the Hindu Kush, since it was more difficult still to cross the Karakorum. Moreover, Bāmiyān lay at the point where two major routes intersected: one leading from China to Iran across the Pamirs, and the other linking the Indus valley with the northern part of Bactria. For this reason it became a flourishing centre of religious life as well as a focal point for travellers and merchants. Generous donations made it possible for impressive monuments to be built there by Buddhist believers, who outnumbered the adherents of Zoroastrianism. Into a high rock-face a large number of small

FIG. 34

caves were hewn, at various levels, extending for some two kilometres. They were connected by internal corridors and flights of steps, and served as chapels or meeting-places for monks. They are of the greatest interest from an architectural point of view, as well as on account of their painted decorations. Particularly impressive are the dome-like ceilings, the figures on which apparently represent the various quarters of heaven and the Buddhas who hold sway over them; some

PLATE
P. 142

of them form a veritable mandala. Between the caves two colossal Buddhas were carved, standing in deep niches. One is 35 metres in height and the other 53 metres. Both of them have been severly damaged, and there is now no trace left of the original coating, which was painted in polychrome, large areas being gilded. The faces were slashed off by Muslim iconoclasts. An idea of the original aspect of these colossi, and the dazzling effect they exerted upon pious pilgrims, can be gained from the description by Hsüan-tsang, a Chinese who still managed to see them during the first half of the 7th century, a few decades before Islam reached Bāmiyān. The life of this town was finally and totally destroyed by the Mongols in 1221.

The art that flourished here was Mahāyānist: this is evident from the links between Bāmiyān and Gandhāra, as well as from the iconography of the colossal Buddhas and the paintings that accompanied them on the walls and vaulted ceilings of their niches. In Mahāyāna art Buddha is conceived as a personification of the universe, as ruler of the world (cosmocrator), and the innumerable Buddhas of all ages are seen as his manifestations. The latter are painted at the side of the larger of the two figures; above the other is a moon-god in a quadriga. Its style clearly displays Sassanid influences, whereas other paintings exhibit greater affinity with Indian art of the Gupta period, evident in the flowing lines and more delicate modelling. A third group has a much more pronounced tendency towards schematization and abstraction. — not unlike the new interpretation of models from Late Antiquity in early medieval European painting. The lines are hard and austere, and preference is given to flat polychrome colouring; in this point there is a very close resemblance to some paintings executed shortly afterwards in Central Asia. A fourth style is closely linked to that of Gandhāran art, with its Late Roman influences. The plastic modelling of the two colossi also reflects two phases of Gandhāran style, one dating from the 3rd or 4th and the other from the 5th centuries. The links with Gandhāran and Gupta art on one hand and with Central Asian painting from about 500–600 on the other make it possible to give an approximate date for the Bāmiyān monuments: the relatively late period between 300 and 600.

Not very far from Bāmiyān is Fondukistan, a site which characteristically enough exhibits Sassanid influences in its painting, and Late Gupta influences in its sculpture. It is on account of the links between these works and those in the mature Indian classical style that Fondukistan can be assigned with some probability to a date not earlier than the 7th century; at the same time they provide evidence of the continual stimulus afforded by India. Together with the plastic works made of stucco at Hadda, which were likewise produced relatively late (4th–5th cent.), and blend so-called Hellenistic and pure Indian features, showing that these traditions lived on here, the Fondukistan finds are among the most original products of this north-western border area. Their subjects and types display the greatest variety and lively modelling of the pliable clay material, whereas in the north-western region there otherwise prevailed a general tendency towards schematization, perpetuating Gandhāran formulae. Appx. PL. 32

The cosmopolitanism evident at these westernmost sites of Buddhist art is also met with at other halting-places along the route through Central Asia, which were discovered between 1900 and 1914 in the course of the important expeditions undertaken by Aurel Stein, Albert Grünwedel, Albert von Le Coq, Paul Pelliot and others. Most of the treasures which they brought back are now housed in museums in London, Paris, New Delhi and Berlin. Although a large part of those in Berlin was destroyed during the war, fortunately a considerable number were saved, and most of the material had long since been made available to scholars in the form of magnificent publications.

These very rewarding sites were situated in oases along the northern and southern rim of the Tarim basin, where rivers and streams rising in the Tien-shan range in the north and the K'un-lun range in the south made it possible to irrigate the foothills, and thus to engage in agriculture with good results. Another source of economic prosperity in these towns was the trade carried on along the two routes mentioned earlier (the so-called 'silk roads'). This commerce flourished throughout most of the 1st millennium A.D. Chinese chronicles convey an impression of the wide range of diplomatic and commercial relations that were carried on, even as far afield as western Asia. The effects are well illustrated by the impressive achievements of Chinese art and civilization. Between the 5th and 10th centuries large numbers of foreign immigrants entered China, bringing with them exotic articles of daily use and luxury goods, as well as art motifs.

But it is the reports of the Chinese pilgrims which constitute the richest source of knowledge about life in these oases — and also about Bāmiyān, the sacred places of India, and even southern Asia. From their accounts many monuments that have

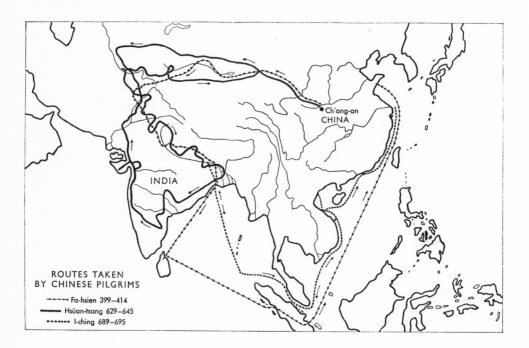

ROUTES TAKEN
BY CHINESE PILGRIMS

----▸ Fa-hsien 399–414
——— Hsüan-tsang 629–645
········· I-ching 689–695

since been destroyed can be reconstructed in broad outline, or an idea gained of the appearance of such damaged works as the colossal Buddhas at Bāmiyān; we can imagine the temples and monasteries bustling with activity, and fit this into the political, social, economic and cultural context — and all this over a period of some six hundred years (400—1000). The most important pilgrims were those who travelled to India between 400 and 700, for this was a period of decisive significance for the development of Buddhist art in Central Asia and China. Fa-hsien left China in 399 and made his way to Gandhāra by way of Tun-huang and Khotan, then following the river Ganges down to its mouth, since along its middle and lower reaches lay the greatest Buddhist sanctuaries: Bodh Gayā, Benares, etc. Then he continued his journey as far as Ceylon and 'Yavadvīpa (presumably Sumatra), finally returning home by sea in 414. This was a tremendous undertaking for a Chinese of that period. A similar route was taken almost simultaneously (404—424) by Chih-mêng, although after visiting the holy places at Magadha he returned home by land, following the same route as he had taken on the outward journey.

MAP
P. 66

The most important pilgrim of all, whose account is of the utmost value, was Hsüan-tsang (also called San-tsang = Tripitaka, and popularized by an imaginative 16th-century Chinese fairy-tale). He lived between 603 and 664 and spent no less than sixteen years (629—645) on his great journey. He broke it at important places *en route* for lengthy periods, often at the request of the rulers whose territory he crossed, who thought that the spiritual life and religious education of their peoples would benefit by his teaching and blessing. Hsüan-tsang made a number of detours from his route, and so came to know more areas than any of the other pilgrims. He even travelled through southern India, finally returning home by way of Central Asia, making a sweeping arc via the north-west that took him through Samarkand. In China he became one of the great 'Church Fathers' of Buddhism, above all on account of his indefatigable work as a translator of, and commentator on, the many sacred scriptures which he brought with him. His example shows how important the personal contacts were between this area and India, the birth-place of Buddhism. At the same time his journey, like those of the other pilgrims, served to pass on forms of ritual and works of art used in the sacred cult.

Similarly, many Indians, Iranians and inhabitants of Central Asia came to China and took part in translation and missionary work — particularly during the early period. The best known of them is Kumārajīva (344—413) from Kuchā. To him we owe the Chinese translation of a text that is of fundamental importance for Buddhist art, the *Saddharma-pundarīka-sūtra* ('Lotus of the True Doctrine'). Another great pilgrim was I-ching (635—712), who travelled to India between 671 and 695, going by sea in both directions: via Annam and Shrīvijaya (Sumatra) to the mouth of the Ganges, and from there by land to Pātaliputra, returning by the same route. Strictly speaking, he ought not to be mentioned in this context, but his journey was no less important than those of the other pilgrims in enlarging our knowledge of Buddhism in Indonesia and Indochina, about which he provided most useful information. The last pilgrim who made his way to the Holy Land was Chi-yeh (964–976). Later these journeys ceased to have any purpose, since Buddhism had become almost extinct in its native land, and was beginning to decline in China as well. Another reason was that communications by land and sea had by this time either broken down or become extremely difficult. By the year 1000 the golden age of Asian culture, when trade and the Buddhist religion gave it a cosmopolitan character, was over.

The oasis towns of Central Asia were, during those six centuries, both trading centres and the capitals of states and principalities of varying size. Those that were

MAP IV,
P. 311

of special importance for the history of Buddhist art were (from west to east): Kashgar, situated at the western end of the two routes; Khotan, on the southern route; Kuchā and Turfan on the northern route; and Tun-huang at the eastern end of the two routes. In the west — for example, in the Khotan area, the population was very mixed, with strong Iranian and Indian elements. Kuchā was inhabited by the so-called Tocharians, a people with blue eyes and reddish-blond complexion, who spoke an Indo-European language. Turfan was the centre of the Uighur Empire, which was of Turkic origin. These ethnic types are vividly represented in figures of donors in wall-paintings. The costumes they wear and the arms they carry also give us an insight into the culture and history of these peoples. These costumes and weapons vary from area to area, whereas the Buddha, of course, and the other sacred figures keep to the lines laid down by the Indian canon. All these centres had important monasteries, which were often magnificent establishments. The best known are the rock-cut sanctuaries, with their abundance of wall-paintings. As a result of gifts by princes and merchants they were splendidly embellished, and could often boast scholars who had something of value to give even a man so learned as Hsüan-tsang.

In this area of inter-cultural contact and cross-fertilization, as in Indochina, there is a border-line between the spheres of Hīnayāna and Mahāyāna. The western part, around Kashgar, and the northern part, extending eastwards beyond Kuchā, are areas of Hīnayāna; Mahāyāna, on the other hand, is to be found at places along the southern route, in particular Khotan, as well as in the north-eastern part around Turfan. This is clearly evident from the iconography of their art. With such close links existing between Tun-huang and China, it is not surprising that Mahāyānism should be dominant there. Together with the distinction between doctrine and cult there is a parallel distinction between spheres of artistic influence: the further west, the more pronounced are the Gandhāran, Iranian and Indian elements; correspondingly, the further east, the greater the influence of China. But it would be wrong to conclude from this that the 'western' styles were strictly linked to the Hīnayāna doctrine. We know that this was not the case: Gandhāra and Gupta art are essentially Mahāyānist in character, whereas the art of Iran is not Buddhist at all. We must therefore conclude that certain styles or repertoires of motifs are not directly dependent upon particular doctrines, and that the development of styles and motifs was frequently determined by completely different factors: by political, social and economic forces, and by mutual cultural links between the major centres. On the other hand, it is evident that in Central Asian art the 'western' elements (including the Indian ones, which were introduced from the west) are to be found on monuments of an earlier date than the 'eastern' (i.e. Chinese) ones. For the movement of Buddhist art is one from west to east, and the greater the distance in time and space from its country of origin, the Kushān Empire, with its main centres at Mathurā and Gandhāra, the more its models faded. The more Buddhist art falls within the orbit of Chinese culture, the more Chinese it becomes. Such Chinese influences were particularly marked on Central Asian Buddhism during the second half of the 1st millennium.

This development was of course not so straightforward and consistent as the foregoing might suggest. In the first place it must be pointed out that, of all the sites in Central Asia, the one where affinities with Late Antique models are most obvious, and which can be ascribed to the earliest date (i.e. the 3rd or 4th centuries), is situated some way to the east: Mirān, on the southern route, which is nearer Tun-huang than Khotan. The paintings discovered there, on the walls of a round chapel with a stūpa inside, show heads of Buddha and his disciples, as well as angelic putti, the style of which is evidently Late Antique. The smooth round faces and wide-open eyes, which have a visionary look in them, are somewhat reminiscent of mummy portraits. It is interesting to note that one inscription here mentions a painter by the name of Tita — apparently Titus, who may well have been a Roman from the Near Eastern provinces, or a citizen of western Asia, who had been trained in the 'classical' school. From the standpoint of subject-matter and style, of course, Mirān art is derived from that of Gandhāra. The monuments at Khotan, in the west — especially the many fragmentary relief figures on the stūpa at Rawak — also exhibit close affinities with classical Gandhāran art. On the other hand, pictures discovered at Dandan Uiliq, not far distant, are in a strikingly pure Gupta style — although it is true that among them, as in the entire Khotan area, there are some of different stylistic origin. At Tumshuk, north of Khotan and east of Kashgar, Gandhāran style is again predominant, and occurs in conjunction with influences from Fondukistan. Thus we see that in the western part of Central Asia, especially along the southern route, Gandhāresque styles prevail, and that Gupta, Indian and Iranian styles are occasionally added, but that this so-called 'western part' of Central Asia may extend quite far eastwards.

APPX.
PL. 5

69

Along the northern route, too, Gandhāran style survives for a long time, and penetrates far to the east (although this is more true of sculpture than it is of painting). Thus it is wrong to adhere to an over-simplified geographical and historical scheme. Gandhāran influence is found, for example, at Kyzyl (situated in the area of Kuchā, approximately half-way along the northern route) from about 500 to 650, but also even further east, at Khocho (Chotscho: now Kara-Chodja), in the area of Turfan, at a much later date — the 8th or 9th centuries.

APPX.
PL. 17

At times the style exhibits more or less 'classical' traits and has close affinities with that of Khotan; at other times it is a highly schematized and abstract variant of Gandhāran style (as, for example, at Shorchuk to the west of Khocho). Owing to the lack of suitable stone, some of these works were modelled in clay over a rough

PLATE
P. 143

frame of wood or reeds, partly with the aid of moulds, and then given a poly-chrome coating. From a stylistic point of view they seem to constitute a link be-tween Gandhāran style and the so-called Wei style in China (5th–6th cent.) —

APPX.
PL. 16-18

although they are of more recent date than the latter works are. Once again we may note that there is no direct line of succession from one style to another. The old Gandhāran types survived in Central Asia for a considerable length of time. Centres such as Khotan or Mirān were influenced by Gandhāra at an early date; and it was presumably from them that these influences were transmitted to the art of 4th- or 5th-century China, where they gave rise to something entirely different and definitely Chinese.

The paintings in the cave-temples along the northern route are more modern (by the standards of the time), and also more varied in style and more cosmopolitan than was the case with works of sculpture, which remained heavily dependent on Gandhāra, and were later influenced by China. The most important caves are those of Ming Oï, 'the Thousand Cells', at Kyzyl (Kuchā area), those at Bezeklik and Khocho (Turfan area), and finally those at Kumtura. The paintings are executed on walls covered with plaster, in a tempera technique. A real fresco technique is also to be found, but only on floors, where it was essential that the pigments should adhere firmly to the surface. These cells, hermitages and chapels were hewn out of the rock on the faces of sheer cliffs, and were embellished with works of sculpture and painting; frequently they had a stūpa in the shape of a pillar as their centre. The idea of rock-sanctuaries came from India — we see them, for example, at Ajantā — and was transmitted to this area by way of such centres as Bāmiyān. The Buddhist themes and iconography likewise remained for the most part identical with those in India. As well as illustrations from the life of Buddha and from the Jātaka legends, which were especially popular at Kuchā, there are scenes showing the Buddha preaching the doctrine surrounded by large groups of holy persons.

APPX.
PL. 3

Especially characteristic of Turfan are the Pranidhi scenes. These show Shākya-muni in his former incarnations encountering the Buddhas of that bygone era, worshipping them and vowing to them that he will also become a Buddha (*pranidhāna* = desire, vow).

Such themes as these, the representation of the 'Thousand Buddhas' of all aeons, and especially the large group compositions showing the Buddha in his realm in the beyond, accompanied by Bodhisattvas, monks and worshippers — all these show that Turfan art is typical Mahāyāna art. It stands in contrast to that found at Kuchā, in which such themes are unknown: in this case we are dealing with typical Hīnayāna art, where particular importance is attached to representation of 'the story', i.e. to narrative illustration of the Buddha legend. Here at Kuchā, the westernmost of these sites, in the earlier of the two phases that have been discovered, Indian styles at first prevail; Iranian elements, it is true, also occur in this phase, but mainly in ornamentation and in the portrayal of secular figures and their costume. Thus one may single out a 'first Indo-Iranian style' (approx. 500 A.D.), in which Indian elements predominate, particularly in the close relation between bodily forms and garments, in the sensitivity of the modelling, effected by linear as well as painterly means, and in the smooth blending of the colours, which are seldom contrasted sharply. On the other hand, in the 'second Indo-Iranian style' (approx. 600–700) this realistic and in some way 'classical' form is abandoned: there is a greater tendency to abstraction; the lines become harder and much more ornamental; the picture has a pronounced two-dimensional character and bright contrasting colours (frequently without regard for the natural colour of the object represented); and the modelling is schematic and devoid of realism. This style thus gives the impression of being typically 'medieval'; as an expression of a transcendental spiritual outlook it stands in contrast to the style of the first phase, which is more realistic, treats the subject-matter in an organic and animated fashion, and seeks to create a greater sense of illusion.

FIG. 64

At near-by Kumtura — an enclave of Mahāyāna art — we find Chinese influences at work in the 8th and 9th centuries which may have been transplanted from the Turfan area. For it was here, and especially at Khocho, the Uighur capital, and in near-by Bezeklik, that traditional Mahāyāna themes were strongly influenced by the style of eastern Asia — or to be more precise, that of the mature T'ang art (7th and 8th cents.). China extended its political power to this area during the first half of the 7th century, conquering Turfan in 640 and Kuchā in 647. This made it possible for Chinese art to make itself felt there, especially since it followed the Mahāyānist doctrine. Even when the Uighurs founded an empire of their own, in the 8th century, there was little change, since they acknowledged China's cultural hegemony. We find types of figure, ways of line-drawing, a range of colour, and a technique of modelling that in many instances closely resemble similar Chinese works, such as those at Tun-huang. Elsewhere, however — as, for example, in the Pranidhi scenes mentioned above — we encounter a strict stylization, hard

APPX. PL. 3

lines, and an ornamental tendency in composition unknown in Chinese art at that time. The idiom of Central Asia still translates Gandhāran formulae into its own dialect, giving these pictorial representations a singular character even where the iconographic and formal vocabulary is largely derived from China. Through the intermediacy of Central Asia this highly cosmopolitan T'ang art had itself assimilated all manner of western influences — that is to say, influences from Gupta India and from Iran. But this occurred a little earlier; and if we still come across typical T'ang art at Turfan between the 8th and 10th centuries (which is already a relatively late period for Buddhist art in China), this must be seen as a kind of backlash from the great wave of the Buddhist cultural advance. The chronological evidence does not support the view that Turfan works transmitted certain 'western' elements, or Buddhist art as such, to China. China had received its stimulus from the west much earlier — i.e. from the 3rd and 4th centuries onwards, when it had led to the development of Buddhist art in that country. These influences had then been absorbed and worked upon independently; and now, as a consequence of the political power it enjoyed, it was China's turn to exert a strong cultural influence upon those parts of 'barbarian' Central Asia that lay within its reach.

The caves at Tun-huang in particular show that the Chinese produced magnificent Buddhist paintings already at an early date — earlier than all the paintings that have survived between Bāmiyān and Turfan, except at Mirān. The roads to the west gained steadily in importance from the Han period onwards, and Tun-huang was a vital military, political and commercial centre on the Chinese border. As it grew in wealth, and as its cultural level rose, so Buddhism began to flourish as well. Between 250 and 500 A.D. religion and commerce joined hands to bring wave after wave of material and spiritual influences to China from the west. Early Chinese Buddhist art would be inconceivable without this stimulus, which in the last instance came from Gandhāra, but it cannot be explained solely as the fruit of these borrowings. In 366 the monk Lo Tsun had a vision of the 'Thousand Buddhas' appearing on the summits of the mountain peaks at Tun-huang; and subsequently one cave after another was hewn into the soft sedimentary rock there. They are situated over one another, in several storeys, and in former times were connected by wooden porches, galleries and flights of steps. At the end of the 7th century (in 698) 'more than one thousand caves' are said to have been in existence. This is of course a vast exaggeration, and is probably connected with the concept of the 'Thousand Buddhas', which gave to this spot the name Ch'ien-fo-tung ('Caves of the Thousand Buddhas'). According to the latest survey carried out under the auspices of the research institute at Tun-huang, the number of caves is 486. This is impressive enough, especially in view of the fact that all of them were painted throughout and frequently also furnished with large groups of sculptured sacred images.

The earliest paintings that have been preserved date from the latter half of the 5th century — immediately after the Chinese persecution of the Buddhist in 445-6. From that time onwards, right up to the close of the 8th century — i.e. into the later T'ang period — work was carried on unceasingly under the patronage of the Li, a family from which the local governors were recruited. Between 777 and 848, when Tun-huang was under Tibetan rule, little was produced, but immediately afterwards, once the Chinese persecution of the Buddhists in 845 was over, Tun-huang was again carefully looked after and expanded in size. It enjoyed the patronage of the Chang and Ts'ao families from 850 to 1035. The latter date falls some way into the Sung period, but although here as elsewhere in China Buddhist art now began to decline, the production of pious works did not cease. It continued until about 1300. In addition the older caves were restored at that time and again afterwards, although fortunately only on a limited scale. Thus Tun-huang provides us with an almost complete collection of Buddhist painting (and also sculpture) from approx. 400—500 to 1300, i.e. for a period of more than eight centuries. But this was not all: its discoverers, Aurel Stein and Paul Pelliot (from 1907), found, in a chamber that had been walled up for security reasons in or about 1035, a vast number of paintings on silk or paper in a fairly good state of preservation. Thus in addition to the great collection of wall-paintings Tun-huang yielded an equally valuable collection of scrolls and drawings. Most of these works originate from the T'ang period, an era from which only a few other original paintings have survived. The history of Buddhist art in China during those centuries would have remained much more obscure than it is had it not been for the discoveries made at Tun-huang. Prior to this extremely little was known about basic problems of Chinese painting during the 500 years prior to the accession of the Sung Dynasty: the development of landscape painting, of three-dimensional representation, or of the colour-schemes used, and much else besides. Among the drawings found there were also sketches for Buddhist paintings in which the outlines of the figures are perforated, so that the composition could easily be transferred to another surface with the aid of coal-dust or some such substance. This provides evidence of one of the methods used to transmit certain types of painting, styles or iconographic traditions across vast expanses of territory.

PLATES
PP. 38,
166, 195,
212, 254,
271

From an architectural point of view the caves at Tun-huang are much less complex than others in Central Asia. Most of them are simple cubic-shaped chambers, of moderate or small size. The largest chapels measure approximately 18 by 15 metres, and most of them are considerably smaller than this. They consist of a vestibule and the shrine proper. The latter has a ceiling that slopes upwards to a central square; along the rear wall there is usually a framed niche or a pedestal on which the sacred images are placed. Less frequently these caves have stūpa pillars in the centre, with an ambulatory around them, which was used in the rite of circumambulation *(pradakshinā)*. They have neither domes nor barrel-vaulting, but in some cases an imitation, painted with decorative designs, of the 'lantern cupola' found in other sanctuaries. Almost the only embellishment was in the form of paintings: the walls were divided into registers and panels, some larger than others, on which were painted, using a tempera technique on plaster, compositions of many figures. Very popular were countless 'realms of Buddha' and lengthy cycles of Buddhist legends (especially Jātakas). These colourful paintings must have made a dazzling impression upon the pious visitor: they will have stimulated his religious imagination, and made it possible for him to feel as though he were transported into a visionary realm, inhabited by sacred beings. Since the iconographic programmes came from China, this was pure Mahāyāna art. The ceilings, too, frequently feature representations of figures: in many cases imaginary celestial beings or the Thousand Buddhas, and above all ornamented panels resembling carpets. The latter were executed either in the austere, often geometric, style of the Six Dynasties period, which incorporated Iranian and Late Antique motifs, or alternatively in the exuberant and lavishly ornamented style of the T'ang or the immediately subsequent periods, with their motifs inspired by organic life.

PLATE
P. 274
By examining the treatment of identical or similar themes, we can obtain a clear idea of the course of stylistic development: in pictorial representations from the early phase, that of the Northern and Western Wei Dynasty (386—556) the style was still archaic, abstract, linear and two-dimensional; we can then trace all the changes that took place in the Sui and T'ang periods, right up to the Sung period. Of special interest are the motifs and elements from Central and western Asia (especially the Sassanid ones) that can be observed in T'ang painting, here as elsewhere; these are, however, neatly integrated into a harmonious whole. Of special interest are the differences between the Late T'ang style at Tun-huang and the corresponding paintings at Turfan, which modify this style in several respects and do not quite live up to its standards in point of quality. There may not be any outstanding masterpieces among the Tun-huang paintings, but technically and artistically they frequently attain a remarkable level. There are some vast, yet exquisitely worked, compositions which portray vividly the religious ideas expressed in them, and at the same time contain a wealth of most delightful detail. They combine lively draughtsmanship with brilliant but harmoniously arranged colours. For this reason one cannot under any circumstances consider Tun-huang art provincial or mediocre, despite the great distance that separated it from the main centres of Chinese art.

The numerous cave sanctuaries of Central Asia have yielded a vast treasure of art. The interest which these works have for the student of cultural history is often even greater than their artistic value. Their ramifications extend across the whole of Asia, from the Antique world and the Near East to China, and embrace the

PLATE 9 – FIVE-STOREYED PAGODA OF MURŌ-JI near Nara, Japan. Wood and plaster, with roofs made of cypress shingles *(hinoki)*. 9th cent. Length of sides at ground-floor level 2.48 m.; height, including bronze finial, 16.2 m. This finely-articulated Japanese pagoda is built in a strict yet elegant style. It is unusually small, but bears all the characteristic features of such edifices in eastern Asia. On the ground floor is a small chapel.

PLATE 10 – RĀHULA BEFORE HIS FATHER, THE BUDDHA. Medallion in relief, from the stone railing of a stūpa at Amarāvatī. Greenish limestone. Approx. 2nd cent. A.D. Diameter 86 cm. *Archaeological Museum, Amarāvatī*. The scene represented took place when the Enlightened One visited his family, whom he had formerly deserted: his wife Yashodarā (also called Gopā) presents to him her son Rāhula so that he may assume his father's inheritance; but the Buddha resolves that he should rather become a monk, thus obtaining a much greater treasure, namely Enlightenment and Nirvāna. His son thus becomes one of his disciples. In the midst of a lively scene with an abundance of figures the Buddha is represented in aniconic form, by means of symbols: the empty throne, the footprints with the Wheel of the Doctrine, and the Blazing Pillar (symbolizing the world axis), topped by the Wheel of the Doctrine and the trident representing the Three Jewels (*triratna:* the Buddha, the doctrine and the community). On the left Rāhula is being led in, raising his hands to his father in veneration; around this central group are worshippers. The relief – which originally may have had a polychrome finish and was partly gilded – is encircled by a stylized lotus.

PLATE 11 – BUDDHA SEATED ON A THRONE. FROM MATHURĀ. Fragment of a relief: red sandstone speckled with yellow. Originally the coating was probably polychrome, and in part gilded. 2nd cent. A.D. Height 68 cm. *Museum für Völkerkunde, Munich.*

One has to imagine the legs, in yoga posture. On the socle-shaped throne there were presumably figures of lions. The left hand rests on the left knee, while the right hand performs the *abhaya-mudrā;* on the palm is incised the Wheel of the Doctrine *(dharmacakra).* The closely-fitting garment covers the whole body except for the right shoulder, right arm and feet. The *ushnīsha* is in the form of a coiled top-knot, shaped like a snail's shell. On the right behind the Buddha is a worshipping deity (probably Brahmā), and on the left fragments of the corresponding figure (probably of Indra); at the rear there should be a large circular aureole.

PLATE 12 – BUDDHA PREACHING. FROM LORIYAN TANGAI, Western Pakistan (Gandhāra). Schist, originally probably with a polychrome and gilded coating. Relief, but almost in the round. 2nd–3rd cent. A.D. or later. Height 85 cm. *Indian Museum, Calcutta.*
The Buddha is seated upon the thalamus of a lotus and holds his hands in the symbolic gesture of teaching, of 'turning the Wheel of the Doctrine' *(dharmacakra-mudrā)*; with this iconographic type the right shoulder is usually bare. *Ushnīsha, ūrnā,* nimbus.

southern part of the continent as well, on account of the religious and stylistic affinities with India. Equally informative and varied finds, with equally extensive international ramifications, have been made in the fields of ornamentation and the applied arts. We can trace the path taken by some types and motifs all the way from Roman provincial art and from Mesopotamia, through Persia and Central Asia, to China and Japan. A similar picture results from study of the vast quantities FIGS. of manuscripts discovered at various sites in Central Asia — especially at Turfan 71-73 and Tun-huang. These are written in seventeen languages and twenty-four systems of script, and are of the utmost importance for the study of linguistics and the history of religion, since they give us an unexpected insight into such long-forgotten languages as Tocharian, or into such obscure religious faiths as Manichaeism. And it is a significant coincidence that the oldest extant printed book in the world, which in addition contains the world's oldest extant wood-cut, should have been discovered at Tun-huang. But it is no coincidence that this very book should be FIG. 1 a Buddhist one, for the discovery and development of the art of printing was very closely connected with Buddhism.

This five-metre-long scroll, kept in the British Museum, is printed with the

Fig. 1 — Frontispiece and beginning of text of a printed sūtra scroll from Tun-huang. Dated 868 A.D. British Museum. (Facsimile wood-cut by Jung Pao-chi, approx. 1960)

79

aid of wood-blocks, and contains one of the most important Mahāyāna texts: the translation of the *Diamond Sūtra*. This belongs to the group of *Prajnāpāramitā* scriptures, which were of fundamental importance for the whole world of Mahāyāna Buddhism. It was translated in China by Kumārajīva, who was of Central Asian origin. The Indian original was written in Sanskrit. The donor has added an exact date — 11.5.868 — at the end of the book, which was designed to multiply the blessings of the holy scripture, in the literal sense, by means of the printed word. The wood-cut frontispiece of the scroll shows a group of Bodhisattvas, celestial beings and monks, with the Buddha preaching in their midst. Its technical and stylistic maturity make it clear that the art of printing texts and illustrations was at that time by no means a novel discovery or at an experimental stage of development. Many other wood-cuts have also been brought to light at Tun-huang: namely, small 'icons' for distribution among the faithful. The printed and illustrated scroll is an impressive symbol of the crucial significance which Buddhism possessed, as a spiritual and artistic force uniting cultures in many widely-scattered areas of Asia, and also of the part which Tun-huang played as a pivot in this extensive traffic.

VI. CHINA

Our study of Tun-huang introduced us to an important monument of Chinese Buddhist art at the height of its development, when it had already come to exert an influence upon Central Asia, the area from which it had previously derived so many varied stimuli. But how did Chinese Buddhist art reach this level of development and become so influential?

The Chinese apparently became familiar with Buddhism during the 1st century A.D., during the period of the Han Dynasty. Although the well-known dream which the Emperor Ming had between the years 60 and 68 has been shown to be a pious falsification dating from the period between the 3rd and 5th centuries, we have indisputable evidence of the existence of Buddhist communities in the year 65 — although there were presumably only very few of them. In 130 we hear of Buddhist monks in the capital of Ch'ang-an. But they were still foreigners who attracted groups of lay followers; Chinese citizens were not permitted to become clergy until the 4th century. These foreigners of course came from the west, from Central Asia and in many cases also from India. The direction taken by Buddhism in China ran from the north-west to the heart of the Han Empire, the area around Ch'ang-an and Lo-yang, where Buddhist communities may have existed from the middle of the 1st century. From this area it continued along the ancient trading routes towards the south-east, to the province of Kiangsu, i.e. to the neighbourhood of Nanking. It was from here, in the empire of the Wu Dynasty (220–284), the power of which extended as far as Tongking, that trade was carried on with South-east Asia. Possibly some knowledge of Buddhism may have come from this area already at an early date, and a few isolated works of Buddhist art may even have reached China from this quarter as well. It is known that already during the Later Han period (to 220) links existed with Tongking and the northern part of Indochina.

The disintegration of the Han Empire was followed by a period of political chaos and spiritual confusion. This may have provided an environment suitable for the acceptance of the new religion, which introduced novel ideas and ways of thought. Chinese philosophy was at first concerned exclusively with the interpretation and ordering of the terrestrial world. Their concept of the universe embraced the two spheres of the divine and of the forces of nature, but it did not have an eschatology, or any means whereby the individual soul could attain salvation. It was unusual for Chinese brought up in this way of thinking to accept the Indian concept of karma, the doctrine of re-birth according to a man's good or evil actions, and of a path leading to salvation through and ultimately beyond the cycle of samsāra.

The foreign Buddhist missionaries and their Chinese followers at first sought to circumvent the difficulties caused by the alien character of their faith by linking it with certain philosophical ideas of Taoism. They also sought to emulate Taoism in the field of magical practices; indeed, Taoist terms were even put to use in translating Buddhist scriptures from Sanskrit into Chinese, which was a completely different kind of language. Afterwards Buddhists found it no easy matter to free themselves from the all too cramping embrace of Taoist ways of thought, which at first proved helpful but later on became more and more of a hindrance. In this they finally succeeded, once closer links had been established (particularly in northern China, during the 3rd century) with Central Asia and India, the source of their faith. This made possible a truer understanding of Buddhism and the Buddhist texts; it also fostered a desire to ensure that the various doctrines were pure and authentic. In spite of this, the typical adaptability of Mahāyāna led to a certain amalgamation with fundamental concepts of Taoist philosophy, which did indeed have something in common with Buddhism: for example, its concept of nature, of the universal Law (Tao), of 'Nought', and the desire to transcend the dualisms inherent in all empirically-perceived existence. This development was to prove of crucial significance for the whole future of Buddhism in China; and it was also especially instrumental in the later emergence of Ch'an (Zen) Buddhism.

From the 3rd century onwards Buddhist teaching, and with it Buddhist art, spread from Central Asia through northern China, especially in the cities, which were way-stations along the trading routes and at the same time centres of cultural life. At first Buddhist monks failed to gain any adherents among the educated upper class. This took place not earlier than the year 300 or thereabouts, and during the 4th century. At this time, owing to the conquest of northern China by the barbarian Hsiung-nu (311), many educated Chinese emigrated to the south, where the Eastern Chin Dynasty established itself (in Nanking) from 317 to 420 A.D. Here a rich culture flourished, in which ancient Chinese traditions were deliberately nurtured. Shortly after the year 300 — a decisive turning-point in the history of Buddhism — the clergy penetrated into the so-called 'gentry', the class of land-owning families, with large or fairly large estates, which played a leading role in politics, administration, and philosophy, as well as in literary and artistic life. This process virtually came to an end during the early part of the 5th century. This alone ensured that Buddhism was taken seriously and became socially accept-able — even to members of the ruling dynasties. The chief reason for this was that it effectively promoted the well-being of the state; another was that followers of Confucius welcomed the co-operation of Buddhists in their ancestor worship, which took the form of 'masses for the dead' and pious offerings to obtain salvation. It thus received powerful material as well as intellectual support. Generous donations made possible the building, between the 4th and 6th centuries, of Buddhist temples and monasteries on a lavish scale. Some of these early monuments in the south were magnificent edifices, but unfortunately only a few remains of them have survived. However, the latest finds from the Ch'eng-tu (Szechuan) area, which are ascribed to the 5th and 6th century and bear traces of influences from India and the Indian colonies in South-east Asia, lead one to hope that the large amount of work now being done by the Chinese in the archaeological field will fill many of the gaps in our knowledge. Some of the oldest Buddha images now known likewise originate from southern China (Szechuan, Chekiang), and date from as early as the 3rd and 4th centuries.

FIGS. 55, 56

In northern China Buddhism developed along somewhat different lines. It met with a particularly favourable response among the 'barbarian' foreign rulers: in the first instance with the Hsiung-nu; later, and more especially, with the Turkic T'o-pa. The latter, who founded the Northern Wei Dynasty (386-535), after undertaking campaigns as far afield as Kuchā, maintained very close links with Central Asia. In the 6th century they also received embassies from Persia, Kashmir, Gandhāra and India itself; by 400 or thereabouts the pilgrim Fa-hsien had already undertaken his great journey. Thus northern China was much closer to the source of Buddhist culture than the southern part of the country, which was more isolated in this respect. In this area the process was one of rapid sinicization, whereas the north experienced one wave of western influence after another. This is shown very distinctly in Buddhist art. Already during the 4th century there were almost two hundred monasteries at Ch'ang-an and Lo-yang. Here, thanks to the constant contact maintained with the west, and the collaboration of foreign monks, the translation of *sūtra* texts was carried on with great zeal. The Sanskrit terms were now rendered into Chinese with greater fidelity to the original meaning, free of any Taoist interpretation.

During the course of the 4th century Buddhism spread in this area as well among educated people who knew how to combine it with traditional Confucianism and Taoism — a combination that must have been most welcome to Buddhists. For it was at first by no means easy for them to vie with these philosophical doctrines, and with the whole social, ethical and political system of Chinese society, so tightly closed and inward-looking, so convinced of its own superiority; and Buddhists had to fight hard to justify their existence. The main reproaches levelled against them were: that they were politically unreliable and economically harmful, for the members of their monastic orders evaded the authority of the state, military service, labour obligations, and payment of taxes; they were unproductive, since they lived by begging and accumulated too much money by soliciting donations; that Buddhism was a non-Chinese, 'barbarian' doctrine, which had not sprung from ancient sacred Chinese tradition, but had been imported from less cultured foreign lands; and above all that it violated the fundamental principle whereby the individual should observe a model pattern of social behaviour, as a member of his clan, because the Buddhist divorced himself from clan ties — in particular through his celibacy — and renounced his duty to worship his ancestors.

Now it was of course true that Buddhist thought extended far beyond the sphere of this ideology, with its utilitarian outlook, enforcement of social ethics and emphasis on national culture. And this explains why Buddhism obtained such a large and loyal following, especially during these centuries of constant political insecurity, when men were questing for new solutions to their problems: for its new philosophical concepts and religious prophecies could greatly enrich and fertilize Chinese spiritual life, by opening up unexplored fields of logic, the theory of cognition, psychology and metaphysics; furthermore, Buddhism satisfied a desire for individual salvation, and in general raised Chinese thought to the high standard set by Indian philosophy. It was natural that the foreign rulers in northern China should support it precisely because it was so 'un-Chinese'. The very fact that it had come from the west, with which they maintained such close relations, was a point in its favour; since it did not serve the interests of any foreign political power, it was not dangerous; the fact that foreign monks were not allowed to belong to the Chinese social system made Buddhism a suitable religion for those who found themselves in the same position; since monks were free from clan ties, they were reliable; the unpopularity of the Buddhists among many followers of Confucius, who were also opposed to their foreign rulers, was another reason for supporting them; and finally, because its doctrine taught a universal religion and ethic, it contained none of the deeply-rooted Chinese ideology and tradition, so suspicious of everything foreign.

These considerations have to be mentioned here in such detail because Buddhism, on its journey through Asia, found itself faced in China with a critical situation. For the first time it had come into contact with a highly advanced culture that could boast of ancient traditions and a firmly established *Weltanschauung* and social structure, which was at first very different from its own, and in many respects even opposed to it. If those processes of adaptation and symbiosis which we have referred to had not taken place, Buddhism could not have been absorbed so easily, or have played the preponderant role it did. If the Chinese had not been ready to learn from abroad, and to harmonize what was alien with what was native, Buddhism might never have exercised the tremendous spiritual force it did in eastern Asia, and the history of this area would have taken a very different course. One may add that much Buddhist art would not have been produced either.

Thus in northern China, apart from two brief periods of persecution, Buddhism was fostered very energetically by the ruling dynasties (Northern, Eastern and Western Wei Dynasties) during the 5th and 6th centuries; and the rulers' example was followed by the Chinese themselves, who made generous donations for the building and embellishment of temples. But the most important monuments of Buddhist art to be found in the north are those associated with the court and the state power. Among them are the huge cave sanctuaries at Yünkang, Lungmên, Kung-hsien and Mai-chi-shan (latter half of 5th cent. to middle of 6th cent., and in part later as well). From this first flowering period of Buddhist art in China relatively little else has survived. In the first place we have stone sculptures, some of which have been broken away from the cave-temples, and others in the form of votive stelae bearing lavish representations in relief, which are of the utmost significance from the iconographic and stylistic points of view. They frequently carry precise dates. In the second place we have large numbers of bronze figures, mainly of small size, which in most cases were probably used for private ritual. This explains why they were more likely to survive than the monumental bronze figures used in the temple cult, the fate of which will be discussed below. These small bronzes were frequently of the utmost perfection, but often they were no more than handicraft products. They also played an important part in transmitting styles and rituals to other countries in eastern Asia.

Map
p. 153

Appx. pl.
14, 24
Appx. pl. 4

Plate
p. 144

Towards the close of this epoch, from about the middle of the 6th century onwards, the north and south began to exert a cultural influence upon one another. This foreshadowed the impending re-unification of the country under the Sui Dynasty (581—618). In art this process is reflected, for example, in the southern Chinese stylistic influences noticeable in the cave-temples at Hsiang-t'ang-shan (built under the Northern Ch'i, between 550 and 577). Since most of the works from southern China have been lost — and they must have been important ones — our evidence about the first flowering of Buddhist art in China comes mainly from the northern part of the country. It is the work of those non-Chinese dynasties during whose tenure of power, incidentally, the first caves at Tun-huang were built. In this so-called Wei style one can detect a very strong influence of Gandhāra, transmitted by way of Central Asia, and also of Iranian elements, but it is equally true to say that within a short span of time it became sinicized. This process may be clearly traced in the monuments mentioned — for example, in the type of figure and face, in the garments, and in the formal expression. This is closely connected with the move of the Wei capital to Lo-yang (494), i.e. the move of the T'o-pa rulers from the northern borderlands whence they originated to the south, into the heartland of Chinese culture in the Yellow River area. This change had important consequences: by about 600 scarcely any affinities with the original model can be observed. Similarly, during the latter half of the 6th century, when the links between northern China and India through Central Asia were interrupted, elements of Amarāvatī and Gupta art were likewise wholly absorbed. The latter had penetrated into southern China by way of South-east Asia (chiefly, it seems, via Funan, Champa and Tongking), and from there they reached northern China. It is only recently that scholars have begun to study these elements somewhat more closely.

As a result there develops, from the Sui Dynasty onwards, a mature style which effects a synthesis between all the foreign elements both from the west and from the south, which are worked upon in a creative fashion to form an independent style. This reaches its apogee, its classical era, in the T'ang period (618—906). The art of the Six Dynasties period had been archaic, austere and hard: its sacred figures were symbols, almost entirely abstract, remote from this world. Between the early

PLATE
P. 193

6th and the mid-8th centuries this art gave way to a completely different style. This style went through a process of steady transformation, involving many transitional phases, which resulted in a complete antithesis of the original form: perfect control of the human body and close familiarity with the phenomena of the empirically-

APPX.
PL. 31

perceived world made possible the organic treatment of form; there was a more natural relationship between body and garments; movement became freer, and the modelling more supple, following the living surfaces; the expression conveys delicate nuances of mood; and the whole figure is a rhythmic symphony of flowing planes and lines. But there is no 'realism' in the proper sense of the term: this feeling for living reality, this human element and sense of harmonious form, serve a religion that transcends all empirical reality, which sees in everything that exists the Absolute, the 'Buddha Essence' — a philosophical doctrine formulated by the most mature and comprehensive systems of Mahāyāna. It was supplemented by devout and more emotional veneration of the power of mercy and salvation possessed by Buddhas and Bodhisattvas, who no longer appear as impersonal symbols, but as kindly, though sublime, beings. T'ang art combines a human charm with a superhuman majesty; it has a suggestion of the transcendental about it. It expresses truly the mature Mahāyāna doctrine that had evolved during preceding centuries; it is the product of a search for a mature art form capable of conveying these subtle ideas.

As in India itself, and other Asian countries, so also in China the doctrines of Hīnayāna and Mahāyāna at first existed side by side. Already at the close of the 3rd century a number of texts of both trends appeared in translation. This was in the main due to Dharmaraksha (Fa-hu, active from approx. 266 to 308), an Indo-Scythian from Tun-huang who was educated in China. Among other works he translated a *Prajñāpāramitā* text which popularized some of the most important concepts of Mahāyāna. His work greatly assisted this trend to strike root in northern China. It was continued by Kumārajīva. From 402 onwards, with the assistance of a translation institute organized almost on modern lines, he did a great deal to introduce Mādhyamika, the doctrine of the 'Middle Path' founded by Nāgārjuna. At a very early date a translation was also made of the *sūtra* of the Lotus of the True Doctrine (*Saddharma-pundarīka-sūtra*; Chinese: *Fa-hua-ching*; Japanese: *Hokke-kyō*). This is a text which provided more themes than any other for early

Buddhist art in China, and became the main text of the T'ien-t'ai school. The MAP V, P. 311 latter was named after one of the sacred mountains of Chinese Buddhism, where its principal monastery was situated. Particularly under Chih-k'ai (or Chih-i, 538—597) it developed Indian basic principles along independent lines. It is the most comprehensive system of Mahāyāna Buddhism, which attempts to bring about harmony between all, even the most contradictory, doctrines; it may truly be called a scholastic *summa* from the standpoint of its aim as well as of its structure; for that reason it became an authoritative model for the whole of eastern Asia, and especially for Japan.

In addition to this strictly philosophical system, which provided the theoretical basis for Buddhist art in eastern Asia, there appeared at an early date the belief in the Buddha Amitābha, the Redeemer. It began to exert an influence in the latter half of the 4th century and was zealously promoted by Hui Yüan (334—417). According to this faith the pious believer is promised joyous re-birth in the 'Pure Land (*sukhāvatī*) in the West': it is thus a non-intellectual form of Buddhism, which involves an attitude of complete and enthusiastic devotion (*bhakti*). It was destined to have the utmost success throughout eastern Asia, and also had a great fertilizing effect upon art. This doctrine gave rise to one of the most magnificent concepts in Buddhist imagery: the splendid 'Pure Land' of Amitābha, who is represented amidst hosts of Bodhisattvas and celestial palaces — a vision which is frequently represented on the walls of the caves at Tun-huang; it exerted an in- FIG. 60 fluence as far afield as Japan, where it served as a model. This eschatologically- oriented piety also led to the worship of the Buddha of the Future, the 'messiah' APPX. PL. 24 Maitreya. He plays an important role in the Wei art of northern China — as, for example, in the caves at Yünkang, as well as in the corresponding phases of Korean and Japanese art. This belief flourished especially between the 4th and 7th centu- ries. We cannot discuss here the complex problem whether the concepts of PLATE P. 192 Amitābha and his realm, or the figure of Maitreya, reached China from the west (i.e. from the Near East and especially from Iran, by way of Gandhāra) as some modern scholars are inclined to believe.

During the late 5th century (in or about 475) the Indian Bodhidharma came to PLATE P. 251 southern China. Later he worked for many years in the north, where he died about 530. He is the most deeply venerated founding father of the eastern Asian form of Ch'an (Zen) Buddhism, and is the subject of numerous legends. He initiated a tradition that was to endure for centuries, gradually giving rise to many subsidiary branches, and is still a living force in the Japan of today. Ch'an Bud- dhism is the antithesis of the belief in Amitābha: man ought not to surrender to a blind trust in the redeeming power of someone else, i.e. of Amitābha and his assistant, the Bodhisattva Avalokiteshvara (Kuanyin); instead he should devote himself to the task of securing insight into the true nature of all things, thereby achieving a sense of inner freedom and of detachment from worldly things, by applying his own strength, in a constant life-and-death struggle, by ceaseless meditation and strict self-discipline, but without seeking knowledge in books or performing rites. In contrast to the easy and popular way this one was difficult and aristocratic, but in spite of this it had a wide appeal in China, Korea and Japan, particularly to men of strong character. In China the Ch'an school saw its greatest development under the T'ang Dynasty, but it also prospered under Sung rule, and it was then that it began to exert a real effect upon art, especially upon ink-painting.

PLATE
P. 232

The last of the great schools of Mahāyāna Buddhism to be introduced by teachers from India and Central Asia was the Tantric 'secret school' (Mi-tsung), or 'School of the True Word' (Chên-yên). It first became known at the beginning of the 7th century and flourished during the 8th and 9th centuries. Shubhākarasimha, Vajrabodhi and Amoghavajra, all of whom lived and worked during the 8th century, were the great patriarchs of this sect. It was they who succeeded in giving it a preponderant position by translating and interpreting the basic texts, and by handing on its ritual practices. In this case we are dealing with a Chinese variant of the Tantrism that developed in north-eastern India and reached Nepal and Tibet from the Pāla Empire; it is a combination of mystical speculations and magic secret rites, expressed in a complicated symbolism. These speculations concern the relationship between empirical reality and true essence, illustrated by a hierarchy of sacred figures, culminating in the Absolute (Ādi) Buddha. The meditations, rites and symbols serve to realize in practice the identity believed to exist between the believer and the Buddha Nature latent within him. A particularly important role in these meditations and rites is played by mystical syllables (mantra) and

FIG. 70
FIG. 53
FIG. 68

magical spells (dhāranī), symbolic characters (siddham) and meaningful gestures (mūdra). The name Vajrayāna is derived from its principal symbol, vajra, the 'thunderbolt' or 'diamond' which destroys everything illusory or evil by the power of Absolute Truth. It already acquired this name in India, where it developed by assimilating elements of Hinduism. Shaktism is likewise of Hindu origin. Its doctrines, practices and symbols, which are associated with sexual magic, came to play an important part in various countries of Asia, especially in Tibet; it did not, however, obtain any notable following in China or Japan.

Tantrism or Vajrayāna, which is incidentally also one of the basic principles of the T'ien-t'ai school, has produced what is probably the most comprehensive iconographic pantheon known in Buddhism. In this a large number of personages are

FIG. 58

arranged systematically, according to their ontological rank, in mandalas. This trend exerted a particularly fruitful influence upon art, but it may also have fettered it to a certain degree by the all too complex apparatus of iconographic rules which it introduced. Some other schools such as Amitābha and Ch'an Buddhism were strongly opposed to these ritualistic tendencies and to the pictorial and symbolic magic they expressed. These schools, too, provided artists with plenty of stimulus, and a vast repertoire of pictorial concepts as well. The result was that probably all the important religious concepts to which Buddhism gave rise found artistic expression in some form or other. Since all these schools developed in China between the 4th and 8th centuries, by the time T'ang rule reached its zenith all the philosophical systems had been fully assimilated and given artistic formulation. Since, in the ultimate instance, both the ideas and the pictorial concepts of all these schools originated in India and Central Asia, and were developed further, adapted and modified in China, Buddhist thought and art during the T'ang era summarizes, so to speak, the whole trend of development up to that time. And it is all the more regrettable that, shortly after this classical art had attained full maturity, it came to a tragic end — of which more will be said below.

By this period the spirit of Buddhism had penetrated deeply into the consciousness of all classes of the Chinese population and had become a firmly established part of its civilization. T'ang culture remained decidedly cosmopolitan in character right up to the mid-8th century, if not later. But at the same time it was completely self-assured, and confident of its own fully-fledged creative powers; it therefore had no difficulty in absorbing one wave of alien influence after another from India, western and Central Asia, and assimilating them smoothly into its own cultural pattern, which gained greatly thereby. Incidentally, these elements also included innumerable imported wares, such as handicraft products, and with these came a large number of ornamental motifs. These likewise greatly enriched the art of the T'ang period. For Buddhist sculpture it was of particular importance that there should be a new vigorous influx of Indian styles, especially those of the Gupta Empire in and after its phase of maturity. This is shown especially clearly in the caves at T'ien-lung-shan, the most important monument of this type in the T'ang period. The figures here have soft, rounded supple bodies, and are often depicted in dance-like postures (which are indeed derived from Indian dancing). This new wave of Indian influence was promoted by the journeys to that country of pilgrims, who had the opportunity to see these monuments with their own eyes, and also apparently by the import on a large scale of original statuettes, paintings and sketches.

PLATE
P. 193

APPX.
PL. 31

Monks from India and Central Asia constituted an important group among the foreigners living in the capital, Ch'ang-an — at that time probably the most civilized city in the world, with a truly cosmopolitan atmosphere. We encounter such monks, with their sharply-profiled, spirited, and often ascetic features, in Buddhist paintings such as those at Tun-huang, or at Hōryūji Temple near Nara in Japan which are representative of the advanced T'ang style. During the 7th century in particular there were also a considerable number of artists from Iran, India and Central

Asia who fulfilled commissions for Buddhist patrons; at least one of them, Wei-ch'ih I-sêng, emerges as a less nebulous figure than the others, thanks to a lucky discovery. The numerous monasteries with their temple halls were scattered across the face of the entire empire. Some of them, built with the aid of very generous donations, were of monumental proportions: majestic cult and assembly halls and stately towering pagodas, lavishly embellished with figures, ritual implements, wall-paintings and ornamental decoration. The architecture of the hall and the pagoda, which will be discussed in detail later, attained a level of great perfection, and the same was true of sculpture, painting and craft products. They reached a standard that was never surpassed in later ages, from the standpoint of technique and aesthetic quality as well as religious content. In painting great masters appeared who were to be venerated as genii in later centuries, such as Wu Tao-tse (active *circa* 720–760), of whose work no originals or reliable copies have, however, survived. Thus T'ang art came to serve as a model over wide areas of Asia by reason of its classical maturity and power of synthesis — just as was the case with the Indian art of the Late Āndhra or Gupta periods in South-east Asia. This was also due to the fact that the T'ang Empire exercised a magnetic attraction as a leading political and cultural power. Its influence upon the art of Central Asia has already been mentioned. Much more pronounced, and of greater historical consequence, was its impact upon Korea and in particular upon Japan. To both these countries it transmitted simultaneously the entire heritage of Buddhist cultural and artistic tradition. Right up to the 8th century both countries were willing pupils of China — at first under the Six Dynasties and later under the Sui and T'ang. Their early Buddhist art is thus a true echo of Chinese art, and their works form a sort of substitute for the lost treasures of Chinese classical Buddhist art.

For with the exception of relatively few remains (chiefly in the form of stone sculptures and small bronze figures, and the work executed at Tun-huang) this entire splendid achievement was destroyed during the persecution of the Buddhists between 843 and 845 — one of the worst catastrophes in the whole cultural history of mankind. In the middle of the 8th century the extensive contacts maintained with western and southern Asia were broken off, mainly as a result of the Arab victory over the Chinese army on the River Talas (751), in western Turkestan (in what is now part of Russia). At this time Buddhism was gradually losing its earlier important position in India itself. All this spelled the end of the cosmopolitan spirit that had prevailed hitherto in China. Another factor was the revolt of An Lu-shan (755), which undermined the power of the T'ang Empire. China turned in on herself and sought security by reviving her national traditions. Confucianism gained a new lease of life; Taoism made itself felt more strongly (not without having assimilated some elements of Buddhism in order to compete with it); and it was their adherents who, using all the old arguments against the Buddhists, prevailed upon Emperor Wu-tsung to prohibit this religion. As a consequence thousands of monasteries and temples were destroyed, with all the irreplaceable treasures they contained, and their considerable property confiscated. Hundreds of thousands of monks and nuns were compelled to return to secular life — i.e. to engage in 'productive' labour, pay taxes and bear progeny. The melting down of the gilded bronze statues yielded welcome metal for minting coins; wealthy people frequently invested their fortunes in this form. The Japanese monk Ennin, who was studying in China at this time, and found himself in the midst of the catastrophe, kept a diary in which he gives an extremely vivid description of the magnificence of classical Chinese Buddhist culture and art during its very last moments. It must be stressed, however, that these and other persecutions of Buddhism were not really motivated by religious reasons, rooted in certain dogmas or rituals; they were thus not due to a real spirit of intolerance, but were designed to strike Buddhism as a political, economic and social system that was alien to the Chinese. In part the persecutions may have been a reaction against a certain unhealthy hypertrophy of monasticism and the widely accepted practice of making donations to monasteries: so far as art is concerned, however, puritanical austerity has never proved fruitful. In any case we must reconcile ourselves to the tragic fact that we have lost the most important works produced at the peak of the flourishing period of Chinese Buddhist art and culture: the monumental bronze statues and wall-paintings found in the principal temples of the major cities and the important monasteries on the sacred mountains. Only very recently have discoveries been made at various isolated sites of remains of this art, which by some quirk of fate managed to survive the holocaust.

Although this prohibition was very soon rescinded (which could not, of course, restore any of the monuments, statuary or libraries that had been destroyed), Chinese Buddhism never really managed to recover from this blow, especially since its economic basis had been undermined. Shortly afterwards the T'ang Empire collapsed. When the Sung Dynasty once more brought about political unity and a high level of culture, Buddhism continued to exist — notably the Ch'an school, which was then the most prominent trend. But the principal spiritual force in China was Confucianism. It had been revived as a social and political ethic by Chu Hsi. True, it could only play this part by studying Buddhist philosophy thoroughly, and evolving a comprehensive metaphysical system; it was this that enabled it to compete with Buddhism. Wealthy educated people now took an interest in, and made donations to, Confucian rather than Buddhist schools and other cultural institutions, although on a much more modest scale. This was bound to have a considerable effect upon artistic production. On the other hand, among the broad masses of the population this repression of Buddhism caused it to decline to a relatively low level. It became closely associated with popular myths and cults, as well as with a vulgarized form of Taoism, in which belief in alchemy and magic played an important part. From the Sung period onwards the Buddhist pantheon was increasingly penetrated by Chinese gods and legendary figures, so that it finally 'was the victim of its own adaptability' (Wright). In this connection the figure of the Bodhisattva Avalokiteshvara (Kuanyin), for example, was re-interpreted in a specifically Chinese way. From the Mongol period onwards (Yüan Dynasty, 1278–1368) great influence was exercised by Tantric Lamaism. This developed in Tibet and spread widely, with official support, particularly in northern China; but generally speaking it produced no really outstanding works of Buddhist art.

After 1300 or thereabouts Buddhist art lost its vigour. Although we do have, dating from this late period, a large number of colossal temples, furnished with impressive images and magnificent decoration, these cannot be compared with the classical works of the earlier period, since their spiritual content is usually trite and their form more or less crude and superficial. There are only relatively few Buddhist works of sculpture from the Sung and Ming periods that still bear witness to the true Buddhist spirit and also develop new modes of artistic expression. Among them one may note the Arhat (Lohan) figures, which were especially popular

APPX.
PL. 34 among adherents of Ch'an Buddhism, since they conformed to the ideal that monks should attain the state of nirvāna by their own efforts.[17] In painting Ch'an Buddhism also registered important achievements, at least from the Sung period onwards, with its rendering of personages imbued with the pervasive power of Enlightenment; but these are surpassed by its landscapes, and other representations of nature, which suggest a sublime vision of the world. In this way, leaving out of account some stragglers of little consequence during later centuries, Buddhist art in China comes to a close with yet another magnificent peak of prowess: Sung ink-painting (in so far as this is Ch'an Buddhist in spirit). But this art form would have been unthinkable without a strong infusion of the old Taoist mystical view of nature. Ch'an art was non-ritualistic in character; it developed entirely out of direct personal experience, and therefore used quite different means of expression from those of its antithesis, classical T'ang art, which was markedly ritualistic, and developed out of Mahāyāna scholasticism. But the two had one thing in common: they both exerted a tremendous influence on Korea, and especially on Japan.

[17] W. Speiser, *China* (London, 1960), p. 160.

VII. KOREA

Korea's geographical position as such suggests that this country was fated to play the part of cultural intermediary. The fact that this process took place in a west-east direction may be explained by the difference in cultural niveau between the China of the Han and Wei Dynasties and Japan, at that time still in the earliest phase of its history, i.e. the late Neolithic. Korea was influenced by China in many crucial ways; it assimilated these influences, and then re-transmitted them to Japan. In this way Buddhist art was able to take a particularly important step forward on its great march through Asia. In studying the role of Korea as an intermediary scholars have usually failed to investigate the question of the part played by autochthonous, i.e. specifically Korean, elements. It is only very recently that a beginning has been made with research into the spirit of Korean art (as distinct from mere compilation of archaeological facts). This native element has hitherto been identified most clearly in Korean ceramic ware, especially in the type originating from the Koryo period (932—1392), which does indeed constitute one of the apogees of this branch of art — one which in any case reached the highest peaks of accomplishment in eastern Asia. It is not easy to do justice to Korean Buddhist art, especially its sculpture, because the Chinese prototypes upon which it was directly modelled, and which served it as a guide, are all as good as lost; thus it is hard to estimate the extent to which the Korean works were imitations or original products. It seems certain, however, that a work of art such as the superb Maitreya (or Shākyamuni) housed in the Duksoo Palace at Seoul expresses this specific Korean element distinctly; but for the present, in view of the lack of really comparable Chinese objects, it would be impossible to describe these features with due scholarly precision. For this reason we must be content with a brief historical sketch, relating Korean Buddhist art to that of China and giving it its place in our general survey.

PLATE
P. 192

Under the Han, between 108 B.C. and 313 A.D., there was a Chinese colony at Lo-lang (Korean: Nang-nang; Japanese: Raku-rō), in northern Korea. It has yielded finds in graves that were of the greatest significance for Han art. There also existed three Korean states during the first three centuries A.D.: one in the north (i.e. in the south-eastern part of Manchuria and in northern Korea), called Koguryo (Japanese: Kokuri or Koma); a second in the south-western part of the peninsula, known as Paekche (Japanese: Kudara); and a third in the south-eastern part, called Silla (Japanese: Shiragi). (We have given the Japanese forms of these names as well because they were generally used in the excellent works published by Japanese archaeologists on the excavations carried out before 1945 while Korea was under Japanese rule.) The origins of all three states, which can be dated back to the pre-Christian era, are shrouded in obscurity. They could only develop along more independent lines once Koguryo had occupied the Chinese colony of Lo-lang. It was no coincidence that this event took place almost simultaneously with the conquest of northern China by the Hsiung-nu. (Buddhism played no part in Lo-lang, since it did not spread extensively in China itself until the 4th century.) From this time onwards cultural development took rapid strides forward. Koguryo, which bordered on China, came most under its influence and also assimilated Buddhism earlier than the others (in 372). Paekche followed its example shortly afterwards (384), and finally Silla, which was in a more isolated position, did so as well (424; officially not until 524). However, the native religion — a combination of a cult of the sun, earth and natural forces with ancestor worship and shamanism — survived beneath the surface and still exists at the present day. A great influence was exerted by the Buddhist culture of the Northern Wei Dynasty which ruled at the same time, and it was this stylistic trend that influenced the earliest Korean works. Those that have been preserved are in the main small bronze statues. On account of its geographical position Paekche had maritime links with southern China, and cultural influences may have reached this area indirectly along this route from South-east Asia and India. But for the present we must remain content with hypotheses in this respect. This is particularly regrettable, since it was Paekche which (looking for a moment in the other direction) established contact with Japan, and in the mid-6th century transmitted to it closer acquaintance with Buddhist doctrine and art. From the point of view of art history this problem is rendered still more difficult by the fact that very few works of Buddhist art have survived from this period in Paekche (as is also the case in Koguryo). They were destroyed during subsequent wars with Silla. The consequence is that we have to draw inferences from works extant in Japan that are executed in the 'Kudara style'; and this style in turn is difficult to define, since there are no objects available from Korea that could serve as a means of comparison ... This vicious circle is a serious obstacle to any attempt to clarify the events that occurred, and the connection between them, in the history of early Buddhist art in China, Korea and Japan. In Koguryo, too, which experienced its golden age between approx. 550 and 620, only

PLATE 13 — STANDING BUDDHA. Bronze with a core of cement-like material; *ushnīsha* (in gold) added later to replace one in bronze; the right foot has also been replaced. Found in eastern Java, but probably produced in Ceylon. Approx. 3rd cent. A.D. Height 42 cm. *Museum van Aziatische Kunst, Amsterdam.*
Right hand in the *abhaya(?)-mudrā* (gesture of teaching), left hand in a variant of the *vitarka-mudrā* (gesture of teaching). The iconographic and stylistic prototype of this figure is to be found in the art of the Late Āndhra period at Amarāvatī (3rd cent.). In many respects this figure bears a resemblance to a huge bronze Buddha found at Dong-duong (Annam, approx. 300) which may either have been produced there or else may originate from Ceylon; the heads of these two figures, however, are distinctly different. The narrow face with the pointed nose looks southern Indian.

PLATE 14 – TORSO OF A STANDING BUDDHA. Red sandstone. From Mathurā. Gupta period, approx. 5th cent. Height 111 cm. *Archaeological Museum, Mathurā.*

The head may have resembled that shown in Plate 6 (Appx.). The right hand was presumably raised, with the palm facing outwards, in the gesture of affording protection *(abhaya-mudrā)*; the left hand holds the hem of the garment. The latter covers both shoulders and therefore hangs down in almost symmetrical parallel folds. Beneath this thin outer garment *(sanghāti)* one can see the under-garment *(dhoti)* shimmering through: it hangs down from the belt, reaching to the feet.

96

independent lines, basing itself upon the rich legacy inherited from China during earlier centuries, which had now been fully assimilated. In architecture and sculpture the classical style of Silla art continues, but shows a tendency to decline. Its most important achievement, which at the same time displays markedly independent features, is its ceramic ware, a thoroughly aristocratic form of art in exquisite taste, suggestive of a high degree of aesthetic refinement.

The last dynasty to rule in Korea bore the name of Yi (Chinese: Li; Japanese: Ri). Its hegemony lasted from 1392 until Korea was annexed by Japan in 1910. It banned Buddhism from court and educated society, and ceased to afford it any support, since it moulded the nation's social and spiritual life on a Confucian pattern closely modelled on that of the Ming Dynasty in China. Among the broad masses Buddhism lived on, but in an impoverished form; its spiritual level steadily declined, and it came to approximate ever more closely to primitive popular beliefs. It is clear that under these circumstances it was no longer possible to create any significant works of Buddhist art. Art developed along different lines. Those educated in Chinese Confucianism, who followed the Wên-jên ideal, executed paintings of a secular character, especially landscapes, which owed much to the close contact established with various Chinese groups and schools. The simple folk, on the other hand, produced ceramic ware of modest technical expertise, but which, judged aesthetically, had a charming rustic character; this ware either had bold painted decoration or was devoid of any embellishment whatsoever. From the 16th century onwards it exerted a decisive influence upon Japanese tea-ware, partly because entire colonies of potters were abducted to Japan. As a result of these political and cultural developments, after the 15th century Buddhist art was paralysed in Korea, as it was in many other Asian countries.

Buddhist art in Japan extends over almost the same span of time. The great phases of development were generally speaking much the same: it began with imitation of Chinese models; then attained an unmistakably independent character through sovereign control of the ideas and styles that had been adopted; and finally ended with a period of languid decline. This process was, however, much more clearly marked in Japan than in Korea, on account of the former country's greater creative potential.

VIII. JAPAN

In the beginning the Japanese led an almost isolated existence at a late Neolithic level of development. Writing was unknown, and religious beliefs took the form of the native cult of natural forces and ancestors later called Shintō. In the middle of the 6th century (552, perhaps as early as 538) — through the intermediacy of Korea, but with hardly any preparation, or at least after only sporadic contact — it encountered the mature and highly developed form of Chinese Buddhism, and thus found itself faced with a far superior civilization. It is known that Japan (by which is meant the aristocracy and the priesthood, which was of noble origin) adopted this new and alien pattern of thought with astonishing aptitude. During the 4th or 5th centuries some acquaintance may have already been made with Buddhist ideas and other elements of Chinese culture, but only on a limited scale.

Fig. 56 Buddhist figures have been found in Japan dating from approximately 300, featured on bronze mirrors of the so-called post-Han type; but it is doubtful whether their significance was really understood. The conversion of Japan to Buddhism got under way only after the mid-6th century. It was to a large extent the work of Korean monks and artists (architects, casters of statues, and painters) from Paekche, who either visited Japan or settled there.

A leading role in this process, and in the absorption of Chinese culture generally, was played by Prince Shōtoku (574–622). As regent of the empire and a devout Buddhist, he did a great deal to help the new religion, and the art and culture associated with it, to strike root in Japanese society. He had to overcome fierce resistance on the part of those who clung to native traditions and the Shintō cult in his efforts to establish this alien religion, and a system of administration and government based on the Chinese pattern. But it was only by this means that Japan could progress from an archaic to a high culture, and so become part of the Chinese cultural sphere and the Buddhist *oikoumene*. Shōtoku, one of the founders of Japanese culture, imbued with the noble spirit of Chinese ethics and Buddhist piety, still lives on today in the Hōryūji, near Nara. This is the oldest Buddhist Figs. 18, 42, 59 Plate p. 194 temple in Japan (and indeed in the whole of eastern Asia) of which the main parts have survived. It was founded in 607, and is a treasure-house of immense value for this early phase of art, of which so little has been preserved in China and Korea. The main image in this temple bears the date 623. It was the work of a caster of statues named Tori, who was descended from Chinese immigrants. It represents Appx. Pl. 25 a type of Wei art that became extinct in China: large bronze statues. Together with the large number of small bronze figures that have survived, and some wooden ones, it is in an 'archaic' style which served as the basis and starting-point of all subsequent development. Considering that this was the first phase of Buddhist art in eastern Asia, it attained a high degree of perfection in form, as well as in spiritual depth.

The city of Nara was laid out in imitation of Ch'ang-an in China, and was the residence of the emperor. It gave its name to the Nara period (8th cent.), when Buddhism almost became Japan's national religion, with the dangerous political consequence of excessive influence on the part of the priesthood. Encouraged by the pious zeal of the ruling dynasty, Buddhists were responsible for magnificent achievements in the field of culture and art: in architecture, sculpture, painting, and also in works of craftsmanship. Even today Nara is still the most impressive site in Japan that survives from this flourishing period of Buddhist art. Although most of its former splendour has vanished, it conveys a vivid impression of this religion and art. As direct contact now existed with China — a large number of Japanese monks and lay 'students' went to the mainland; similarly, Chinese clergy and artists came to Japan — Chinese influence came to prevail over Korean.

Artistic trends followed those of the T'ang style, which in the meantime had reached its apogee and become the model for the whole of eastern Asia. It was imitated so faithfully that Japanese works such as the large statues of Buddhas and Bodhisattvas executed in bronze or dry lacquer (in the Yakushiji, Tōshōdaiji and other temples) can more or less serve as a substitute for those Chinese works that have been lost. They were not, however, copied slavishly. The spiritual basis of this art was provided by the doctrines of all the important Buddhist schools that existed in T'ang China, the influence of which made themselves felt very rapidly in Japan. Among them was the Avatamsaka school (Japanese: Ke-gon), which also exercised great influence in Silla, and was particularly productive in the field of fine arts. It was to this school that the Tōdaiji belonged, the largest temple at Nara and the one most lavishly supported by the imperial house. The figure of its central Buddha — Vairocana, the primeval or all-embracing Buddha of the mature Mahāyāna doctrine — is a colossal bronze statue completed in 752, measuring almost 18 metres in height. It has since been damaged and restored several times.

Appx.
Pl. 20

There are other temples at or near Nara that also date from the 8th century, both as regards their layout and the actual buildings, some of which are still extant. Of the statues, both large and small, that were executed in bronze, clay or dry lacquer *(kanshitsu)* an amazing number of outstanding masterpieces have survived. At the Hōryūji the wall-paintings of the Golden Hall, executed in or about 710, represented the classical Buddhist art of monumental painting, of which no examples are left in China. Unfortunately in 1949 fire broke out as a result of negligence, and now only a few shadowy fragments remain.

Fig. 40

Plate
p. 194

In the treasury of the Tōdaiji, the Shōsōin, many thousands of craft products have survived, dating from about 750. They either belonged to the pious Emperor

Shōmu, or were used in the consecration ceremony for the Great Buddha, and are representative of the best work done in this field during the period when the T'ang style flourished — of which only a few examples have been preserved elsewhere. Some of them were imported from China; others were the work of Chinese artisans in Japan, or of their Japanese pupils. Here again the oecumenical function of Buddhism proved its value, for under its inspiration, in the service of its ritual and traditions works have been handed down that are in the universal style of the T'ang period, which in itself was linked in many ways with India, the Near East and Central Asia.

These epochs, which saw the absorption of vital and fundamental elements of Buddhism, were followed by the Heian or Fujiwara period. Heian is the name of the imperial metropolis, founded at the close of the 8th century, now known by its modern name of Kyōto; it remained the capital of Japan until 1868. Fujiwara is the name of the powerful aristocratic family which, with its extensive ramifications, practically ruled the country and shaped its cultural life from the middle of the 9th century until the close of the 12th. During this period, especially after contact with China had been broken off around 900, a synthesis took place between the Chinese Buddhist outlook and views that were indigenous to Japan. There thus

PLATES
PP. 163,
170

APPX.
PL. 29

developed a culture of the utmost charm and aesthetic refinement, which was promoted by the aristocracy. This culture finds expression in the poetic *Tales of Prince Genji,* and last but not least in art (Buddhist art included); it led to some highly accomplished works.

Buddhism continued to be the dominant spiritual force in the country. It enjoyed support from the leading families on a generous scale. Large monasteries flourished, especially those built at various remote points in mountainous areas, in imitation of those in China, such as Hiei-zan near Kyōto and Kōya-san. Here, and also in magnificent temple compounds in the capital and its environs, there developed a new universal system of doctrine and ritual. It was introduced from China by Japanese priests, among whom pride of place is taken by Saichō (Dengyō Daishi, 767—822) and Kūkai (Kōbō Daishi, 774—835). These doctrines — the T'ien-t'ai (Japanese: Ten-dai) and Mi-tsung or Chên-yên (Japanese: Mikkyō or Shingon) — carried to a climax the Mahāyāna interpretation of the world.

They also proved a most fertile source for medieval Japanese art. They solved in a simple and harmonious manner an issue that had been acute for a long time: the relationship between Buddhism and Shintō, the indigenous Japanese cult of natural forces, ancestors and the state. This solution consisted in interpreting the Shintō gods as incarnations or manifestations (*avatāras*) of Buddhas and Bodhisattvas, who were thought to form their original essence, their true nature. This helped to enlarge the pantheon considerably, to make the doctrine still more complicated, and the ritual harder to understand. However, there began to spread at this time a growing sense of decadence, expressed in the doctrine of 'the end of Universal Law' (or of the Buddha's doctrine), according to which the present cosmic age was in its final decline *(mappō)*. This led to the rise among the broad mass of the population of a simpler form of religious belief. It concentrated almost exclusively upon the Buddha Amitābha (Japanese: Amida) and the Bodhisattva Avalokiteshvara (Japanese: Kannon). Its adherents derived strength and hope from their belief in the redeeming power of this Buddha, and in their re-birth in his 'Pure Land in the West', the realm of bliss.

At first, during the early period and even well into the age of maturity of eastern Asian Buddhism, this doctrine was closely linked, in China as well as in Japan, with other systems. The most important of them was the T'ien-t'ai school, whose followers also devoted intense worship and meditation to Amitābha. It was only later that the Amitābha schools split away from the other schools. In Japan this occurred under the leadership of Hōnen (1133–1212). They objected to their highly complicated speculative and liturgical systems, which simple believers were unable to understand, and to their superficial expression in ostentation and splendour, justified by the doctrine that salvation could be attained through pious works, as distinct from mere faith. The iconography of the Amitābha cult, which was at first adopted from China (where it has left most traces at Tun-huang), received an important contribution from Japan, although this was a development of earlier ideas rather than a new conception: the vision of Amitābha (Amida-Raigō) PLATE P. 179 approaching in a hovering state, accompanied by his host of Bodhisattvas, and leading the believer to his realm at the hour of his death. This became a very popular piece of imagery. The main monument of Amitābha art preserved from the Fujiwara period is the 'Phoenix Hall' (Hōōdo, 1053) at Uji, near Kyōto. The whole temple depicts the palace in the Pure Land of Buddha on earth, and contains, in the cult statue of Amida, a masterpiece by Jōchō, the greatest wood- APPX. PL. 29 carver of his time, as well as lyrical and elegant wall-paintings on the theme of Raigō, executed in the delightful style of this epoch. Unfortunately the latter have been badly damaged.

This simple piety, which sought salvation in faith alone, was bound to have a strong appeal during the next major epoch as well. This was the Kamakura period (1185–1336), when an important cultural role was played by the new class of feudal warriors or knights *(samurai* or *busshi),* who were opposed to the court aristocracy at Heian, now in the process of gradual decline. The knights established a new centre of government and culture, situated far distant from Heian. It was at Kamakura, south of Tokyo and Yokohama. Even today it is still one of the most important centres of Buddhist art in Japan (the others being Nara and Kyōto). The art of this epoch was characterized by vigorous representation of reality. In Kamakura, as well as in ancient Nara and many other places, charming variants

PLATE
P. 164
APPX.
PL. 33

APPX.
PL. 35

of traditional temples were produced (some being built under fresh influences from Sung China). In particular many magnificent works of sculpture were executed. This was the last flowering of this branch of art in the history of Japanese Buddhism. Its climax came with the work of Unkei and his pupils, who were active around 1200 and during the first few decades of the 13th century. Seeking spiritual freedom and security beyond life and death, the knights felt themselves attracted, to a greater extent even than by belief in Amida, by Ch'an or Zen Buddhism, which had been introduced from China.

The first Zen monastery was founded in 1191 by Eisai (1141—1215), on his return from China, at Hakata in the south-western island of Kyūshū. Shortly afterwards a second one was built at Kyōto (Kenninji, 1202), and these were followed by many others there as well as at Kamakura and other places. Since then Zen has become one of the most important spiritual forces in Japanese life. From an artistic point of view its effects were not felt so strongly in the Kamakura period, but rather in the ink-paintings of the Ashikaga or Muromachi period (1336—1573), in which the culture of the samurai became reconciled with that of the court. An example of this is the extensive work done by the Zen monk Sesshū (1420—1506). This was the last time that Buddhism expressed itself in artistic form on a significant scale, for in Japan as elsewhere it was unable to produce anything original after the 16th century — except for a late flowering during the Tokugawa period (1603—1868), among Zen monk-painters such as Hakuin or Sengai, and the poet-painters. The latter produced paintings based on the *haiku,* a short poem consisting of seventeen syllables, which was greatly influenced by Zen. During this period Confucianism, vigorously supported by the Tokugawa shōguns (regents), also began to play an important part in the life of the burgher class in the fast-growing cities, which now became active culturally. At the same time Buddhism, aided by Zen, also penetrated into many aspects of the secular culture of the broad masses: into poetry, the tea cult, the building of houses and gardens, and flower arrangement. Thus modern Japanese art is extensively influenced by the Buddhist ideal of natural simplicity, sober restraint, and utmost candour. In many important spheres of activity it helped to eliminate the dividing-line between the religious and the secular.

In Japan the movement of Buddhist art through Asia came to a halt: for it could travel no further than the eastern limits of the continent. Japanese art, however, is not simply a late offshot, a marginal phenomenon. The impassioned piety and artistic talent found among the Japanese enabled their art to attain a high peak of achievement, on the basis of previous accomplishments in China and Korea, but of a specific character and of superior quality. Since Japan is also a country where love of tradition is extremely strong, it has constantly done its best to preserve and foster its cultural heritage, and to maintain consistency and continuity in its development. For this reason in Japan a great deal survived which elsewhere was neglected or destroyed much earlier. Japan has rightly been called a storehouse of eastern Asian culture, since it was here that the influences pouring in from Asia over the centuries were amassed and accumulated, with results that are still visible today. This makes it possible to gain many useful insights into the stratification of Asian culture. For example, the history of Asian music, of the theatre and of ritual dancing can only be studied with the aid of Japanese material, and one can find beneath the surface of Japanese culture strata bearing the imprint of Korean, Chinese, Central Asian, western Asian and Indian influences.

In the visual arts the position is similar with regard to sculpture, painting, and — last but not least — the wealth of motifs found in ornamentation. Each work of Buddhist art in Japan contains these strata, or at any rate some of them. Its spiritual basis is Indian, and this is also mainly true of its iconography, in so far as Chinese influences are not involved instead; its style is primarily and principally moulded by China — which of course had already absorbed features from India, western and Central Asia; but the mode of expression is first skilfully adopted, and then translated into a Japanese idiom, thereby obtaining an unmistakable *cachet*. Exact analysis of a Japanese work can often reveal the different strata concealed in it. Frequently the whole iconographic, symbolic and stylistic 'vocabulary' is derived from foreign sources — from various geographical areas and stages of historical development; and only the final artistic formulation, perhaps no more than a delicate nuance, is really Japanese. Nevertheless, it is this which makes it original and determines its quality.

Figs.
72, 73

IX. RETROSPECT

The history of Buddhist art covers an extensive area and a long period of time — roughly speaking, from the first centuries B.C. until approx. 1500. But seen as a whole it is one vast process, which takes its origin from a single source and then branches out in various directions. To a varying degree it stimulated the cultures with which it came into contact either to produce works of their own or to imitate those produced elsewhere. The main initial phases of this process follow one another in fairly rapid succession, so that already at an early date important works of Buddhist art appeared simultaneously in areas situated far apart from each other.

The preparatory period covers the last centuries B.C. and the first centuries A.D. Full artistic development begins with the production of the Buddha image and Mahāyāna iconography, i.e. in the 2nd and 3rd centuries. The period from the 2nd to the 5th–6th centuries includes the first creative epochs at Gandhāra, Mathurā, Amarāvatī and in the Gupta Empire. This period was the basis for everything that came later, and may be divided into two phases: an earlier, formative phase, during the 2nd and 3rd centuries, and a later phase, one of elaboration, lasting from the 4th to the 6th century. Already at this time, however, Buddhist art begins to evolve in Indonesia and Indochina. Owing to the speed with which influences were transmitted across Central Asia, even China reaches its first peak of achievement, so far as Buddhist art is concerned, between 300 and 600. Then the wave spreads rapidly to Korea (4th–6th cents.) and Japan (6th and 7th cents.). India is always one phase ahead: between 450 and 600–650, when the prevalent style in China, Korea and Japan was the 'archaic' style of the Six Dynasties period, which in the last instance originated from Gandhāra (although in a greatly modified form), India had already gone on to the classical Gupta style. Later, between 600 and 750, when this phase had reached eastern Asia, Buddhist art in India was already starting to draw to a close.

If in these formative epochs we can speak of a rapid sequence of events over wide distances, the second phase presents the impressive picture of a universal flowering of Buddhist art all over Asia. This art is mature and rests securely at the high level it has attained. Between 600 and 800, with the apogee in the 8th century, we find in India the Late Gupta and Pāla styles already showing slight signs of decadence, while in Indonesia this is the age of Central Javanese art, and in Indochina of Dvāravatī and early Khmer art, in China of classical T'ang, in Korea of Silla, and in Japan of Nara art. To mention a few examples: the Borobudur in Java, the caves at T'ien-lung-shan in China, the sanctuary of Sokkul-am in Korea, and the

Great Buddha of the Tōdaiji Temple at Nara: all these were built at roughly the same time, i.e. about the middle of the 8th century, and exhibit features associated with a period of high classic art. This is because they are mature works, built on solid foundations laid, and rapidly evolved, in all these areas during earlier centuries. In the 7th and 8th centuries there exists a mode of expression in Buddhist art, as regards both iconography and style, that is international — common to the whole of Asia — in which one may only distinguish regional 'dialects'. And everywhere this was once again a time for laying foundations for the future, evolving standards and establishing models on which subsequent generations and other regions could build, and which they could develop further with varying degrees of success and independence.

Whereas Buddhist art in India became extinct by 1200, if not earlier, in several other areas there followed, between 1000 and 1400, a third great phase of development — a late flowering. This was the case, for example, in Indonesia, in the Khmer Empire, in Sukhothai, in Sung China, in the Korea of the Koryo period, and in the Japan of the Fujiwara and Kamakura periods. But at this stage there no longer existed a universal style, inspired by classical Gupta in the Indian cultural sphere and classical T'ang in eastern Asia. Instead, regional characteristics emerge ever more clearly, and the lines of development tend to diverge further. Another reason for this is that in the meantime the contacts formerly maintained between all parts of Asia had become much weaker, or even had broken off entirely, with the result that it was only within a limited adjacent area that tangible influences were exerted

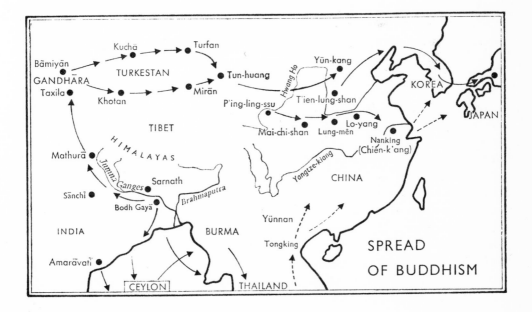

(e.g. between Sung China and Kamakura or Ashikaga Japan). Buddhist art of this phase still reached a high level where some potent spiritual movement existed, such as Ch'an (Zen) Buddhism. This did not exercise any real influence upon Chinese ink-painting until the 13th century, and was particularly effective in Japan between the 14th and 16th centuries. It enjoyed, incidentally, powerful support from those opposed to traditional art, which was essentially ritualistic and hieratic in character. In contrast Ch'an stimulates artists by presenting them with a completely different concept of the tasks and functions that a work of art should fulfil. Significant achievements are registered even in late phases, wherever a people that comes within the orbit of an ancient civilization subsequently produces characteristic types of religious imagery — as was the case, for example, with the Thai in the 14th and 15th centuries, whose art rested upon foundations laid by Dvāravatī and Khmer.

A few isolated exceptions apart, the last, fourth phase, from 1400 or 1500 onwards, is everywhere characterized by lack of originality, by a flagging of creative power, by a tendency to repeat classical models, and by loss of deeper spiritual content and true vitality in the mode of expression. This was due to the fate experienced by Buddhism itself, which outside as well as inside India was compelled either to yield gradually to indigenous spiritual forces, such as Hinduism or Confucianism, or else, in areas where it lived on as a popular or national religion, as it did in the Hīnayāna countries, to preserve itself by repeating old and proven formulae.

PART II

CHANGING TYPES AND FORMS

I. FROM THE STŪPA TO THE PAGODA

The chief Buddhist religious sanctuary is the monastery. It was here, cut off from the secular environment, that works of Buddhist art were produced. The monastic community, often small in numbers, is the basic nucleus of the whole community of Buddhist believers. Each monastery has to have a sacred centre, where rites can be performed. In the earliest times this was not a temple with a sacred image — for originally the Buddhist cult had no use for such figures, and it was only at a relatively late date that a need arose for buildings to house them; instead, this centre was at first a stūpa. In all the Asian countries monasteries, and later temples, went through considerable changes in design, but the architectural type of the stūpa remains basically the same throughout. Although at first sight it does seem as though it changes radically, these modifications are really no more than a metamorphosis of a type that remained essentially unchanged. The reason for this is that the stūpa was the Buddhist 'holy of holies', and performed this function over a long period of time, whereas all other religious buildings were added later in a secondary stage of evolution, and in a form that varied from one region to another.

The original meaning of the word *stūpa* was 'topknot'. This became 'vertex', then 'peak', and finally came to mean 'mound'. The stūpa is a sepulchral mound or tumulus, and dates back to prehistoric times. In its monumental form, as used for the burial of princes, it had the shape of a large hemisphere. Already at an early date this kind of tomb developed into a general commemorative monument, and was adopted by Buddhism as one of its main symbols, and as the centre of religious buildings. On one hand the stūpa was an actual sepulchre, placed over the earthly remains *(sharīra)* of the historical Buddha, of other holy men, or of legendary Buddhas of the past. A stūpa of this type is called *sharīraka* (= corporeal); is belongs to a special category if it is erected over the implements left behind by a Buddha, such as his begging-bowl *(paribhogika)*. On the other hand, a stūpa may be *uddesika,* i.e. a symbol to commemorate some sacred place; such stūpas are to be found at sites which played an important part in the life of Shākyamuni (cf. p. 26). Since the stūpa is primarily a sepulchral and reliquary monument, it always played a crucial role as the very symbol of nirvāna, of final redemption — in other words, the goal of every Buddhist. The close relationship existing in principle between the monument and the holy person concerned, and the relics of the

Buddha (each Buddha) embodying that person, has survived up to the present day.

The Indian ruler Ashoka, a pious promoter of Buddhism, is said to have erected 84,000 stūpas (84 is a symbolic figure) over the relics of Shākyamuni, scattered throughout his empire. Ever since a monument of this type has been an almost indispensable element of every monastery or temple in Asia, either in the ancient form of the Indian stūpa or its variants, or in the eastern Asian form of a pagoda. Although it was not strictly requisite for a stūpa or pagoda to contain a relic, this practice was widely followed. This was possible only if the term 'relic' was interpreted very freely indeed, and was extended to include sacred texts *(sūtras)* and spells *(dhāranī)* as the word-body of the Buddha, as well as statuary, representing his corporeal manifestations — all of which may afford such a sanctuary a holy substance. Since the Buddha was deemed to be present there, the stūpa became an object of worship already at an early stage in its development. An ancient Indian rite was carried out, in which the worshippers circumambulated the stūpa following the path of the sun (rite of *pradakshinā*),[1] making all manner of offerings and ritual performances *(pūjā)*. The stūpa never lost the shape appropriate to a free-standing monument, even when it formed part of a chapel or hall.

It may be assumed that stūpas were the earliest Buddhist sacred buildings, since the monks were at first content with temporary shelter in caves or lightly-built huts; it was not until much later, with the development of Mahāyāna, that the possibility and necessity arose of erecting proper buildings for ritual purposes, adorned with statuary. The first evidence we have of stūpas dates from the Ashoka period. The core of the Great Stūpa at

PLATE P. 1 Sānchī (no. 1) probably originates from the 3rd century B.C. In many Indian and Indonesian stūpas the original building was later encased in a mass of earth and stone; for when the building was enlarged (and its size testified to the piety and prestige of its patron) it was the custom not to commit the sacrilege of destroying the original monument, but instead to encase it in a succession of stone coverings, the space between which was filled in with earth and rubble. The stūpas at Sānchī are representative of the oldest type of such a structure. They are mainly still in their primeval state, despite the lavish decoration they bear. Upon the circular base *(medhi)* rises the massive hemispherical dome (*anda* = egg, i.e. cosmic egg; or *garbha* = womb) ; on the crown of the dome, which is slightly flattened, is a square stone railing *(vedikā);* from this there rises a short mast, sup-

[1] B. P. Groslier, op. cit., p. 214.

porting three flattened circular umbrellas *(chatra)*. Elsewhere this square railing is frequently given the shape of a box *(harmikā)*, topped by three or more slabs, one resting upon and projecting over the other. The umbrellas, which increase in number as time goes on, serve as a mark of distinction and honour, i.e. as a baldachin or canopy. These umbrellas and the mast supporting them came to play an important role in the gradual evolution of the type. On the base, around the hemispherical dome, is a narrow path, along which the procession moved *(pradakshinā-patha)*; it is accessible by two flights of stairs. There is a second path at ground level. The latter is enclosed within a tall stone railing *(vedikā)*, which isolates this sanctuary from the outside world as a sacred area, or *temenos*. Access to it is gained through four monumental gateways *(torana)*,[2] some ten metres in height, the uprights and crossbars of which are lavishly carved. The building faces all four points of the compass — a feature that is emphasized still more strongly in later stūpas. Monuments of this type have survived at Bhārhut and Sānchī, as well as other places, from the period between the 3rd century B.C. and the 1st century A.D.; there are also a few that are more recent. A lavishly decorated structure such as 'Stūpa I' at Sānchī took decades to complete. Of course we no longer see these monuments in their former splendour, with their smooth white or gaily-coloured plaster exteriors and sculpted decoration with polychrome painting. The massive drums of the stūpas frequently contain a system of concentric or radial supporting walls, the Figs. 2, 3 spaces between which were filled in with loosely packed material. In many cases the way in which these walls were arranged was determined by considerations other than those of a technical nature: they faced the different points of the compass, and represented rays leading out from the centre, in a diagram in the form of a mandala; this was not visible from the outside, but was of crucial importance for the sacred substance of the monument.

In many of the ancient Indian stūpas finds have been made of containers for relics, located in various parts of the building: on the base of the hemispherical dome, on its crown, or elsewhere. In most cases, but by no means invariably, they are found on the central axis. Fig. 2, the hypothetical reconstruction of the stūpa at Ghantashālā, near Amarāvatī, shows very clearly the core of such a monument: a medial axis, running all the way through the building, the top of which is formed by the mast with the umbrellas; it contains a cavity in which the relics were kept. In

---

[2] H. Goetz, op. cit., p. 58.

PLATE P. 35
FIG. 21

India and in other Buddhist lands these relics — the 'seeds' *(bīja)* in the 'womb' *(garbha)* of the stūpa — were usually kept in tiny receptacles made of very precious material, such as gold or rock crystal; these in turn were enclosed in other containers, which are of decreasing value. For example, there would be first a silver jar, then one of bronze, and finally a stone or ceramic urn. These containers in turn are frequently in the shape of a stūpa.

FIG. 2 ET SEQ.

All other forms of stūpa and pagoda, in all the Buddhist countries of Asia, are directly or indirectly derived from the basic type of building which we have described. The process of evolution is remarkably consistent, and affords a splendid example of the way in which an art type lives and grows, according to an inherent law dictated by its meaning, its purpose, and the cultural climate in which it exists. The first stages of

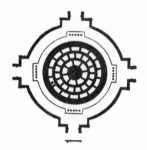

Fig. 3 — Ground-plan of Mahācetiya stūpa, Nāgārjunakonda. Diameter approx. 35 m. The cross denotes the site where the relic was found

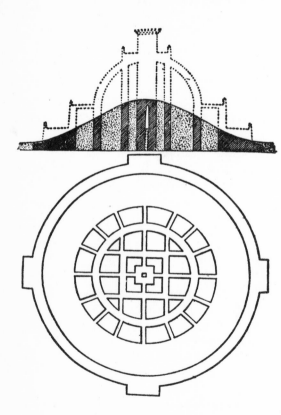

Fig. 2 — Ground-plan and elevation of the stūpa at Ghantashālā (southern India, near Amarāvatī): reconstruction

Fig. 4 — Votive stūpa from Gandhāra

Fig. 5 — Stūpa in a cave-temple at Ajantā

development may be seen to advantage at Gandhāra and its environs, as well as in the region of Amarāvatī, and in the cave-temples in western India (Bedsā and Kārlī: their dates must now be ascribed to the period 50—100 A.D. and approx. 120 A.D. respectively). At first the circular base is elongated, which gives the shape of a cylinder; it is then attenuated to a varying degree, and divided into zones. By this means the hemispherical dome is also raised, so that it becomes smaller in proportion to the base. These zones or storeys are set off from one another by cornices. At Gandhāra, under Late Antique influence, they are articulated in an architectonic fashion by means of pilasters, arcades and niches. Since by this time the Buddha image had been created, and Buddhist representational art had developed on a lavish scale, these rows of niches served to accommodate statues and narrative reliefs; the believers passed by them as they walked round in their processional rite, using them as 'stations' for meditation or prayer. The superstructure took on a more attenuated form; the umbrellas steadily increased in number and were crowded more closely together; the top gradually tapered off, until it eventually formed a cone, which was in some cases squat and in others slender, and consisted of a number of discs or layers. The dome itself may also be attenuated (as at Nāgārjunakonda and Ghantashālā, and in the 6th century, during the Gupta period, in the Dhamekh stūpa at Sārnāth). Alternatively, it may shrink to form a flatter structure, in the shape of a bowl turned upside down. The result of all these changes is a fairly slender tower-like structure, highly articulated, in which the original main part, the hemispherical dome, loses steadily in importance, while interest shifts to those parts that at first played a secondary role.

In addition to this a new element was added at Gandhāra already at an early stage: the circular base found in the earlier type was replaced by a square socle, which soon consisted of several layers, with flights of steps on all four sides leading up to the processional path at the foot of the stūpa proper; this socle is likewise articulated by pilasters, arcades, and niches with figures. On a substructure of this kind there rises the actual stūpa, with its cylindrical basements below and hemispherical dome above (e.g., Bhamāla near Taxila, Top-i-Rustam at Balkh, and the Rawak stūpa near Khotan). These popular types of stūpa were built between approx. 150 and 400 A.D.: they may be of monumental proportions, or alternatively small or average-sized votive stūpas; they are also to be found in

Fig. 5a — *Reconstruction of Top-i-Rustam stūpa at Balkh*

Central Asia. The motif of the square stepped socle with flights of stairs — which we find taken to an extreme monumental form in the Mesopotamian ziggurats — may have reached Gandhāra from the Near East by way of Parthia; in Gandhāran art it inaugurated a separate trend from approx. 100 A.D. onwards. But this type of stūpa also exerted an influence upon the east and south, making itself felt even far beyond the confines of India — as, for example, in the Borobudur in Java, or the non-Buddhist buildings in Cambodia,[3] where we find again the combination of a stepped pyramid and a crowning central shrine. It did not spread to the region of Amarāvatī, which kept to the customary cylindrical, moderately elongated, hemispherical stūpa, with emphasis laid on the entrances with their lavish sculptured decoration.

The stūpas in Ceylon and Indochina, and especially those in Thailand, are derived from the original type, with almost no regard for all the metamorphoses that took place in the north. Here, too, there is a tendency towards verticality, leading to impressively monumental forms, but for all the slight differences in detail there is no divergence from the basic type, consisting of hemispherical dome and crowning superstructure upon a rather low circular base; in the latter there are four entrances, facing the four points of the compass, as in the stūpa at Sānchī. The proportions between base, dome and crown are such that emphasis is laid on the dome, despite the strong tendency towards attenuation. A characteristic is the outline flowing smoothly from the top to the base, thus producing a concave moulding and an overall shape reminiscent of a (European) bell. We find it again in the Borobudur. This feature, and also the very slender needle-like spire, the elegant curve of the easily rising outline, yet the base firmly planted on the ground in a state of absolute repose — all these characteristics distinguish the southern Asian stūpa to a marked degree from the Indian as well as from the Far Eastern pagoda. The Lamaist pagoda of Tibet and China likewise still retains the essential characteristics of the old Indian stūpa, with emphasis laid mainly on the dome.

Another, completely different type of Buddhist religious monument in Ceylon and Indochina is the slender step tower, consisting of cubes placed one above the other, gradually decreasing in size. The walls are vertical, with niches framed by pilasters, in which large Buddha figures are placed.

PLATE P. 56
FIG. 24

PLATE P. 55

FIGS. 6-8

PLATE P. 36

FIG. 9

[3] B. P. Groslier, op. cit., pp. 96, 105.

This type of building is to be found, for example, at Wat Phra Pathom and Wat Kukut (Dvāravatī),[4] as well as in the Sat Mahal Pāsāda at Polonnāruwa, Ceylon, which originate from the 12th century; the latter was influenced by Dvāravatī. It is based either on the old architectural concept of the Khmer temple-mountain, or upon the tower with superimposed storeys, which had already developed in India; alternatively, all these types of building may be based upon the widely familiar idea of the stepped pyramid. These are problems that still await clarification. Some of these stepped towers in southern Asia even exhibit affinities with a much older type of the Chinese pagoda, dating from the 8th century at the latest, in which cube-shaped blocks are placed one upon another. An example of this is the 'Great Gander Pagoda' at Ch'ang-an (Sian-fu, 701—705), which likewise probably belongs to this widely disseminated type. But the pagodas of eastern Asia for the most part assumed quite different forms. (The word 'pagoda' has not yet been explained satisfactorily.)

How was this type of building, which appears to be so completely differ-

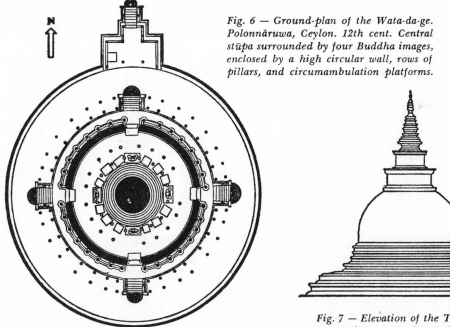

Fig. 6 — *Ground-plan of the Wata-da-ge. Polonnāruwa, Ceylon. 12th cent. Central stūpa surrounded by four Buddha images, enclosed by a high circular wall, rows of pillars, and circumambulation platforms.*

Fig. 7 — *Elevation of the Thūpārāma. Anurādhapura, Ceylon. 3rd cent. B.C.— 13th cent. A.D.*

[4] B. P. Groslier, op. cit., p. 209.

Fig. 8 — Stūpa at Ayuthia, Thailand.

FIGS. 10, 11

FIGS. 12, 18

ent from the Indian stūpa, derived from it? In actuality it was just a logical continuation of a line of development that was already under way: the tendency towards verticality was intensified by increasing the number of steps or tiers of the substructure, which gradually came to take on the character of storeys; the cornices dividing them developed into roof projections of varying width; the pronounced contrast between the base with sharply defined steps on one hand and, on the other, the hemispherical dome resting upon it, is resolved by assimilating the storeys to one another and placing them firmly upon each other to give a gradual tapering effect; the hemispherical dome of the stūpa becomes more and more dwarfed, until in the end it only exists in a scarcely visible rudimentary form, as the base of the finial — the mast with discs or rings, derived from ritual umbrellas. But it never disappeared completely, and may still be recognized under the bronze finial in some of the Chinese (and especially Japanese) wooden pagodas, where it occasionally occurs in conjunction with the *harmikā,* a box-like form which rests upon it. The orientation

Fig. 9 — Types of Lamaist stūpa in China

towards the four points of the compass, making for a square ground-plan, was already a usual feature at Gandhāra; the eastern Asian pagoda adopts this principle — if for no other reason, on account of the fundamentally cosmological Chinese world-outlook — although the number of sides is greatly increased; this eventually results in a building that is polygonal in plan, a type especially popular in China.

PLATE P. 57

It may be that the metamorphosis of the stūpa into the pagoda, with its several storeys, was also influenced by another type of building: the tower, of which there is already some evidence in Indian Buddhist art from the 2nd century A.D. onwards. It apparently existed along with, and quite independently of, the stūpa proper as a Buddhist cult building. What purpose it served is not yet clear. Reliefs at Mathurā and Amarāvatī dating from the 2nd or 3rd centuries feature towers of this kind. Like the Gandhāran stūpas, they have an architectonic articulation of the basement by means of cornices and niches, but lack the hemispherical dome and the combination, in a clearly visible form, of a stepped base and a stūpa in the old style. The terracotta plaque of Kumrahar, dating from the 1st or 2nd century A.D., shows a tower structure of this kind, with a cult image in the basement chapel (not representing, incidentally, as has been presumed hitherto, the Mahābodhi, or Temple of Enlightenment, at Bodh Gayā). It is topped by a superstructure just like the later eastern Asian pagodas, and already has the same proportions: as we can clearly see, it has the dwarfed hemispherical dome of a stūpa with *harmikā* and umbrellas. This type of building, like the Far Eastern pagoda, may thus be classified as a storeyed tower plus a stūpa. The problem is whether the tower part can simply be derived from an enlargement and enrichment of the base of the stūpa with its tiers, or whether we have to assume that some part in this development was played by an independent type of tower. The storeys shown on this plaque have a number of niches (as on the substructure of many stūpas at Gandhāra, and on some Chinese pagodas), in which no doubt Buddha figures were meant to be placed. Many later examples of towers of this type are also known, dating from the Gupta period in central and eastern India (4th–6th or 7th cents.). It is represented, in a monumental form, by the original Mahābodhi Temple at Bodh Gayā,[5] which dates from the 6th century, or even the 5th, but has been restored on several occasions. Nālandā, the city of monasteries, also boasted many magnificent towers, of which Hsüan-tsang says that they were lost to view in the morning mist. This type of building

FIG. 13

APPX. PL. I

FIGS. 14, 15

[5] H. Goetz, op. cit., p. 91.

Fig. 10 — Evolution of the Indian stūpa into the Far Eastern pagoda. From left to right: basic Indian type; later Indian type (Gandhāra); Chinese multi-storeyed stone pagoda; multi-storeyed pagoda with wood and tiled roofs (from a relief at Yünkang, northern China)

then develops into the *shikhara,* the tower-like temple of northern India. This served at first the Buddhist as well as the Hindu cult, but subsequently became entirely Hindu.

These later forms may, however, have been of little consequence in the actual evolution of the Chinese pagoda, for the latter already appears in a fully-fledged form shortly after 450 or 500, represented in the reliefs at

FIG. 11   Yünkang and Lungmên in northern China. Literary sources speak of multi-storeyed wooden pagodas from the same period, and indeed as early as the middle of the 4th century; and we know for certain that during

Fig. 11 — Evolution of Chinese pagoda from the Indian stūpa (after Willetts). From left to right: ceramic model of a watch-tower, Han period; Stūpa I at Sānchī; reliquary in the shape of a stūpa, Gandhāra; two representations of pagodas on wall-paintings at Tun-huang (5th—6th cents.); representation in relief of a Chinese multi-storeyed pagoda in Cave II at Yünkang (early 6th cent.). Cf. Fig. 10, text p. 117.

the 6th and 7th centuries a large number of pagodas, of most complex design and by no means 'primitive', were built in China, Korea and Japan. In Japan specimens are still extant from the 7th century (Hōryūji and Hōkiji near Nara). In China only one particular type of building recalls the late Indian prototypes: the pagoda on the Sung-shan, dating from 523; it has the same dense piling up of storeys, some similar details in the decoration, and especially a parabolic outline. In later times, too, pagodas were continually being built with their storeys and cornices set close together. It is not easy to see how this type derived from its predecessors in China and Gandhāra. It may have reached China directly from India, and thus represent a separate form of development, although the main route taken from Gandhāra lay through Central Asia, and it was this route that the evolution of the pagoda followed. In this way it was possible for architects in eastern Asia to obtain, through pilgrims and missionaries, a personal view of such monuments, or exact descriptions, or above all models and drawings of them.

One monument in particular, very well known from accounts by pilgrims in the 6th and 7th centuries, played a very important role. This was the so-called Kanishka stūpa at Peshāwar: a wooden tower, said to have measured 130 metres in height, resting upon a stone substructure 50 metres high (its foundations have been excavated, and the sides are 100 metres long), topped by an iron mast 10 metres high, with gilded metal discs. This was regarded at the time as one of the wonders of the world. It bore the most lavish decoration over the whole exterior, and inside was furnished with innumerable implements used in ritual and votive offerings. But unfortunately the form and construction of this building were not described in sufficient detail; and it may also be the case that the original Kanishka stūpa, from the 2nd century, looked quite different: that it was either a hemispherical stūpa with an attenuated base and long finial, or else a tall cylindrical stūpa, of monumental size, on a square multi-stepped terraced base. Another possibility would be a storeyed structure in wood, built around a circular stūpa. In any case we know that towers with rows of niches in their numerous storeys were widely spread over the Kushān Empire.

All this, however, does not provide an adequate explanation of the specifically Chinese features of the eastern Asian pagoda: its wooden

Fig. 13 — Tower. From a torana relief, Mathurā

Fig. 14 — Mahābodhi Temple, Bodh Gayā

construction (frequently translated into stone) and the characteristic shape of the roof. The basic type was surely imported from India or Central Asia, but not these details of the technique or the stylistic idiom. One might say that the Chinese translated the foreign architectural type into a form they had known for many centuries, which accorded with the principles of their own building techniques. But in addition to this two native types of building must have played at least a minor part. In the first place, we have in mind the multi-storeyed watch-tower, recorded in representations and ceramic models from the Han period, and authenticated in literature even earlier. This type of watch-tower was rectangular or square in plan, and had roofs that projected far outwards, supported by a system of superimposed bracket-arms, with small galleries in each storey. In the second place, we have in mind the multi-storeyed polygonal pavilion, which has a close affinity with the watch-tower. Chinese architects have always been fond of polygonal forms; and perhaps the great popularity of the pagoda may be explained by the fact that the stimuli from India encountered in China a related type of structure, in which the technical problems involved in a wooden building had already long since been solved — for in this case a circular building in the shape of the Indian stūpa was not feasible, and all the details were in conformity with Chinese taste. Later, between the 5th and 8th centuries, the Chinese pagoda became the standard prototype for those in Korea and Japan, but these two countries contented themselves with a far narrower range of types than did the Chinese.

There is a remarkable affinity in the basic features, although not in the details, between the wooden pagoda in eastern Asia and the so-called *meru,* which occurs on Bali, and also in Nepal and Burma. The latter consists of a slender tower symbolizing the structure of the world, with tiers of wooden roofs that project far outwards.[6] It may have developed from Indian models in the same way as the eastern Asian pagoda, but this is a question that still needs further detailed study.

The earliest identifiable type of Chinese pagoda confronts us from the reliefs at Yünkang and Lungmên (around 500). Later many variants developed, as did regional differences. Striking features include the pre-

Fig. 15 — Stūpa on top of the Mahābodhi Temple, Bodh Gayā

6 F. A. Wagner, op. cit., p. 193.
H. Goetz, op. cit., p. 140.

dilection for a polygonal ground-plan, the solid structure of brick or quarried stone, the wealth of sculpted decoration, the strong colour effect (produced by the tiles, which are frequently gaily coloured), and the boldly curved roofs — the latter found mainly in the south. With most of PLATE P. 57 the monumental pagodas either the whole structure consists of masonry, in which case the roofs project forward only slightly, in the manner of cornices; or it has a core of stone encased in a wooden structure containing galleries and roofs jutting far outwards. In each case the structure has, resting upon the small hemispherical base, a mast of varying height, which supports several discs or rings; these may be made either of stone or metal. Chains with small bells are often suspended from the top of the mast, which hang down to touch the corners of the uppermost roof. Other small bells, along the roof-edges of the other storeys, sometimes serve to proclaim the word of the holy doctrine further afield. The same purpose was originally served by the popular practice, which originated in India, of illuminating pagodas with large numbers of lamps, in accordance with their meaning as 'lighthouses of the doctrine'.

Chinese pagodas sometimes have in the centre a massive pillar running from top to bottom; around it is an ascending staircase, which can also FIG. 17 be used for the ritual circumambulation around the centre. Alternatively they may contain a shaft, in the centre of which is a Buddha figure, standing free for purposes of circumambulation; from this shaft narrow corridors like tunnels in each storey run towards the exterior, terminating in windows. In this solid structure spaces may also be left for other corridors, niches, and even small chapels which contain statues. All this shows that the pagoda is basically a plastic structure, expanding out in all directions from a distinct, self-contained core; it does not actually enclose an inner space, but is hollowed out as though sculpted. This core is formed by the Buddha statue or the central pillar, which rises from the base upwards through the whole structure, culminating in the finial. Built into it are the relics, and leaning against it are Buddha images, which face outwards, in the direction of the four (or eight) points of the compass, from the end of the radial corridors — as though to enlighten the universe. The Buddha statue, the body of Buddha in the form of a relic (either physical or spiritual, i.e. *sūtras* and sacred formulae), and the pillar in the centre may be substituted for one another, since they are identical in meaning. Many pagodas also have on their external walls a large number of Buddha figures in relief. These represent the 'Thousand Buddhas' of

Fig. 16 — Meru at Mandalay, Burma

the universe, which manifest themselves in visions to those who meditate upon them. In the course of time, however, the Chinese pagoda also began to play an important role outside the Buddhist sphere — in Taoist cosmosophy, and especially in geomancy (*feng-shui:* 'wind and water'). Innumerable pagodas are designed to exert a favourable influence upon the geomantic conditions of a particular place or area, by radiating their blessing over it. For this reason they blend so harmoniously with the landscape; often they serve to enhance and complement the natural beauty of their surroundings.

PLATE P. 58 In Korea two main types of pagoda are known: the stone pagoda already mentioned and the wooden storeyed pagoda. The former was inspired by China, but developed to a great extent along independent lines; the other type copied the Chinese model without, it appears, making any notable contribution of its own. In most important details the Japanese pagoda, too, followed foreign models: at first Korean, and later Chinese — although some remarkable special features of its own were added as well. The Japanese demonstrated their independence by the fact that they chose, from among the fairly extensive repertoire of types which China already had to offer during the 6th and 7th centuries, two for which they showed an almost exclusive predilection, and to which they adhered from then onwards. One of them, at least, they virtually monopolized: the square wooden pagoda with storeys and galleries (mostly with five, often with three, occasionally with seven or nine storeys). It has roofs that project far outwards, topped by a tall bronze finial, usually with nine rings; the same type also occurred with a polygonal ground-plan, but this was less frequent. This narrow selection was no doubt also due to technical reasons

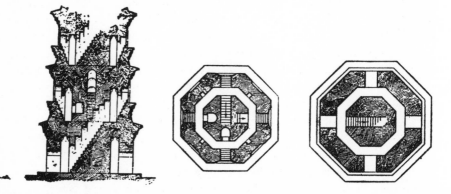

Fig. 17 — Ground-plan, section and elevation of the pagoda at Ling-yen-sse, Shantung, China. 8th cent., renovated during 11th cent. Height 51.60 m.

— to the considerable danger of earthquakes, which would destroy a stone building, and to the difficulty experienced in erecting polygonal wooden structures. But a contributory factor must have been the aversion on the part of the Japanese to massive compact stone buildings and their fondness for elegant and finely articulated structures. They paid no attention either to sculpted decoration or polychrome tiles, but limited themselves to painting, with the utmost restraint, the wood-work (mainly in red), the walls being coated with white plaster and the roofs covered with silvery-grey tiles or brownish shingles. This basic and most common type of Japanese pagoda was imported in ready-made form from China by way of Korea. We still have an extant specimen in the 7th-century Hōryūji pagoda, which is apparently based on a Korean (and, ultimately, a Chinese) one dating from the 5th or 6th centuries. A large number of pagodas continued to be built right up to the 18th and 19th centuries.

The most important single feature of the Japanese wooden pagoda is the central or 'heart' pillar. This was evidently likewise adopted from China, but there, in the case of wooden structures, it was only preserved in rudimentary fashion, i.e. in the uppermost storey. This pillar resembles a huge mast, resting upon a foundation-stone sunk deep into the earth. Its chief function is to support the very high (in the case of the Hōryūji pagoda, almost 10 metres) and heavy bronze finial, to take the weight off the finely articulated wooden structure, and to ensure that it is borne by the foundation-stone. Structurally, the storeys are not connected with the central pillar, but encircle it, leaving a narrow space around it, so that the complex structure is not endangered by the gentle shaking it is likely to receive in the event of a typhoon or earthquake. In contrast to the Chinese pagodas, the upper storeys are never accessible; their interior consists of a tangle of structural members, transverse beams, king-posts and rafters. Only the lowest storey contains a chapel, very small and cramped, but embellished with elaborate care and evoking a sense of intimacy: in it are four Buddha figures, or groups of figures, leaning against the central pillar; the walls and pillars frequently feature many painted figures of a mandala or some other iconographic programme. As in China and other Buddhist lands, so also in Japan there exists an 'identity' between the building, the relic and the Buddha figure: for in a depression in the foundation-stone, at the base of the central pillar, are the relics, like seeds, housed in several precious receptacles, one inside the other.

In addition to the multi-storeyed pagoda there is in Japan — as there was, to judge by pictorial representations, also in China — a special type of

FIG. 18

FIG. 21

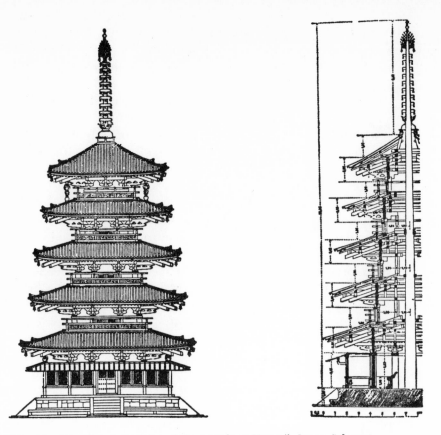

Fig. 18 — Elevation and section of the pagoda at Hōryūji, Japan. 7th cent. Height 33.55 m.

Fig. 11

Fig. 20

pagoda, usually called by its Japanese name of *tahōtō*, or 'Pagoda of Many Treasures'. This refers to the Buddha Prabhūtaratna ('Many Treasures'), who appears at a crucial point in the *Saddharma-pundarīka-sūtra*, the 'Lotus Sūtra'. Particularly from the 8th and 9th centuries onwards, this type of pagoda plays an important part in the esoteric Buddhism of the T'ien-t'ai and Chên-yên (Japanese: Tendai, Shingon) schools, symbolizing the absolute wisdom embodied in the Ādi-Buddha Vairocana. The image in which he manifests himself, surrounded by the Buddhas of the four points of the compass, forms the centre of a pagoda of this type. So far as its form is concerned, it took over more features from the ancient Indian stūpa than the storeyed pagoda did. On a square substructure, topped by a roof, rises a truncated hemisphere, coated with white plaster (a sham construction giving merely the outer appearance of a dome); it is derived directly from the main part of the Indian stūpa. It has a round neck with a small false gallery, over which is a square upper roof, jutting far outwards and crowned by the usual bronze mast with rings. In this case the 'heart pillar' rises only from a point above the chapel in the substructure; instead of a pillar (i.e. physically replacing it) stands the central statue of Vairocana on a socle, representing the cosmic mountain Sumeru. Old drawings and the traditional miniature *tahōtōs* FIGS. 19, 23 (reliquaries, sepulchres, etc.) show an uncovered cylindrical main part under a single roof: in this case the affinity with Indian prototypes, the PLATE P. 55 Amarāvatī and Gupta stūpas, is even clearer, and it may be assumed that the square wooden sub-structure, including its roof, was only added as a secondary feature, probably either for climatic or ritual reasons.

Throughout Asia the stūpa or pagoda is also to be found in miniature form. These objects serve various kinds of sacred purposes: as votive PLATE P. 56 offerings, sepulchres, reliquaries, censers, or for private devotion. Although these objects vary greatly in appearance, they are all derived from the FIG. 23 basic type of stūpa, prominence being given now to one element (base, dome or superstructure), now to another. One type of sepulchre and reliquary that is particularly popular in Japan is the so-called *gorintō*. FIG. 22 This is a close copy of a stūpa: its five parts represent, firstly, the five elements (earth, water, fire, wind and void), which are ultimately identical with Vairocana, the supreme all-embracing Buddha, and secondly (as the product of involved speculation), various aspects of existing phenomena

Fig. 19 — Tahōtō. Drawing from a Japanese mandala

Fig. 20 — Elevation and section of the Tahōtō. Ishiyama-dera, Japan. Approx. 1200. Height 15.50 m.

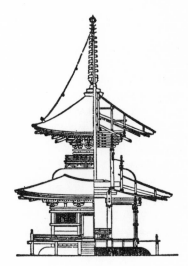

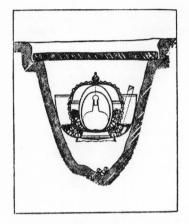

Fig. 21 — *Reliquary in basement of the pagoda at Hōryūji. Bronze bowl, bronze urn, egg-shaped receptacles of silver and gold, small green glass flask. Height approx. 14 cm.*

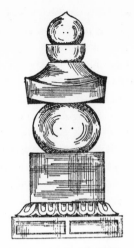

Fig. 22 — *Gorintō, Japan*

and absolute reality, and the degrees to which this reality can be apprehended.

Sacred buildings always have some deeper meaning. The Buddhist monument that we know as a stūpa or pagoda, in so many variants of a basically consistent type, is heavily laden with religious symbolism. In the form of a reliquary the stūpa, or the central pillar of a pagoda, encloses the body, the very essence of the Enlightened One: it represents the Buddha in the state of nirvāna, and itself becomes a symbol of nirvāna, i.e. of the Absolute. In Mahāyāna this concept is made manifest in the Buddha figure, which may thus serve as the centre of a stūpa. If, for example, we find a Buddha figure on stūpas in the later Indian *caitya* halls (as at Ajantā or

FIGS. 6, 31

Elūrā), or in representations of stūpas, it is invariably designed to be the central core of the monument in question, and not merely to stand *before* it, as part of its façade. Therefore a Buddha may form the centre of a pagoda — as is clearly shown in the *tahōtō* — and his body may constitute the central pillar. For the Buddha, and particularly the Ādi-Buddha Vairocana, as well as the axis of the stūpa or pagoda, are deemed to be in the centre of the cosmos; this cosmic axis rests deeply in the ground and rises, by numerous gradations, to the heights of heaven. Leading off from the centre are the four points of the compass. In Mahāyāna Buddhism these correspond with various Buddhas, and the structure of the stūpa or pagoda is also related to them: the ancient stūpa with its four gateways and flights of steps, and the eastern Asian pagoda with its design of square or polygonal sides.

This arrangement around the centre, closely related to the four or eight Fig. 58 points of the compass, re-appears in the mandala. It is not fortuitous that the ground-plan of a stūpa or pagoda often bears great affinity to this metaphysical world-diagram. In the interior of Japanese pagodas we find wall-paintings which, taken in conjunction with the cult statues in the chapel in the basement, form a mandala. The octagonal radiation outwards from the centre corresponds to the eight-petalled lotus, which in turn is a very ancient cosmic symbol. The symbol of the wheel — of the universe, world rule, and the doctrine of Buddha — also plays a part here. The pattern of the ground-plan is supplemented by the vertical arrangement: the terraces, tiers and umbrellas on the stūpa, and the storeys and rings on top of the pagoda, represent the cosmic spheres, superimposed upon one another: the spheres of deities and Bodhisattvas, which must be interpreted as planes of cosmic existence, and at the same time as *bhūmi:* stages of consciousness, meditation, maturation, and enlighten-

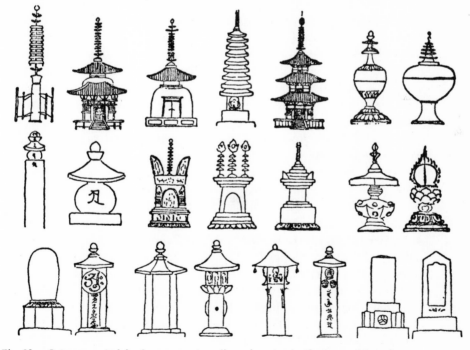

Fig. 23 — Japanese sepulchral monuments, reliquaries, etc., in the form of pagodas

ment; seen in the temporal sense, they are successive stages on the path to redemption leading ultimately beyond the limits of time and space. In this way the stūpa or pagoda takes over the ancient Indian cosmological interpretation of the world mountain Sumeru, which is related to the widely disseminated image of the cosmic pillar or tree — the latter, again, is 'identical' with the Tree of Enlightenment. This cosmic axis is repre-

FIGS. 2, 3

sented by the axis of the ancient Indian stūpa, which in many cases runs through the whole structure; but in some buildings it is merely repre- sented by the mast with umbrellas. On account of the importance attached to this symbolism, when building a pagoda great care was always taken to

FIGS. 17, 18, 20

retain the central pillar. Thus the characteristic Hīnayāna monument, which was originally linked with the earthly life of Shākyamuni and other holy men, gradually became an image of the cosmos that included all the ideas of advanced Mahāyāna scholasticism, and was also sometimes asso- ciated with the symbolism of universal rule, of happiness and prosperity.

The Borobudur in Java is undoubtedly the finest example of this type of

FIGS. 24, 25

building and its iconological symbolism. It consists of five terraces which are square in plan and sharply gradated; on these terraces rise three cir-

PLATES PP. 36, 139, 252

cular platforms, encircling a last and highest platform: in all there are thus nine tiers. The square terraces are surrounded by corridor-like ambu- latories, with high walls: these walls, stretching for several kilometres, are covered with reliefs and bear numerous figures of Buddhas. The circular terraces, on the other hand, are exposed to the sky: on them rise 72 (32 + 24 + 16) bell-shaped stūpas; in the centre of this colossal monument, and crowning it, is a larger stūpa, with a slender finial (which has been damaged). The general outline of the monument, despite the stepped terraces, forms a hemispherical dome, i.e. the original shape of a stūpa.[7] While the building was still being erected, probably for statical reasons, the lowest terrace was encased within a retaining wall, which at the same time provided a conveniently broad processional path *(pradakshinā- patha);* we know of this from the fact that some of the reliefs at the very bottom are unfinished. Access to the upper terraces is gained by means of staircases in the centre of each side. The combination of the two main parts — the square stepped pyramid, which faces, and slightly projects towards, all points of the compass, and the circular superstructure of the stūpa — recalls Indian prototypes, particularly those developed at Gandhāra; but here the basic scheme is greatly enriched.

FIG. 5a

Thus the Borobudur, like other monuments of this type, is both cosmic

F. A. Wagner, op. cit., p. 90.

mountain and stūpa, and at the same time has the form of a mandala. This is evident not only from the pattern whereby a circle is placed within a system of squares, but also from its expressly iconographic formulation. Each of the first four square terraces have, on each side, an identical Buddha figure, i.e. the Buddhas of the four points of the compass: in the east Akshobhya, with the gesture of touching the earth *(bhūmisparsha-mudrā);* in the south Ratnasambhava, with the gesture of granting a wish *(varada-mudrā);* in the west Amitābha, with the gesture of meditation *(dhyāna-mudrā);* in the north Amoghasiddhi, with the gesture of fearless-ness *(abhaya-mudrā)*. That is to say, they are arranged in a similar way as they are depicted in the mandala of Vajrayāna or the group of figures in the Tahōtō. The main Buddha of the mandala is Vairocana. In the Borobudur he appears in the first place on all sides of the fifth square terrace, making one of the gestures of teaching *(vitarka-mudrā);* the fact that he is to be found on all sides, and not merely on one, indicates that he is not related to a single point of the compass, and thus subject to spatial limitations. In addition, Vairocana is also represented seated upon the three circular terraces in the interior of all the stūpas, making a different gesture of teaching *(dharmacakra-mudrā)* — in other words, here he occurs 72 times in all. (The Borobudur has, or rather had, a total of 505 Buddha figures: 92 Buddhas of the four points of the compass, on each of the first four terraces; 64 Vairocana figures, on the fifth terrace; 72 figures in the small stūpas; and one in the great stūpa in the centre.) The state of preservation of the central stūpa is unfortunately far from good, and the unfinished Akshobhya (or Shākyamuni?) figure found there, with the *bhūmisparsha-mudrā,* is not likely to be the original one. It is an open question which Buddha this was, or whether the stūpa may not have been left empty. The iconographic programme as a whole would suggest the most sublime form of Vairocana, Vajrasattva; but it would also be appropriate for this closed chamber in the heart of the monument to be completely empty.

PLATE P. 139

FIG. 58

The central stūpa has a solid wall, whereas those of the 72 smaller stūpas are perforated with a lattice-like pattern, so that the Buddhas seated inside them are half visible and half invisible. This may perhaps be interpreted symbolically, as indicating the transition from the phenomenal world to the world of nirvāna, of imperceptible Void. For the pilgrim starts at the bottom, in the terrestrial world, and then, as he ascends the terraced path, reaches planes of ever greater Enlightenment, until he finds himself in the purity of the spiritual world. The lowest terrace (which was covered up later) had 160 reliefs showing the world of desires *(kāmadhātu),* which

PLATE P. 252

leads to all manner of misdeeds and punishments, and the purgatory in which men had to atone for their sins, i.e. the sorrowful cycle of *samsāra*, bound by karma. The next one, on the other hand, represents in 120 reliefs the life of Shākyamuni and the way by which he attained Buddhahood, i.e. liberation from the bonds of *samsāra* (according to the *Lalita Vistara*, ending with the First Sermon), and also the Jātakas and Avadānas — legends that tell of all his good deeds and his readiness for self-sacrifice during his countless former incarnations: this shows the believer the exemplary path which he may follow to Buddhahood. The reliefs on the next terraces illustrate *sūtra* texts, which likewise describe successful endeavours to attain the highest form of Enlightenment. They include the tale, in the *Gandhavyūha* (or *Avatamsaka Sūtra*), about the pious boy Sudhāna. The choice of this theme and its continuation in the legendary biography of the philosopher Asanga (4th century) show that the Borobudur is a monument of the Yogācāra or Vijnāna doctrine, founded by Asanga. In some respects it is related to the Mādhyamika doctrine of Nāgārjuna, and is thus of fundamental significance for the whole of later

Fig. 24 — Ground-plan of the Borobudur, Java. Length of sides 123 m.

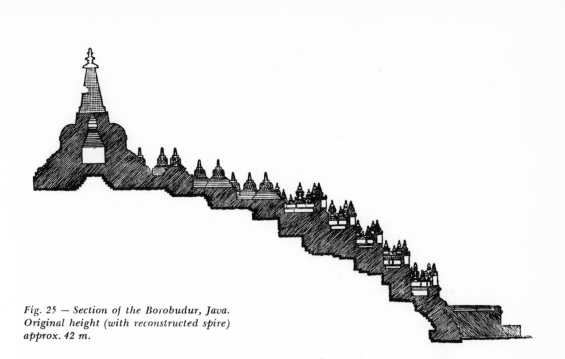

Fig. 25 — Section of the Borobudur, Java.
Original height (with reconstructed spire)
approx. 42 m.

Mahāyāna. These representations lead on naturally to the sphere of the upper circular terraces, and the central stūpa, which symbolize the 'Void' *(shūnyatā)* or 'Suchness' *(tathatā)*, the ultimate truth than can no longer be described or represented, but can only be recognized by a pure unconditioned conscience.

This sharp transition to a completely different sphere (despite all the gradual preparation for it) could hardly have been made more dramatic than it is here: first the reliefs depicting legendary themes afford a rich feast for the eye; then the Buddha figures become more spiritual; and finally they are only partly visible or not visible at all, hidden in the pure symbolic signs of the stūpas. The spiritual message is still more effectively conveyed by means of geometric forms: by the transition from square to circle. A square occupies certain definite limits in space, and symbolizes the phenomenal world, with its essentially relative and conditional nature. The circle is all-embracing, lacking in direction, and infinite; it thus symbolizes the Absolute, which may be attained in nirvāna. For this reason Borobudur has rightly been called a psychophysical pilgrim's path: the terraces lead the pilgrim through the different cosmic spheres, levels of apprehension, and stages of redemption. It is an initiation course into the Buddhist faith, executed in stone.

II. MONASTERIES AND TEMPLES

As we have seen, the stūpa underwent a metamorphosis in its form, yet remained basically unchanged. It continued to serve the same function and to retain the same meaning, despite the fact that it gradually accumulated more and more iconological symbolism. This shows very clearly the oecumenical character of Buddhist art. But temples and monasteries, on the other hand, are to a greater degree the result of the efforts made by particular regions to solve certain functional tasks by which they were confronted, and development of their form is only to a certain extent connected 'genetically', as it were. To put the same point differently: a Chinese temple or monastery does indeed have a functional affinity with ancient Indian monasteries, and must therefore observe certain common principles, but its design is derived from completely different prototypes; it develops along independent lines and appears in numerous variations in its form within the eastern Asian cultural sphere.

The prototype of the Indian monastery is a cave or hut, in which a single monk lived, especially during the rainy season. It was only gradually that groups of monks came to require accommodation in common. This was built around a centre where rites were performed, in most cases a stūpa; the basic element was the single cell, not a communal dormitory. From this resulted the typical Buddhist *vihāra*, such as we see plainly at Gandhāra (Taxila, etc.): an open court, rectangular in plan, frequently with a stūpa in the middle, and surrounded on several or all sides by rows of
FIG. 27 very simple cells. The latter could be replaced by niches or chapels that held small stūpas, and later images of deities (once the cult of such images had been introduced). A large number of votive or commemorative stūpas, varying in size, are frequently used to fill in the spaces between them.
FIG. 26 Occasionally the cells and chapels are arranged in a circle around the

Fig. 26 — Monastery at Taxila, Gandhāra: stūpa surrounded by cells

Fig. 27 — Monastery at Jamālgarhī, Gandhāra: stūpa surrounded by cells

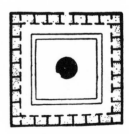

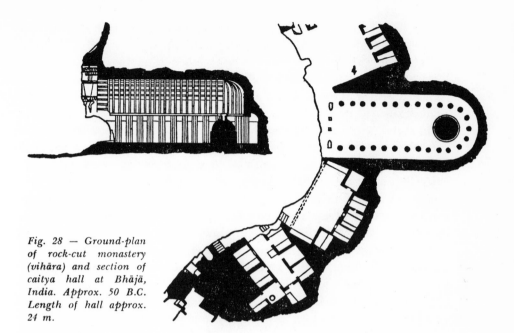

Fig. 28 — Ground-plan
of rock-cut monastery
(vihāra) and section of
caitya hall at Bhājā,
India. Approx. 50 B.C.
Length of hall approx.
24 m.

stūpa, as though it exerted some magnetic force of attraction upon them. Groups of cells of this kind, arranged around a central area, were sometimes hewn out of the rock. This practice was especially popular in western India. The effect produced is that of a complex of buildings thrust into the mountain side. Occasionally these subterranean monasteries even had several storeys, arranged around a central hall.

The Indian cave sanctuary has a long history — from the pre-Christian era to the Late Gupta period — and its influence also spread throughout Asia, as far afield as China and Japan, by way of Central Asia.

The layout of the old Indian *vihāra* is based upon that of a secular house. It is built around a courtyard, with a ring of cells facing inwards. Sometimes the court of the stūpa and that of the cells are separated, in which case they are situated either behind or alongside one another; there may also be fairly large assembly halls and refectories. On the walls of the monasteries at Gandhāra there were murals with appropriate representations, as well as stone or stucco figures and compositions in relief. The cave-temples at Ajantā, dating from the period between the 2nd century B.C. and the 8th century A.D., are especially lavishly decorated with magnificent murals. This is not only the most splendid monument of Buddhist painting in India, but is also very interesting to the art historian,

FIG. 29

PLATES PP.
97, 180

since the development of styles here extends over a whole millennium. The great monasteries are important centres of ritual as well as places of pilgrimage and learning; they join together a number of *vihāras*, or group them loosely around the central point where the rites are per-

FIG. 32

formed, which in the course of time came to include a hall to contain the cult image.

But this type of building already had a history of its own. The courts of the monasteries contained small niche- or chamber-like chapels designed to hold stūpas; and in the rock-hewn monasteries in particular there developed a monumental form known as the *caitya* hall. (*Caitya* is a general word for a sacred object, i.e. not only buildings, including stūpas, but also sacred trees, statues, etc.; it was only in a secondary sense that it

FIGS. 28, 30, 31

came to denote a shrine, chapel or temple.) In most cases this hall is rectangular in plan and consists of a nave and two aisles, with rows of columns and an apse. It is somewhat reminiscent of a Christian basilica, although for chronological reasons alone there can have been no connection between them. It also contains, as its sacred centre, a stūpa; the apse and side-aisles result from the circumambulation around the stūpa. This advanced form is apparently composed of an accretion of two distinct elements: a circular chapel with a stūpa and an assembly hall situated in front of it (prototype: Sudāmā Cave at Barābar, Maurya period). In these halls the false vault was hollowed out of the rock and had many transverse ribs affixed that were either made of wood or hewn out of the

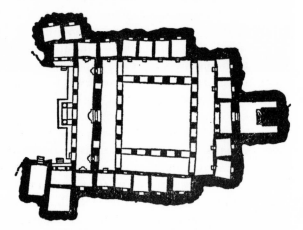

Fig. 29 — Ground-plan of Cave I, Ajantā. 7th cent. Length approx. 40 m. From left to right: vestibule; interior hall in the form of a courtyard, surrounded by ambulatory and rows of cells; on the right, chapel containing cult image. Cf. Plate 32

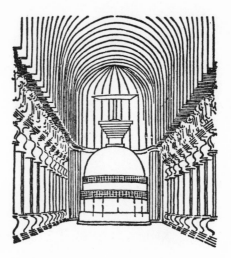

Fig. 30 — Caitya hall at Kārlī. Approx. 120 A.D. Height slightly over 15 m.

rock in imitation of a wooden building. The front was embellished with huge doors and ogee windows; Buddha statues and figures were later added as well. Among the most important *caitya* halls, situated near Bombay, are: Bhājā (approx. 50 B.C.), Bedsā (mid-1st cent. — close of 1st cent. A.D.), Kārlī (approx. 120 A.D.), Ajantā (Cave X: 1st cent. B.C.; Cave XIX: early 6th cent.; Cave XXVI: early 7th cent.), Elūrā (8th cent.; here there are Jain and Hindu caves as well as Buddhist ones). The hall at Kārlī, for example, measures 41 metres in length, 15 metres in width, and 15 metres in height. In some of these halls it is possible to trace clearly the stages in the evolution of the stūpa right up to the time when the Buddha image appeared on this originally aniconic symbol.

The *caitya* halls are thus an expression in monumental form of the primitive hermit's cave. The latter, which had no artistic form, was developed into a magnificent shrine where sacred relics could be kept and venerated. The two archetypes of the Indian sanctuary, the cave and the mountain, are represented by the grotto or cave-temple and by the stūpa; both of them develop along independent lines, but meet up on repeated occasions: the cave-temple contains a stūpa (a 'mountain' in a 'cave'), and the stūpa contains the hollow for the relic (a 'cave' in a 'mountain'). The tower-like temple which appeared later, first of all as a Buddhist and then as a predominantly Hindu building, is in turn a combination of these two types, for in this case the cosmic mountain is erected above the *cella* to hold the cult image or symbol. By nature the stūpa forms a self-contained monument, with a compact body, radiating outwards in all directions from the

Fig. 31

Figs. 30, 31

Fig. 31 — Caitya hall at Elūrā. Early 8th cent. Height slightly over 11 m.

centre; it is thus 'spaceless', also from the standpoint of its religious significance, since it represents the Absolute; only in a secondary capacity is it
associated with spatial elements, as when it becomes the centre of a *vihāra*
court or *caitya* hall, i.e. the life and ritual of a monastic community.

In addition to the *caitya* cave there also developed the free-standing *caitya*
hall, which is identical in plan but has a barrel-vaulted roof, built either
of stone or wood (there is a well-preserved one at Chezarla, dating from
the Gupta period). This very ancient type is represented, for example, in

FIG. 32   the *vihāras* at Nāgārjunakonda (2nd or 3rd cents.) where, in connection
with the development of the cult image, two chapels of this kind were
erected, facing each other as cult centres of equal status: one of them
contains a stūpa and the other a Buddha statue; they are built along one
side of the square formed by the monastery, the interior court of which
now frequently takes the form of a pillared hall with a wooden roof. (In
the so-called university at Nāgārjunakonda the statue contained a tiny
reliquary in gold.) Shortly afterwards, however, the *caitya* hall lost its
popularity. Later a tower was erected above the apse of these chapels and
the old *caitya* hall became an offering-chamber in front of the main structure, which was built over the holy of holies (the stūpa or cult image). But
the characteristic Indian tower-like temple was derived, not from this type
of building, but probably from independent free-standing towers, such as
we find recorded in reliefs already at an early stage: they are square in
plan and have a *cella* on the ground floor; to this *cella* are added niches or
chapels for cult statues, which face the four points of the compass. From

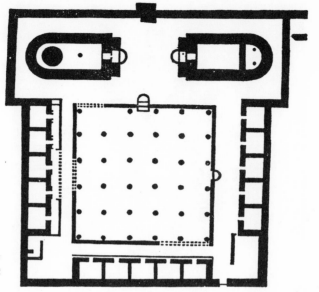

Fig. 32 — Ground-plan of
so-called 'university' at
Nāgārjunakonda

the Late Gupta period onwards, especially in north-eastern India
(Pahârpur and Mainamati in Bengal) centralized monuments of this kind
tend to be placed in the middle of a large *vihāra*, which sometimes consist
of buildings with several storeys. Here the old type of an open square,
with the monks' cells round about it, small enough to convey a sense of
intimacy, is carried to an extreme of monumentality: there are between
one and two hundred cells. But the tower-like temple with its cruciform
ground-plan did not develop to its fullest extent until Buddhism in India
came to be superseded by Hinduism; and for this reason we shall not
trace its subsequent history here.
In Buddhist countries other than India, however, it had important consequences. Just as the tower at Bodh Gayā was copied directly (although
with some variations in form) in Burma, Thailand,[8] Nepal and even in
China, so also this extremely popular type exerted a great influence upon   FIGS. 14, 15
Burma (Pagan temple), Cambodia and other parts of Indochina, and
— last but not least — upon Java. It was in this area that many *tjandis*
appeared, in either simple or highly developed form but based on this
design; the more intricate of them may take the shape of a mandala. The
word *tjandi*, like the word stūpa, formerly meant 'sepulchre', but later

[8] B. P. Groslier, op. cit., p. 213.

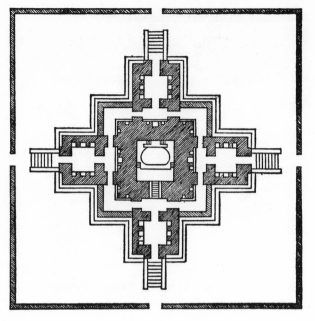

Fig. 33 — Ground-plan of
Tjandi Sewu, Java

came to mean above all a shrine or temple containing images of Buddhas
or deities; there was also a close connection with ancestor worship and the
idea of sacral kingship. The following are among the most outstanding
Buddhist *tjandis:* Tjandi Mendut (approx. 800) has in its central chamber
three magnificent *jīnas* (a Buddha preaching, with the Bodhisattvas Vajrapāni and Lokeshvara), and reliefs closely akin in style to those in the
Borobudur. Tjandi Kalasan (mid-9th cen.) contains one great stūpa
towering over groups of smaller ones. The central temple at Tjandi
Sewu (9th cent.) has side-chapels grouped around, but more isolated from,
the main structure; these chapels apparently contained the four so-called
Dhyāni Buddhas with Vairocana in the centre. Taken in conjunction with
many of the figures in the niches, they formed a Vajrayāna mandala; surrounding the central temple, in four squares, were single statues in 240
small shrines, topped by stūpas. Tjandi Jago (eastern Java, latter half
of 13th cent.) contains the main cult image of the Bodhisattva Amoghapāsha — a form of Avalokiteshvara, depicted with eight arms, which
appears in Japan from the 8th century onwards as Fukūkensaku-Kannon
(Hokkedō, Nara); it is surrounded by a pantheon of Tantric figures.
These Javanese buildings combine monumentality with noble proportions: great masses of stone and a wealth of decoration are handled with

APPX. PL. 8

FIG. 33

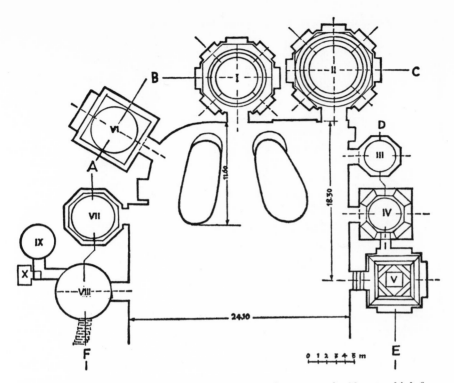

Fig. 34 — Ground-plan of rock-hewn chapels at Bāmiyān, near the 53 metre-high figure of the Buddha. Cf. text, pp. 64 f.

restraint, resulting in a classical beauty that is rare within the Indian cultural sphere.

The type of *vihāra* found in northern and north-western India was also adopted by Buddhist centres in Central Asia, although not universally, and it did not reach eastern Asia. A far more important role as intermediary between India and eastern Asia was played by cave-temples. There is a long chain of them running across the continent, from India all the way to China, passing through Bāmiyān, Kuchā, Turfan and Tun-huang; offshoots are found as far afield as Korea and Japan. We have already discussed Bāmiyān and the Central Asian temples, as well as those at Tun-huang. Most of them are of greater significance for their wall-paintings than for their architecture. So far as the latter is concerned, they do, however, continue many features of Indian cave sanctuaries, such as the central stūpa, often represented as a square central pillar; it bears cult images, and the faithful would walk round it in procession. In the

FIGS. 34, 35

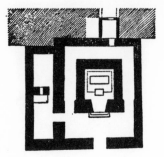

Fig. 35 — Ground-plan of a chapel like a cave-temple built against the rock face at Bezeklik, Turfan area. In the centre is a cella containing cult images, separated from the rest of the structure to permit ritual circumambulation

chapels at Bāmiyān, Kyzyl and elsewhere a striking feature is the popularity of the so-called lantern roof, a panel in the centre which takes the place of the cupola, and is filled in with squares laid diagonally across the corners, diminishing in size towards the top. At Tun-huang panels of this kind are frequently painted. This type of roof, as well as that in the form of a canopy, which occurs at Tun-huang and in temple halls all over eastern Asia, are both based upon the widely disseminated idea of a 'Dome of Heaven'. Thus in this case, too, the sanctuary, with a stūpa (or pillar) or cult images in the centre and a repertoire of figures painted on the walls, in its totality represents the cosmos.

PLATES PP.
38, 274

In China it is possible to trace fairly clearly the route by which Buddhism spread, following the line of cave-temples and the dates ascribed to them. They extend from the Six Dynasties period to the Late T'ang (approx. 350—900). In general terms, from Tun-huang (360—1300) its influence first spread to north-eastern China (Yünkang, approx. 460—540; I-hsien, approx. 490—530), then to the centre, around Loyang (Lungmên, 495—approx. 540 and 580—750; Kung-hsien, approx. 505—540); later some way to the north (Hsian-t'ang-shan, approx. 550—590; T'ien-lung-shan, approx. 540 — after 760) and to the east (T'o-shan and Yün-mên-shan, approx. 580—620), and finally reached the south-west, in the province of Szechuan (Kuang-yüan, approx. 720—895; T'ung-chiang, approx. 740—880). At an early stage, however, one line branched off to the south: it includes

MAP P. 153

FIG. 36

Fig. 36 — Ground-plan of Caves V—XIII, Yünkang

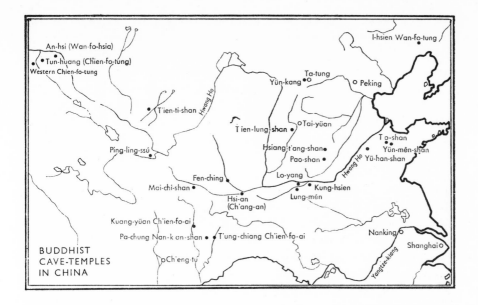

Map labels:
An-hsi (Wan-fo-hsia)
•Tun-huang (Chien-fo-tung)
Western Chien-fo-tung
I-hsien Wan-fo-tung
Ta-tung
Yün-kang •○
○ Peking
•T'ien-ti-shan
Hwang Ho
T'ien-lung-shan
○Tai-yüan
T o-shan
Hsiang-t'ang-shan•
Yün-mên-shan
Pao-shan •
Yü-han-shan
Ping-ling-ssú
Hwang Ho
Fen-ching
Lo-yang
Mai-chi-shan •
• Kung-hsien
Hsi-an
(Ch'ang-an)
Lung-mén
Kuang-yüan Ch'ien-fo-ai
Pa-chung Nan-k an-shan • •T'ung-chiang Ch'ien-fo-ai
Nanking○
Shanghai○
BUDDHIST
CAVE-TEMPLES
IN CHINA
○Ch'eng-tu
Yangtze-kiang

Mai-chi-shan (approx. 480—620 and later) as well as T'ien-ti-shan (approx. 500—535) and Ping-ling-ssu (approx. 500—535 and 640—730). Geographically, cave-temples of this kind are to be found in large numbers in the north-east and in the centre along the River Hwang Ho; chronologically, they date in the main from the period 450—750, i.e. from the golden age of Buddhist sculpture, the iconography and stylistic development of which may be traced in these monuments without interruption; the large number of inscriptions recording the circumstances of their consecration give us some idea of the changes that took place in religious beliefs, expressed in the waxing and waning popularity of certain Buddhas and Bodhisattvas.

In their interior the caves are usually covered with groups of figures, reliefs and ornaments carved out of the living rock; there is in many cases no iconographic system, but amidst the confusion one's eye is caught by spectacular groups in niches, and (at Yünkang and Lungmên in particular) by colossal figures of the Buddha, shown in a seated posture with the accompanying figures represented standing. Here we have a survival of the ancient notion of the all-embracing Buddha, or cosmocrator; this idea also inspired the production of colossi in India, Ceylon, Thailand, Burma and elsewhere, and at the western end of the Buddhist *oikoumene* is represented by the Buddha figures at Bāmiyān. But it seems doubtful whether Bāmiyān served as a model for Yünkang: both monuments may have been carved at about the same time, and the Chinese appear to have

PLATE P. 142

had no knowledge of Bāmiyān; it is more likely that the colossal statue of Maitreya at Darel (on the upper reaches of the Indus, beginning of 3rd cent.?). of which we have literary evidence, served as a source.

FIG. 37   In Korea cave-temples of this type are represented by Sokkul-am, where a huge statue of Shākyamuni forms the centre of a circular chapel. The faithful may walk round it in procession, and it is circumambulated, as it were, by the Bodhisattvas and Arhats featured in the reliefs on the walls. In Japan only unimportant cave sanctuaries were built, usually rather flat niches in the rock containing groups of figures (e.g. Usuki, on the island of Kyūshū). But these provide confirmation of the fact that this type of sanctuary spread as far as the easternmost limits of the Asian continent.

The monasteries and temples of eastern Asia differ greatly in their layout from those of India. It is true that in both cases the nucleus is a square court, often containing a pagoda and a hall with cult images. But the monks' cells are often not built around this court, and the principle of concentric arrangement around a single central point is superseded by one whereby several independent buildings, usually placed transversely, are

FIG. 38   sited along an axis running in most cases from south to north; it is this axis that gives the entire complex a strict symmetry. The believer enters the sacred area through a monumental gateway and walks up the *via sacra* to the centre, which may be either a pagoda or a hall containing the images, or both.

The changes that took place in the type of these buildings, designed be-

FIG. 43   tween 600 and 800, can be followed more easily in Japan than in China, although in essential points they correspond. At first the pagoda still plays the most important role — an 'Indian' feature — and the Buddha hall takes

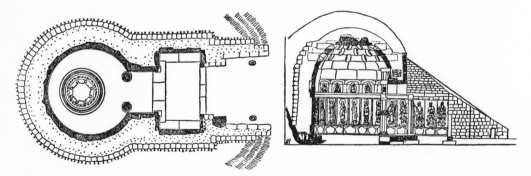

Fig. 37 — Ground-plan and section of the Sokkul-am, near Kyongju, Korea. Approx. 750 A.D.

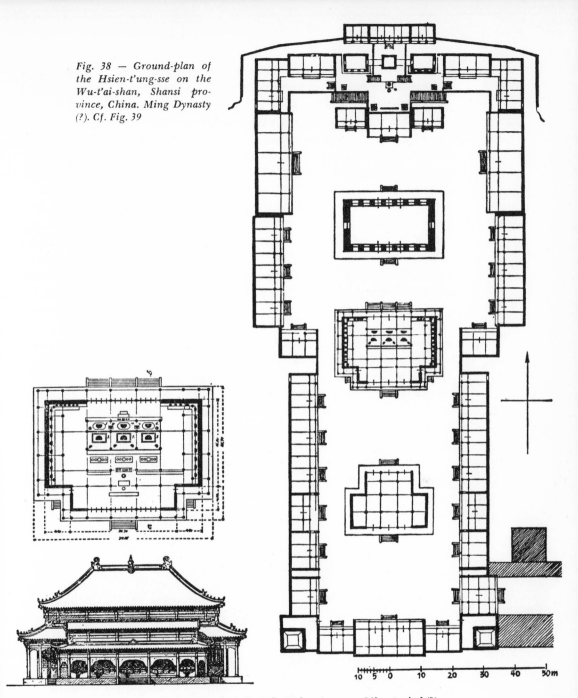

Fig. 38 — Ground-plan of the Hsien-t'ung-sse on the Wu-t'ai-shan, Shansi province, China. Ming Dynasty (?). Cf. Fig. 39

Fig. 39 — Elevation and ground-plan of main hall of the Hsien-t'ung-sse. Ming period (?). Height approx. 18.60 m., width 34.65 m. The ground-plan shows the cult statues and altar tables. Cf. Fig. 38

Fig. 42 second place; it is situated behind the pagoda, but later becomes an equal partner and is to be found next to it. As the ritual grows more and more complex, this hall gains in importance and size, eventually becoming the main building. The pagoda, too, is emphasized more strongly in a visual sense by duplication, but so far as its religious import is concerned it is diminished in value, since it loses its former centrality and uniqueness. Later pagodas are even displaced from the central enclosure and degraded to a mere decorative role along the sides, unless they serve a special function in the cult, as the *tahōtō* does (cf. p. 129) and thus have a special place in the layout of the temple, as the centre of smaller enclosures of their own. In eastern Asian temples the main buildings along the central axis are usually surrounded by an ambulatory; outside this are situated the other monastery buildings, grouped according to a more or less regular pattern. Some of the latter are residential and others administrative buildings; others again are halls used for special purposes (such as the Meditation Hall or the Library), or rooms for welfare work.

In its general layout (enclosed courtyards, with the principal buildings grouped along an axis, and the ancillary ones adjoining them in a symmetrical arrangement), as well as in its architectonic structure, the Chinese temple is based entirely upon the traditional indigenous homestead, and especially on the palace as it developed during the Han period. This model was later copied in Korea and Japan: at first very closely, but then gradually in a modified form, although the changes made were as a rule Fig. 41 not radical ones. From the golden age of Buddhist art in China and Korea only a few buildings other than pagodas have been preserved. Most of

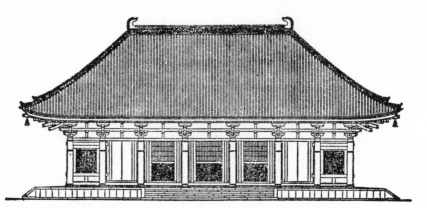

Fig. 40 — Golden Hall (Kondō) of the Tōshōdaiji, Nara, Japan: front elevation. Second half of 8th cent. Height 15.50 m., width 27.60 m. Built in the style of T'ang architecture in China. Cf. Fig. 41

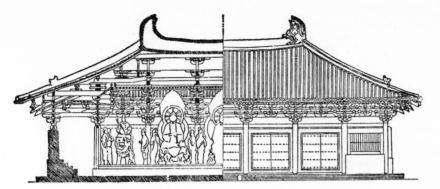

Fig. 41 — Section and elevation of main hall of the Fo-kuang-sse, Wu-t'ai-shan, Shansi province, China. Mid-9th cent. Height approx. 17 m., width at the eaves approx. 43.60 m.

those that are extant at the present time date from recent (and in some cases very recent) centuries. But in Japan there still exist a large number of classical temple buildings — those at Nara, Kyōto and Kamakura in particular — which have maintained, or only slightly modified, their original form; these date from all periods between the 7th and the 17th–18th centuries. This makes it possible, not only to study in detail the development of their style (and thereby also to reconstruct that of Chinese architecture), but also to experience the impressive atmosphere pervading these sanctuaries.

FIG. 40

It is not possible to deal here in detail with the architectonic form and the finer points of style. All we can do is to point to the fact that Buddhist temple architecture adopted the standard wooden frame structure — in

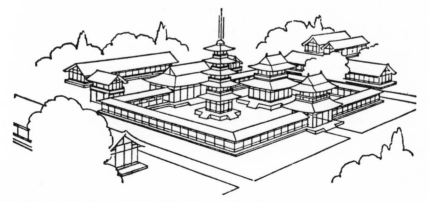

Fig. 42 — Original layout of the Hōryūji, near Nara, Japan

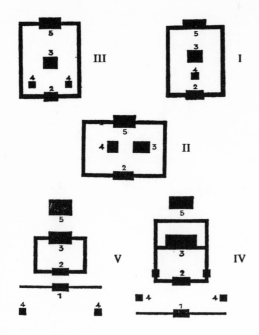

Fig. 43 — *Development of the temple compound in Japan*

China also that of brick masonry — with curved roofs projecting outwards to a varying extent. The latter are supported by an intricate form of bracketing, essential from a structural point of view but also effective as decoration. Whereas Chinese architects tend to build on a grandiose monumental scale and to decorate their temples with a wealth of sculpted ornament, the Japanese, following a line of their own, prefer simplicity and lack of ostentation; their temples are elegant and finely decorated, yet lose none of their religious dignity and do not degenerate into trivial playfulness.

FIGS. 39, 41 The interior of the hall is almost completely taken up by the platform with its cult statues, which are frequently numerous and of very great size. It is the main function of the temple hall to enclose them, so making a shrine, rather than to serve as an assembly hall for a community. Instead, a special hall is set aside for sermons and disputations. In the hall containing the images the main cult statue is in most cases that of a Buddha in a triad or a larger group of figures. It is the centre of the entire temple complex which is most lavishly embellished: the pillars and beams are painted and gilded; the ceiling, in the form of a canopy, represents heaven. Of the greatest importance are the rich murals completing the iconographic programme, which is dominated by the statues. Of these monu-

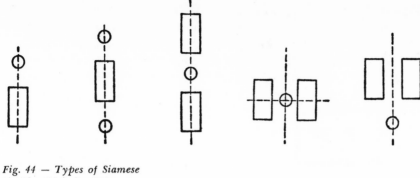

Fig. 44 — Types of Siamese temples, I (circle: stūpa; rectangles: halls for images and cult)

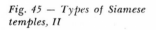

Fig. 45 — Types of Siamese temples, II

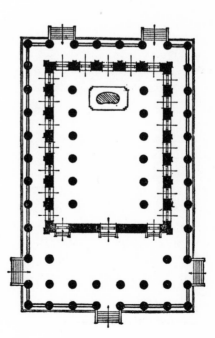

Fig. 46 — Ground-plan of temple hall in the Vat Thephsirin, Bangkok. Length 34 m.

PLATE P. 194

FIG. 60

FIG. 58

FIG. 47

FIGS. 44, 45

FIGS. 46, 47

mental and extremely important paintings unfortunately only a few remnants have survived. The programme of statues and paintings in most cases served to make the temple a terrestrial representation of a Buddha's blissful realm, such as the Sukhāvatī realm of Amitābha, into which the believer was intended to feel himself transported at the sight of the gilded statues, radiating the light on the Buddha's wisdom and mercy. Alternatively, all the figures, whether sculpted or painted, were supposed to combine in a mandala, the centre of which — the centre and axis of the cosmos — is occupied by the Buddha, seated upon his lotus throne. For this reason the temple hall is just as much a 'picture of the cosmos' as is the fully-developed stūpa, the pagoda or the cave-temple.

An interesting special type of temple hall was produced in Thailand. Here the area where the monks lived is separate from the sacred buildings. The latter contain, within surrounding walls or ambulatories, and arranged in various patterns, a stūpa, representing the holy of holies, a hall for the Buddha image, which served as the place for the monks to perform their rites, and a hall for the community of lay brethren; to these were added a hall for preaching, a library, etc., as was also the case in other Buddhist monasteries, as well as votive or sepulchral stūpas, which often occur in large numbers. The characteristic feature of the Siamese temple hall is the fact that it has an oblong ground-plan; the Buddha image stands on one of the shorter sides, with the entrance opposite. Frequently the interior is divided by two rows of pillars to form a nave and two aisles. In both these points it bears a resemblance to the old Indian *caitya* hall; but did a connection really exist between them? Another feature of these buildings is the steep gable-roof, with the ends of the ridge curving upwards; the gables often overlap and telescope. This is probably derived from the architecture of the dwellings built by the local population in southern China and Indochina.[9] With these temples Thailand produced a quite peculiar solution of the problems with which its architects were confronted. This differed from the monasteries and temples of India (and their derivatives) and also from the Chinese type prevailing in eastern Asia. Yet all of them have in common the fact that they contain the basic elements of the Buddhist sanctuary: the stūpa (or pagoda), the monks' cells, and the hall for the cult images and performance of ritual. They have different layouts and styles, but — as a glance at the ground-plans illustrated here shows — contain many elements that are basically the same everywhere: the sacred nucleus consisting of the stūpa (or pagoda), and the ritual hall enclosed within a court. The particular type of arrangement adopted depends on the stage of religious development or on the

9 B. P. Groslier, op. cit., pp. 207, 220.

Buddhist school to which the temple or monastery in question belonged. The choice of alternatives runs the gamut from one extreme to another: from the ascetic and simple Hīnayāna *vihāra*, in which the only cult object is the abstract symbol of the stūpa, without an image of any kind; and at the other extreme the Vajrayāna temple, designed for the worship of a vast pantheon, with a correspondingly complicated liturgy and iconography, and requiring a number of lavishly decorated buildings.

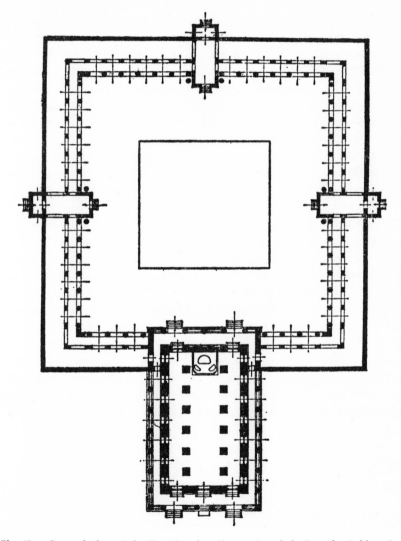

Fig. 47 — Ground-plan of the Vat Mongkut Krasat, Bangkok. Length of sides of square courtyard 52 m., length of hall 28 m.

III. THE BUDDHA IMAGE

The history of the Buddha image, like that of the temple, runs its course between two poles: at one extreme the non-personal symbol, and at the other a highly developed representational art with an abundance of figures. The supreme and central figure, that of the Buddha in his real essence, in the state of complete extinction in nirvāna, presented the artist with a problem that was in principle insoluble: how to represent in visual form something entirely transcending human vision without thereby dragging it down to the level of *samsāra,* of the phenomenal finite world. To suggest the transcendent nature of Buddha a form had to be evolved that was visually impressive, yet spiritualized to an extreme, which in itself transcended the limits of the finite world and passed into the realm of the 'Without Shape'. 'He who (like the sun) has gone to rest is comparable to nothing whatsoever. The notions through which his essence might be expressed are simply not to be found. All ideas are nothing, as bearing upon him; hence all modes of speech are, with respect to him, unavailing (tr. by H. Zimmer)'. This is the way the *Sutta Nipāta,* a text of the Pāli Canon, describes the Buddha after his entry into nirvāna; and what is said about 'modes of speech [being] unavailing' applies equally to representation in art. For this reason the earliest Buddhist art in India, so long as it continued to base itself on the dogma of what was later to be called Hīnayāna, i.e. into the first centuries of the Christian era, always represented the Buddha by symbols alone, and not in person; curiously enough, this custom was also observed in scenes showing the Buddha during his earthly life, prior to his final extinction, and indeed in some cases even before he became the Buddha. This total abstention from pictorial representation was by no means the result of an actual ban, as was the case in Islam, or in Old Testament times. It was in fact no novelty in India, but was a continuation of the old Brahmanic practice of not representing Vedic deities as persons but of worshipping them at best in the form of

PLATE P. 76

PLATE 25 — SHĀKYAMUNI BUDDHA. Section from a hanging scroll: pigments and gold on silk. Approx. 1100. Jingoji, Kyōto, Japan. Total height of painting 159 cm.
The Buddha Shākyamuni (Japanese: Shaka) is seated upon a lotus throne, which rests on an octagonal pedestal (omitted here) symbolizing the 'world mountain' Sumeru. His right hand is raised in the gesture of teaching. The pattern of his garment and other fine details are executed with the utmost care in cut gold-leaf *(kirikane),* while the blazing aureole, transformed into flowers, is painted in gold. An important example of the mature courtly art of the Fujiwara period.

cult symbols (a practice that was gradually superseded by a cult of images during the last five centuries B.C.).

Among the symbols used to suggest the Buddha are: the Tree of Enlightenment, the Wheel of the Doctrine, the throne, the pillar encircled by flames, the footprints, and the stūpa (as a symbolic representation of nirvāna). Most of these symbols have some ancient and widespread cosmological meaning (cosmic axis, cosmic tree, wheel of the sun and life). They may also be combined to form an imaginary body of the Buddha: for example, PLATE P. 76 a stool with footprints, an empty throne, a pillar depicted as a 'backbone', and a wheel rendered as a radiant head; all these are means of representing simultaneously the cosmos (including the earth), the cosmic axis and heaven. Many of these symbols, however, not only denote the Buddha as such, but are related to particular important events in his life: for example, his Enlightenment, his decision to take up preaching, and his entry into nirvāna; they thus at the same time have a 'historical', biographical and narrative function. For this reason they frequently occur in pictorial narratives of the life of Shākyamuni, or of his previous incarnations (Jātakas), and represent his person in the context of a particular story; the other persons concerned in the narrative are portrayed as human beings, while the principal figure in their midst is depicted as a silent symbol, thereby being present in even greater purity, spirituality and predominance. (Even during later periods, far away from the main regions where the old symbolic mode of representation was practised — in Sānchī, Bhārhut, Mathurā, and to some extent at Amarāvatī as well — the Buddha was occasionally shown in an aniconic form amidst iconic historical scenes. An example of this is the drawing on cloth showing the main events of the Buddha's life, found at Kyzyl (7th cent.); in this case the Buddha as FIG. 64 a new-born babe is represented only by the halo around his head and body, and thus ceases to be regarded as a historical figure — since this halo suggests that he had already become a perfect Buddha.

Where a Buddha symbol of this kind is worshipped, what was at first only intended to be an act of homage to the living master is gradually transformed in to a ritual act, performed in honour of a superior being. From this it is but a step to replacing the symbol by an image of this being. There gradually follows a shift in the centre of gravity from the symbol to the image, from the ascetic austerity of an abstraction to the sensitive portrayal of a person, from the honour and respect accorded to a model human being to the veneration accorded to a superhuman power of mercy, a feeling that springs from deep piety and a desire that one's ritual acts should be effective.

For the development of Mahāyāna in the centuries immediately before and after the birth of Christ led to a completely new concept of the Buddha. Of course, it emerged to some extent from within the old form of Buddhism, so that for a time the old and the new doctrines co-existed. Henceforth the Buddha was not a single historical person, Shākyamuni; he was deemed to have been preceded in earlier ages by several (usually seven) Buddhas; Maitreya was seen as his successor. We came across these earlier Buddhas in the reliefs on the *toranas* at Sānchī, where they were represented in an aniconic form, merely suggested by the symbols of their Trees of Enlightenment. Later, in the reliefs at Gandhāra, they are depicted in human form. This idea then evolves into the concept that there were, are, and will be an infinite number of Buddhas ('Thousand, Three Thousand or Ten Thousand Buddhas'), all of them but manifestations of the One Absolute Buddha. The latter is in principle beyond the limits of human vision. According to the *trikāya*, the doctrine of the Three Bodies of the Buddha, his real essence is embodied in the Dharmakāya ('absolute body of the law') ; this is revealed to those possessed of visionary power as the Sambhogakāya ('body of bliss') in the blessed realms beyond the phenomenal world; and it is revealed to those living in the finite world as the Nirmānakāya ('body incarnate'). The *Lalita Vistara* interprets the life of the Buddha on earth as a mere 'game', as the phantasmagoria of a superhuman being, adapted to man's limited understanding, thus representing the point of view expressed in Docetism. According to advanced Mahāyāna doctrine there is no difference between the Absolute or nirvāna personified by the Buddha, and the relative, empirical existence of the world of *samsāra* (although they are not simply identical); their relation is a 'non-duality'. True reality, the 'Nature of Buddha', or 'Suchness' *(tathatā)* is 'void' *(shūnya)*, i.e. it transcends all the categories and limitations of our thinking. All ideas and concepts — including pictorial concepts — of the Buddha are no more than an expedient *(upāya)*, something temporary and non-real, which however can help the individual to attain Enlightenment, to become a Buddha, by meditation *(dhyāna)*, fervent devotion *(bhakti)* and ritual veneration *(pūjā);* for in principle the Absolute Buddha is a nucleus latent in each living being, and ought to find pure and perfect realization. These aids also include the representation of sacred beings, culminating in the Buddha himself. Since, from a transcendental point of view, everything is 'void', in the ultimate resort the realm of *samsāra,* and even the idea of the existence of nirvāna and of the Buddha, are all equally illusory; but for that very reason they may also be interpreted symbolically and represented pictorially — although with the reservation that such a representation cannot attain true reality. The Buddha image is only an illusory reflex of true reality, for this lies beyond all human dimensions and categories: it provides a support and aid in meditation upon this reality, and its form must therefore be such that it transcends itself, makes the beholder forsake all notions limited by *samsāra,* and leads him to that which lies *beyond* all form. It is necessary to understand this fundamental paradox before one can understand the singular form and nature of the Buddha represented as a human being.

These are some of the concepts of the Mahāyāna doctrine that were of fundamental significance in directing the development of the Buddha image. Some of these ideas made themselves felt already at a comparatively early date; others, by contrast, only later. The new concept of the Buddha naturally led to the growth of a mythology. The piety of the broad masses of the population was no doubt one of the strongest driving forces towards the production of cult images. In their eyes the Buddha soon became a merciful redeemer, to whom man could turn in every need, as one could to the deities of the native mythology, whereupon he would help believers to attain nirvāna or a blessed reincarnation in his heavenly realm. To make sacrificial offerings to him, whether of a spiritual or material nature, was considered highly meritorious, as an essential step towards obtaining a better karma. In many texts the Buddha himself is made to declare that the production and veneration of his image is a meritorious act, which would bring its due reward. Eventually the point was reached where the real Buddha was thought to reside in his image; by the 'eye-opening' rite and by depositing sacred objects inside the image, it was believed that the latter could acquire a numinous vitality and even a magical miracle-working power.

Apart from these general reasons for producing a Buddha image, one on the strictly metaphysical plane and the other on that of popular piety, it was also regarded as necessary to justify the portrayal of the Enlightened One by linking his image directly with his historical person, thereby deriving later Buddha images from one authentic archetype. In more recent texts the Buddha is said to have given express permission for his person to be represented and venerated by ritual acts. All manner of legends sprang up about the First Image. The best known, recorded in several versions, runs as follows. When, after this Enlightenment, the Buddha spent some months in the Heaven of the Thirty-three Gods to preach his doctrine to his mother, who had been re-born there, King Udayana of Vatsa (Kausambi), who revered him highly, was inconsolable with worry lest he might not return. He wanted to have at least a picture of the Buddha. At the request of the king the disciple Maudgalyāyana sent an artist (according to another version, 32 artists) up to heaven by magical means, to memorize the Buddha's features and to carve a figure of him in sandalwood, five feet high. When the Buddha returned the statue rose up to welcome him. Thereupon he gave it the task of spreading his teaching among future generations.

A statue with such a legend about its origin did apparently exist in India. Its subsequent history is a tangle of fact and myth that cannot be unravelled, but throughout Asia it was regarded as the authentic Buddha image. The pilgrim Hsüan-tsang brought a replica of it with him to China, where further copies were made. In 985, during his stay in China, the Japanese monk Chōnen had another such replica made, which he took with him to Japan in 987. It still stands today in the temple of

FIG. 54d   Seiryōji, near Kyōto; it in turn served as a model for a large number of other replicas. Of the many figures that existed in India, Central Asia and China now one, now another was regarded as the original, dating from the time of Udayana; Chōnen, on the other hand, was honest enough to admit that his figure was a copy of a Chinese copy. But he afforded it sanctity and potency by depositing in its body relics, pictures, *sūtras,* documents and votive offerings, and even imitations of inner organs made of silk. (There is as yet no answer to the riddle why it shows the Buddha standing, whereas according to texts and pictorial representations of the Udayana legend from Gandhāra the original was conceived as a seated figure.) This statue is of great interest in many respects: it is very well documented and preserved (including its 'content'), and thus affords a fine example of the way in which an image of this kind was made into a 'cult instrument'. It shows further what was understood in medieval Buddhist art by a 'copy' (or rather, a copy many degrees removed) of an 'authentic' original, which could trace its source back to India. It shows how sanctified models of this kind were transmitted from one part of Asia to another, and how the prime concern was to ensure that something of the omnipresent and beneficial essence of the Buddha was contained in it; the main concern was to acquire religious merit, while far less attention was paid to accurate rendering of form. In appearance the image diverges considerably from the type usual at that time (the 10th century) and may come relatively close to the legendary archetype — although this is hard to judge, since it passed through several intermediary stages. It thus still reflects certain stylistic features pertaining to the area whence the entire tradition of Buddhist imagery originated. Elements of the Late Gandhāran style (similar to that of Bāmiyān), in which the draping of the folds is depicted by schematized lines, are modified by Central Asian features, such as occur above all in Turfan (Karashahr, Bezeklik); the latter may, however, already contain an echo of Chinese stylistic features, which exerted a similar influence on some types of the Buddha image of the Silla period in Korea as well as upon the so-called Jōgan style in Japan (9th—10th cents.). But the specific characteristics of *eastern* Asia, especially in the quality of plasticity, are less noticeable in the Seiryōji figure than the ancient austerity evident in the linear treatment of the drapery, which points to Central Asia and Gandhāra; this is a feature that also appears in Gupta figures from Mathurā. This work of sculpture is of course not the only one to have handed on to eastern Asia an Indian type of image, or Indian and Central Asian styles: we know of many others which originated from quite different regions and periods, and spoke, as it were, different stylistic dialects. For example, we have paintings and drawings from Tun-huang which reproduce a whole collection of famous and (in the religious sense of the word) authentic statues from the Holy Land.

Appx. pl. 3

Plate p. 96

We have already dealt in detail with the origin and development of early iconic Buddhist art in India (cf. pp. 28f.). Lack of space prevents us from tracing fully the subsequent phases in its history, or all the transitional stages through which it passed. We shall therefore confine ourselves to a description of the main types of the Buddha image that appeared in the various Asian countries, and indicate briefly how their form was modified in accordance with changes in the religious outlook.

As we know, the Buddha image appeared at roughly the same time in Mathurā and Gandhāra. It was based on various cultural and artistic factors that can be traced further back in native tradition in Mathurā than they can in Gandhāra; these may actually have led to the Buddha being rendered for the first time somewhat earlier, i.e. already during the 1st century A.D. The iconography of these two centres was at first by and large still based upon Hīnayāna; but in Gandhāra the ground is already being prepared for the new concept of the Buddha from which Mahāyāna was later to develop, until it eventually attained its position of predominance during the first centuries A.D. To an ever greater extent a need came to be felt to worship the Enlightened One in his human incarnation. Curiously enough, the trend towards portraying the Buddha as a person came into being as part of the same religious and philosophical development that raised him to the level of a superhuman, supra-personal and 'supra-mundane' being. The reasons for this apparent contradiction have already been discussed. Artists were now faced with the problem of conveying something of his transcendental nature in the human figure — no easy task and one not solved at once.

FIG. 48 The image of the Buddha in a standing posture was to a large extent modelled upon an ancient native type of figure, that of a *yaksha*. The two have in common a block-like compactness, an abundance of vigour, taut tension in the treatment of plastic forms, and similarities in the athletic PLATE P. 77 type. These features also occur in the seated Buddha, emphasized still further by the firmness and stability of the posture, and by the smooth close-fitting robe, almost devoid of any draping folds, which left large expanses of the body uncovered. This type seems to have been inspired by the representation (possibly somewhat earlier) of the Jainist saint, the Jīna. Jīna ('the Victor') is also one of the terms used in referring to the Buddha as well; and indeed it is obvious that these images were intended to express the idea of the victory of the Enlightened One over all doubt, delusion and temptation. The Buddha is depicted as a lion ready to pounce (the lion is a simile for the Buddha), in a heroic pose, with the right hand raised to afford protection and the left resting firmly on the thigh, in the posture of a Yogin — not absorbed in sublime and tranquil contemplation, far removed from worldly concerns, but abounding with the energy of the 'Awakened One' (Buddha), ready to preach to a world in need of redemption. Incidentally, figures shown seated in a yoga posture already occur much earlier. They represent an Indian archetype occurring FIGS. 49, 50 on seals of the Indus Valley culture as early as the 3rd or 2nd millennium B.C., although the feet are shown in a rather different posture.

In the second basic type of Buddha, that from Gandhāra, the figure is interpreted quite differently — rather in the manner of the Yogin as he is

Fig. 48 — *Yaksha figure from Patna (2nd cent. B.C. or later; India Museum, Calcutta) and Buddha from Mathurā (2nd cent. B.C.; Musée Guimet, Paris). After Willetts*

Fig. 49 — Seal from Mohenjo-daro. Indus valley culture (3rd—2nd millennia B.C.)

Fig. 50 — Seal from Mohenjo-daro. Indus valley culture (3rd—2nd millennia B.C.). National Museum, Delhi

described in the *Bhagavadgītā:* in a state of perfect equilibrium, both physically and mentally, free from all desire, concentrating his gaze upon a single point, imbued with the peace of nirvāna, like a lamp burning but not flickering at all. It is true that here, as everywhere else, there is a tendency to represent the Buddha as the Teacher, but he is always shown with that detached introvert attitude of superiority over worldly things, of immunity to all change, of inactivity, which make him a personification of the supreme essence — at least, that is the intention, for the eclectic and hybrid art of Gandhāra does not wholly succeed in accomplishing this task; only too frequently it lapses into lifelessness and spiritual vacuity, yielding mere routine works. The spiritual content of this type of Buddha is in any case purely Indian, and the fact that it looks so Apollinic is due to a superficial resemblance, and to external stylistic influences; these striking alien features serve to give its Indian content a specific *cachet.* But these features do not jar at all: the kindly humanity of the Antique model served to represent the noble benevolence and amiability of the Buddha to which all the texts testify. The idealized beauty evident in figures of the Buddha raised him to a sphere beyond empirical experience, and removed him from the world of *samsāra,* with its ugliness and suffering. The same effect is also produced by the regular, even rhythm in his draped garments, as well as by the way in which the artist's gentle hand instilled a sense of tranquillity into the volumes of which the figure is composed. This makes the face somewhat suggestive of a mask (even if we take into account the fact that the original colouring has disappeared) and greatly reduces the tangible corporeality of the figure.

The same purpose is fulfilled by the strict, and frequently rigid, symmetrical treatment of these cult statues which are represented in frontal view; (we are not speaking here about the Buddha figures that appear in narrative compositions in reliefs). This is a sacred formula denoting

PLATE P. 78
APPX. PL. 5

Fig. 51 — Gold coin of the Kushān king Kanishka, showing Buddha and the inscription BO ΔΔO in Greek. British Museum

majesty, which raises the Buddha above the three-dimensional physical environment and makes him the centre of the cosmos. Thus even the Buddha figures of Gandhāra, which in their external appearance come closest to Antique models, are far removed from them in spiritual content; and in the course of its development this form, which is at first still organic and functional, becomes increasingly spiritualized — i.e. abstract and schematic. The volumes of the body, and especially the face, lose their warm animated soft quality and instead acquire a cool hard smoothness and a schematic regularity. The locks of hair are no longer modelled plastically, with an eye to individual differentiation, but are incised almost graphically, and arranged in a regular pattern. In a number of Buddha heads from Gandhāra one can follow step by step the inner course of this process, which does not necessarily tally with the absolute chronology. The treatment of the robe loses more and more of its former plasticity, suppleness and tangibility; it gradually takes on the form of strictly geometric ridges, spaced at regular intervals and usually running parallel to one another, so that the figure is covered with an ornamental network of lines. In this transformation of the 'classical' style of Late Antiquity a role was played by provincial Roman influences (Palmyra) combined with equally important borrowings from Parthia (Hatra).[10] The ultimate consequence was that the curves formed by the draping were reduced simply to engraved pairs of lines.

In strange contrast to this type of Buddha, with its growing tendency towards abstraction, carried almost to the point where it again became a symbol, is the starkly realistic Buddha image, also produced at Gandhāra, which shows Shākyamuni during his ascetic period, wasted away to a skeleton — a grim picture of the fruitlessness of this road to salvation,

APPX. PL. 5

[10] E. Porada, *Alt-Iran* (Baden-Baden, 1962), p. 189.

PLATE 31 — AMITĀBHA APPEARING FROM BEHIND THE MOUNTAINS (Yamagoshi-Amida). Hanging scroll: ink, pigments and gold on silk. Zenrin-ji, Kyōto, Japan. First half of the 13th cent. Height 138 cm.
Amitābha (Amida) is represented appearing in a golden glow from behind a mountainous landscape, sending his two attendants, the Bodhisattvas Avalokiteshvara (Kannon) and Mahāsthāmaprāpta (Dai-Seishi) to the dying believer, by whose bed a painting of this kind would be customarily suspended. Kannon offers him the lotus in which he is to be carried to a blissful re-birth in the 'Pure Land of the West', where the Buddha reigns. This is a special form of the theme of 'Amitābha arriving to receive the believer (Amida-Raigō)', which was particularly popular in Japan. Top, left: the mystical letter *(siddham)* A, denoting Amitābha. Below: the four celestial kings (Lokapāla; in Japanese: Shi-Tennō) and possibly the gods Indra and Brahmā in courtly attire.

which can perhaps be explained by the great interest taken by Hīnayāna in his life on earth and his spiritual struggles. However, inconsistently enough — or, to put it more precisely: anticipating his transcendental Buddhahood — the figure incorporates features of the Enlightened One, an *ushnīsha* and an *ūrnā*. This type has spread to Central Asian wall-paintings (e.g. at Kuchā), and also occurs occasionally in China; but it never enjoyed great popularity there and was toned down into something harmless.

At Mathurā and Gandhāra there developed iconographic features symbolizing Buddha's supra-human nature as the Enlightened One which remained standard throughout Asia. Even at Gandhāra they are predominantly of Indian origin; only a few seem to be derived from western Asia or the world of classical Antiquity. Texts give a detailed description of the Buddha's bodily appearance, mentioning 32 major and 80 minor features *(lakshana)*. The details are so plentiful that it is practically impossible to reproduce them all in a work of art; usually, therefore, some of the principal features only are shown. The general appearance associated with the Buddha characterizes him partly as a noble human being and ideal ruler *(cakravartin)* and partly as supra-human. All the volumes of his body are perfectly proportioned, symmetrical, smooth and fully rounded; the shoulders are broad, and the hips narrow; the torso is like that of a lion and the legs like those of a gazelle; when he is depicted standing, his arms reach down to the knees; the lobes of his ears are distended (a characteristic feature of rulers, which may be explained by the Indian custom of wearing heavy ear-pendants); and his body emits a wondrous scent. His hair, which he cut to a length of two inches from the scalp after departing from his secular life, and which never grew again, APPX. PL. 6 has small short locks curling towards the right. In most Asian countries ET SEQ. this becomes the canonical form, which distinguishes the Buddha from all

PLATE 33 — BODHISATTVA PADMAPĀNI. Relief. Chunar sandstone. From Sārnāth, near Benares. Approx. 9th cent. (Pāla period). Height 118 cm. *Archaeological Museum, Sārnāth*.
The Bodhisattva is seated upon a lotus throne in the 'comfortable and relaxed' *lalitāsana* attitude often found with Bodhisattvas. It is similar to the attitude of 'royal ease' adopted by princes, and thus approximates more closely to the world of *samsāra* than does the Buddha's strictly hieratic attitude of meditation, the 'diamond seat' *(vajrāsana)*. The right hand is stretched out in the gesture of granting a wish *(varada-mudrā)*; in the left hand the Bodhisattva holds a lotus-stalk, consisting of leaf, bud and blossom — hence the name Padmapāni: 'he who holds a lotus'. On the front of his head-dress appears the Buddha Amitābha, seated in the attitude of meditation. These two attributes distinguish this figure as Avalokiteshvara. On top at the left one can see another Buddha, in the *bhūmisparsha-mudrā*, the gesture of invoking the earth to witness his Buddhahood — for this reason it may perhaps be identified as Shākyamuni. Companion-piece to the Plate on p. 98.

FIG. 52

PLATES PP.
77, 78

PLATES PP. 78,
163, 164, 179

other figures, although — especially during the early period at Gandhāra and Mathurā — we also find a different treatment (in strands, or a coiled top-knot). On the palms of his hands and soles of his feet the Buddha bears the Wheel of the Doctrine. Between the eyebrows is the *ūrnā,* which according to legend is a white lock curled towards the right, from which emanates the light of wisdom illuminating the universe. In works of art this is usually executed as a golden dot, in crystal or some other precious material. It is not to be interpreted as a Third Eye: this only occurs on some figures of Vajrayāna (Tantrism), where it is derived from the Hindu pantheon. Head and body are enclosed within a halo and an aureole, which likewise symbolize the 'Buddha Light', the immeasurable brilliance of truth and wisdom, as does the golden colour of his body. These features were probably introduced into Buddhist iconography from the religion of Iran, with its cult of light. Kushān rulers appear on coins wearing a halo of rays, and a part may also have been played by the image of the deified Roman emperors, which in turn was based on representations from late Antiquity of Helios and other deities. At Gandhāra, and thence also in Wei art in China, there are some Buddha figures with flames shooting out of the shoulders.

Finally, the Buddha's head has an approximately hemispherical elevation, the *ushnīsha,* which symbolizes enlightenment and wisdom. We will not go into the very intricate and much-debated question whether this symbol is a re-interpretation of a hair-dress, such as the ancient Indian hair-knot worn under the turban as a sign of princely status (*ushnīsha* originally meant a turban), or whether, on the other hand, it is derived from the *kroblylos* of Antiquity, such as we find on statues of Apollo, or whether, finally, the towering coiffure found on some Buddha figures from Gandhāra was supposed to conceal this symbol, because it was deemed

FIG. 52

'unnatural'. Ancient Buddha figures from Mathurā have a coiled top-knot. Some of those from Gandhāra have strands of hair, arranged in an orderly manner over the *ushnīsha,* sometimes treated in a rather realistic manner and sometimes in a more schematic way. But other works produced at this time have short locks covering the whole head, including the *ushnīsha;* these were usual at Mathurā and continued until the Gupta period, and

APPX. PL.
12, 13

even later still. On Siamese Buddhas a lotus bud is usually added on top of the *ushnīsha,* or else a pointed flame shoots forth from it.

Buddhist sacred figures are often depicted seated upon a throne or support (*āsana*), which has a symbolic significance. Those of the Buddha have (a few exceptions apart) three different forms. The first is the lion's throne. The lion here is not only the symbol of a ruler, but embodies the victorious

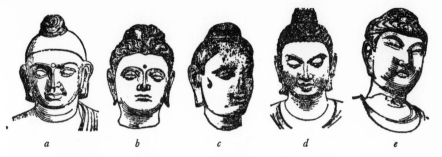

Fig. 52 — Development of the Buddha's head-dress. India: a) coiled top-knot (kapardin type), Mathurā; b) Gandhāran type; c) Gandhāran type showing Mathurā influence; d) type with short 'peppercorn curls' locks (Mathurā, Gandhāra, Gupta and many other parts of Asia); (e—g) China, variants of b—d. After Willetts

power of the Buddhist gospel, which awakens the world in the same way as, in the legend, the roaring of the lion roused its cubs, which seemed to be still-born. The second form of throne is that of a lotus: the main symbol in Buddhism to denote the Buddha nature in man and all things that remained immaculate in its innermost essence, undefiled by the filth encountered in *samsāra*. At the same time the lotus is an ancient Indian symbol for the cosmos, and is thus associated with the Buddha in his capacity as spiritual ruler of the world and embodiment of the Absolute. In art the lotus throne is apparently first met with at Gandhāra, at a relatively late date (3rd or 4th cents.), most frequently on figures of the preaching Buddha. The third form of throne, which is particularly popular in eastern Asia, consists of a rectangular or circular platform which projects on top and at the bottom, but has receding steps in the middle, in imitation of the cosmic mountain Sumeru, which is shaped like an hourglass. Thus here again we have a cosmic symbol.

PLATE P. 163

PLATE P. 166

Many of the symbols to be found in representations of the Buddha are connected with certain events in his biography and indicate the historical place where the event concerned took place. This is the case, for instance, with the nine-headed snake, on whose convoluted body he is seated, with its heads rearing above him to protect him from a storm. This motif is borrowed from the story of Buddha's visit to the palace of the snake king

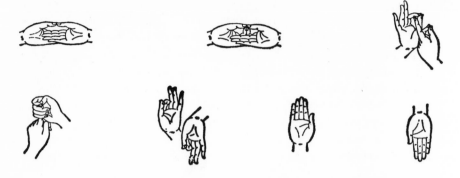

Fig. 53 — Symbolic gestures (mudrās). Above, from left to right: two gestures of meditation (Plates 17, 26) and gesture of teaching (cf. p. 78¹, Appx. Pl. 7). Below, from left to right: gesture of the Buddha Vairocana (p. 146), one of the gestures of Amitābha (p. 166, cf. p. 179), and the gestures of granting protection and fulfilling a wish (both in Plate 191)

PLATE P. 98 Mucilinda, and was particularly popular in Indochina.[11] Other examples are the two gazelles or stags depicted kneeling in front of his throne, often flanking the Wheel of the Doctrine, and hearkening to his preaching: this refers to the First Sermon in the Deer Park at Benares.

But even the most common seated posture of the Buddha, showing him in frontal symmetry, calm and motionless, in the attitude of meditation, is in itself an impressive symbol. It indicates his detachment from all things terrestrial and from the three-dimensional world of phenomena, of human action and suffering. It demonstrates the unshakable nature of absolute truth and wisdom, a state of utter tranquillity from which emanates the Enlightenment that leads the world to salvation. (In cases where the Buddha is represented in a different seated posture, either sitting in 'European' fashion or standing, this suggests abandonment of this detached attitude in favour of action and manifestation.) There is a close connection between such an attitude of absolute detachment, of superiority over all things mundane, and one other symbol of the Buddha which is, so to speak, a negative one: the absence of any attributes or ornaments whatever. This is a principle that is always adhered to, except in a few special instances. Attributes and ornaments, where they occur, serve to denote sacred beings of lower status, such as Bodhisattvas and lesser deities. The Buddha, however, surpasses them all in the silent simplicity of his appearance. From a 'biographical' point of view this may be explained by the fact that he was a monk, and as such was only allowed

[11] B. P. Groslier, op. cit., p. 161.

to wear simple garb, and to possess only a few utensils for everyday use. This was later interpreted in a metaphysical sense, to signify his detachment from the world, his independence from its various phenomena, and his withdrawal into 'a realm of Suchlessness'. At the same time this effectively enhances his figure, making it sublime and monumental. The differences between the various Buddhas in Mahāyāna, between the various states in which he may be represented, or the actions he may perform (meditation, preaching, etc.) are indicated mainly by symbolic gestures of the hands *(mudrā)*, and also by the kind of seated posture adopted. Examples of these are given in Fig. 53 (cf. also the captions to the relevant plates).

This symbolism, so far as the Buddha is concerned, was almost fully developed already in Gandhāran art (and to a lesser extent at Mathurā as well). Thereafter it remained standard in all Buddhist countries. In this respect early Buddhist art combined with Mahāyāna doctrine, then in its first flower, to lay the foundations on which all later art developed, thus uniting the Buddhist *oikoumene* by the firm bonds of common formulae of representation.

At first the two different archetypes of the Buddha, that of Mathurā and that of Gandhāra, are found independently side by side, but they soon begin to influence one another. From the close of the 2nd century A.D. onwards the bulky athletic physique of the Mathurā Buddha gradually acquires a note of slender elegance and delicacy, as in the Gandhāran figure. The closely-fitting robe is superseded by a loosely draped monk's habit *(sanghātī)*, hanging freely from the body. Although it frequently covers the shoulders, it does not conceal the body completely, as was usually the case at Gandhāra, but falls in a fine smooth cascade of ripples, covering the body with a very regular and almost symmetrical system of lines, often executed with sharp, even geometric precision. It is a feature derived from native Indian art, however, that the volumes of the body show through very distinctly beneath the thin robe. Under the influence of the idealism and nobility expressed in the Gandhāran image, the Mathurā Buddha became imbued with a spirit of aristocratic humanity and a harmony of form that it had not possessed before. The counter-influences which Mathurā exerted upon the Gandhāran Buddha are weaker and less readily discernible. Moreover, owing to the absence of an accurate chronology for the statues that have survived, many of the stylistic problems

FIG. 54

Fig. 54 — Development of the Buddha figure: a) Gandhāran type; b) Mathurā type from Sārnāth, showing influence of Gandhāra; c) Gandhāran type, showing influence of Mathurā; d) so-called Udayana figure in the Seiryōji, Kyōto, Japan. After Willetts

involved still await solution. As a result of the synthesis of these two types — the dominant element being Indian and not derived from Antiquity — Mathurā produced the classical Buddha image of the Gupta period.

PLATE P. 96 But prior to this another most important early type developed in the area of Amarāvatī, at approximately the same time, during the 2nd and 3rd centuries. Meanwhile the aniconic principle continued to exist, so that the transition from the earlier to the later concept of the Buddha is especially obvious here. The Amarāvatī Buddha, depicted either in a seated or in a standing posture, bears a close affinity to the Mathurā PLATE P. 55 Buddha, as modified by Gandhāran influences. This is especially evident in the rather stout body and in the treatment of the long robe, which hangs down in smooth, gentle, regularly-spaced curves. The folds of the drapery often lie quite flat on the body, and are sometimes indicated simply by lines; the body itself is only slightly articulated, the softly modelled forms being boldly combined. Where the Buddha is shown raising one hand, or both hands, in a symbolic gesture, the robe hangs down from the wrists in closely-spaced vertical folds, while lower down, by the hem, it swirls out in a wide curve: this is a characteristic feature of this type. It frequently leads to asymmetry, especially where the hanging folds on the left-hand side contrast with the raised right hand and bare right shoulder. This type is based on a very human concept of the Buddha, as a simple monk who has attained a certain sublimity through his role as a great teacher. It is not surprising that it should have proved very influential in the countries where the Hīnayāna doctrine was popular — especially in Ceylon (Anurādhapura), where it attains a rigid and austere monumentality. But its influence was felt in many other areas: in Indo- PLATE P. 95 nesia, and also in Indochina, where there is a particularly fine example in the well-known standing bronze Buddha at Dong-duong (Annam, approx. 300). Indeed, one can detect a faint echo of it even in the Chinese art of the latter half of the 6th century. But its main effect was felt in early Buddhist art.

For it was in the mature Gupta period that a standard concept of the Buddha was formulated that led eventually to one of the truly great Buddha figures of all time, accepted throughout the entire Buddhist PLATE P. 96 world. It is as though in Gupta art all earlier attempts to render the Buddha are epitomized, and developed to full maturity; for this reason it became the classical model over such extensive areas of Asia. The Gupta type of figure evolves chiefly on the basis of that of Mathurā — including, as we have seen, certain Gandhāran elements — but all the forms are ennobled, refined, and purified to the utmost. The body is soft and yet taut; its curves, visible beneath the thin robe, are more rounded; the clearly defined forms of the oval face no longer have the angularity or harsh roughness of the Mathurā type; they appear to be swelling with the breath of life beneath the smooth taut skin. A sense of perfect tranquillity and profound meditation emanates from this figure, which gives an impression of weightlessness; it is compact, but the curves of the robe, which flow together, give it absolute harmony. As in the Amarāvatī type, parts of the robe are held up, so that even deeper hollows appear at the sides of the body; the hem either describes vertical sweeping curves, or else small rippling waves over the ankles; this does not, however, detract from the sublime tranquillity of the figure.

The above mainly concerns the Gupta type of the standing Buddha, as produced at Mathurā. Another type is the seated preaching Buddha of Sārnāth. This figure, clad in a completely smooth garment, resembles the Appx. Pl. 6, 7 old Mathurā Buddha, but it likewise obtains a maximum of aristocratic refinement and perfect harmony — the features that are characteristic of the classic Gupta type. This is due in no small measure to the observance of exact rules of proportion and to the strictly triangular composition. A smooth and rounded form, without any folds of drapery, is also typical of the Sārnāth Buddha figure portrayed in a standing posture. In this case the wide hanging robe forms deep depressions, making sorts of niches about the protruding body;[12] this is modelled in great planes, clearly defined yet smoothly merging, treated with sensitivity and restraint. A perfect specimen of this type, which was to have a great future in Indochina (Dvāravatī and elsewhere), is the copper statue, larger than life-size, Appx. Pl. 11 from Sultanganj and now in Birmingham. The finest Buddha statues of the classical Gupta period, despite their delicate radiant beauty, soft lines and graceful majesty, seem to be withdrawn from the phenomenal world: they appear cool and inaccessible; the eyelids are half-closed, suggesting introspection: it is as though the Buddha is not looking at anything in the physical world but experiencing a vision by deep meditation. In Late Gupta style the figures are softer and fuller, or have an elegant supple form, as is evident from the paintings at Ajantā dating from the 6th or 7th centuries. On the other hand, in the last centuries of Indian Buddhist

[12] H. Goetz, op. cit., p. 96.

art (Pāla, etc.), the Buddha figures, despite their technical excellence and craftsman-like perfection, are schematized and lacking in originality. The

PLATE P. 98 forms are smooth, but seem cold and hard.

The Amarāvatī type of figure, and to an even greater extent the slightly more recent Gupta type, are the starting-points from which the Buddha image of southern Asia developed, whereas the Gandhāran type provided the main stimulus for Central and eastern Asia — a stimulus later developed along quite independent lines in China, Korea and Japan. During its early Buddhist period Indonesia was subjected to the influence of Amarāvatī, which at that time was dominant everywhere in southern Asia. Afterwards the Buddha images of the classical central Javanese period[13]

PLATE P. 139
APPX. PL. 8 were closely linked to the Gupta and post-Gupta type — i.e. the type of Sārnāth, Ajantā and Elūrā, which was devoid of all Gandhāran elements — but adapted it in the direction of yet greater restraint, tranquillity and harmony. The treatment of form is simplified: it often reaches the point where it appears as though figures clad in a monk's robe are naked; yet

APPX. PL. 9 the volumes of the body have a somewhat softer plasticity, with fuller forms; the head is depicted as a broad oval, and the face is animated by a warm kindly humanity. Though the Buddha has an aura of majesty and seems remote from mundane concerns, no attempt is made to convey that degree of aristocratic elegance, cool rigidity of form, and sublime spirituality that we find in masterpieces of Gupta art. It is admirable that the artists who created the innumerable Buddha figures of the Borobudur should have been so successsful in avoiding superficiality and sheer mechanical routine.

The tendency towards monumental simplicity and the fashioning of Buddha figures with large smooth surfaces, originating from the mature and post-Gupta type which we find exemplified at Sārnāth, Ajantā, Elūrā and elsewhere, is continued, and indeed even enhanced further, in Indochinese art. This shows a tendency towards simplification in its iconography as well, since, as it is predominantly Hīnayāna in inspiration, there are relatively few types of Buddha figure. The style of these is very peculiar, and varies only to a limited extent within the various regions. In out-

13 F. A. Wagner, op. cit., p. 111.

PLATE 34 — HEAD OF LOKESHVARA. Sandstone, originally presumably painted. Khmer, Bayon style. Beginning of 13th cent. Height 36 cm. *Museum van Aziatische Kunst, Amsterdam.*
In front of the stylized coiffure, seated in a posture of meditation, is the Buddha Amitābha, of whom the Bodhisattva Lokeshvara (Avalokiteshvara) is a manifestation. In Cambodia Lokeshvara ('Lord of the World') is regarded as the embodiment of the supreme principle of the universe and is deemed to be incarnate in the ruler. Cf. Plate on p. 37.

line three main characteristic types may be distinguished in Indochina: those of Dvāravatī, Khmer and Siam. This order of listing corresponds with their historical sequence. It is not possible to discuss here the preparatory or intermediary stages in their development, or to examine the local variants that existed.

The type of Buddha figure especially characteristic of Dvāravatī is portrayed in a standing posture. We see it to advantage in stone and bronze figures. It developed under the influence of Late Gupta art, from the close of the 6th century onwards, and retains a predominant position right up to the 12th century. It is designed to be viewed in direct frontality and exhibits an almost perfect symmetrical treatment. This results from the *mudrā,* which is normally identical in both hands: they are outstretched, in most cases in the *vitarka-mudrā* of teaching; but even where the *mudrā* is different this symmetry is still found. As with the Gupta type, the upper garment forms a spacious niche for the figure; the smooth and rounded torso and legs protrude from this niche; the hems of the garment hang down from the wrists to the lower part of the legs in an unbroken sweeping curve, but at the bottom there are frequently angular shapes which project outwards — more pronounced in some statues than in others — and are often given animation by means of decorative zigzag folds. Otherwise the figures are smooth and devoid of any ornamentation; the robe clings to the volumes of the body; there is a tendency towards stereometric treatment of certain elements (the legs look like columns, and the upper part of the body is trapezoid in form); and there is also a pronounced angularity in the basic structure, concealed beneath the smooth rounded forms of the surface. The head is almost spherical in shape; the features are dominated by the accentuated horizontal lines of the mouth, shown with full lips, of the eyes and eyebrows; the latter are characteristic of this type, in that they nearly touch above the nose, running at first almost straight, and continued in rising curves. The short curly locks are unusually large and rounded: this enhances the impression of stereometric simplification and vigorous plasticity. The block-like heaviness gives many of these heads a resemblance to the old Mathurā type. Some of them have pronounced ethnic features, with low forehead, full lips and flat nose; others have a finer, more 'Indian' physiognomy. The examples illustrated here of the pure consistent Dvāravatī style suggest a manly seriousness and an almost heroic quality appropriate to Hīnayāna, with their rigidity, clear definition, grandeur and vitality. (These features are also present in the seated Buddha figure, which did not become so important here as it did elsewhere.) The Dvāravatī type is far removed from the classical

Appx. Pl. 10, 11

Gupta type, with its delicate spirituality and serenity, its physical beauty and elegance of form.

Somewhat later, from approximately the 8th century onwards, the characteristic Khmer type comes into being. It developed once early Cambodian art (5th—7th cents.) had received a stimulus from various quarters, especially from the Indian art of the Làte Gupta period and partly also from Dvāravatī, and played a predominant part between the 10th and 13th centuries. Especially popular were two types of Buddha image. One was the Dvāravatī type, shown in a standing posture with both hands outstretched with the same gesture. The other was of Buddha seated in meditation upon the convoluted snake king Mucilinda, with the heads of the seven snakes rearing up and forming a kind of protective canopy over his head.[14] This is based on a well-known episode from the Buddha legend, but here it may also indicate adaptation to the ancient popular cult of the snake, which was even incorporated in the ideology fostered by the court. The Khmer type is characterized by rigid construction of the body with pronounced accentuation of horizontal lines: the legs are spread far apart; the shoulders are fully developed; the mouth is extremely broad and often has full lips; the eyes and eyebrows are rendered almost as straight lines; and the hair-line is often accentuated by a decorative band like a diadem. All these horizontal lines run right across the face. Earlier works[15] have a stern and frequently rigid expression, enhanced by wide-open glaring eyes. The plastic volumes are treated with near-abstract rigidity, without much attention being paid to sensitive modelling; and the hard lines of the planes are often sharply contrasted with one another and are set at an angle. Characteristic features are the fondness for engraved double contour lines to denote lips and eyes, the clear-cut details of hair and ornaments, and the step-like layers of the *ushnisha*. Nothing is left of the sensitivity, animation and supple modelling found in the Indian prototypes; and these Khmer figures, which are rigid, severe, and unapproachable, remote from human concerns, and almost akin to idols, differ markedly even from the Dvāravatī Buddha, which for all its austerity, conveys a strong sense

PLATE P. 191   of humanity. But gradually, towards 1200 or thereabouts,[16] the treatment of form becomes softer and more rounded; the hard angularity gives way to greater suppleness; the facial features become finer and more delicate, and the expression is milder — although the modelling is still executed with the utmost restraint, as though held back behind same unseen barrier

14 B. P. Groslier, op. cit., p. 169.
15 B. P. Groslier, op. cit., p. 129.
16 B. P. Groslier, op. cit., p. 188.

that separates the Buddha from the world about him. It is now that we find the detached smile — which is not really a smile, but a faint reflection of a mood of deep meditation, and of the inner freedom enjoyed by one who has achieved redemption: this is also suggested by the eyes, which are now only half-open. This type, however, soon became a stereotyped cliché, and is found with Bodhisattvas as well as with Buddha figures, so that the two types can only be distinguished by their iconographic features (for example, the small Amitābha figure on the head of Avalokiteshvara). The colossal Lokeshvara heads on the Bayon at Angkor represent an inter- PLATE P. 37 mediary stage between the earlier and later styles. With the transition to Hīnayāna, from the 14th or 15th century onwards, the Dvāravatī type of Buddha — the most influential in the Hīnayāna area — also appears in Cambodia, in slightly modified form.

The specifically Siamese type of Buddha is very different from the other two types. The final stage in its development took place during the Chiengmai, Sukhothai and Ayuthia periods (i.e. during the 14th and 15th centuries), and thereafter it was handed on in a stereotyped form that became increasingly schematized. The material used in this case is almost exclusively bronze, and this exerted a considerable influence upon the treatment of form. The preceding types, those of Dvāravatī and Khmer (the latter also found between the 11th and 15th centuries in its variant at Lopburi) still exert an after-effect during this period, so that all three types sometimes occur simultaneously, and exercise a slight influence upon one another.[17] The Siamese Buddha proper, the most recent of them, appears in several main iconographic types; including all the variants, there are more than thirty of them. The most popular is the seated Buddha, shown executing the *mudrā* of touching the earth *(bhūmisparsha)* — to be precise, in two poses, distinguished by the posture of the legs. The crowning of the *ushnīsha* is also different: in one case it is rendered by a APPX. PL. 12, 13 lotus, and in the other by a flame. The Buddha portrayed in a standing posture appears in an attitude familiar to us from Dvāravatī: the *mudrā* is usually the same on both sides of the figure, but sometimes may be a different one. The Buddha depicted in a recumbent posture — on entering nirvāna, i.e. on his death-bed — is a type that is very popular in southern Asia, but it is only met with in versions of little artistic significance.

Siam appears to have invented the free-standing figure of the 'walking Buddha', which is probably derived from representations in relief depicting the Buddha as he descends from heaven. The main figure was

[17] B. P. Groslier, op. cit., p. 205.

detached from its scenic and illustrative context and made into an independent cult image — a process that occurs frequently in the history of typological development. Some of these high-quality bronze statues are dated to the year 1426. The theme already occurs in the earliest Indian Buddhist works of art: the elegant walking attitude, with the hips curving outwards slightly, and the smooth flowing rhythm of the body and gar-

PLATE P. 35

ment, are features found at Gandhāra and other centres where this theme was treated. In the latter case, of course, it is derived from the classical *contrapposto,* but occasionally also present in mature Gupta art, whence

PLATE P. 97

it may have reached Siam. In the case of figures in which the right shoulder is bare — on account of the gesture made with the right arm — a narrow piece of garment folded like a sash hangs down over the chest from behind the left shoulder. This is a feature of the Siamese Buddha which also occurs at Dvāravatī. It probably originates in Indian art of the Pāla-Sena period.

The classical Siamese type of Buddha figure is sharply distinguished from

APPX. PL. 12, 13

the other types found in Indochina, and also from those of Java, by its slender build, small hips, supple limbs that are softly and smoothly modelled, and flowing curved outline — a typical style suited to modelling and metal-casting. The distinctive features also include a decidedly oval head, with a fine, thin-lipped mouth, a long, slightly curved nose with a sharp ridge, and eyebrows that form a sweeping, clearly defined curve above the distended almond-shaped eyes. All these features make the face seem longer. This effect, enhanced still further by the high crowning of the *ushnīsha,* sometimes produces a rather haughty expression. Incidentally, features of this type are not found among the population of Siam; they may be derived from Burmese, and ultimately from Pāla art, and be designed to make the Buddha's features approximate more closely to the ideal by portraying them as alien. On the smooth planes of the body the few seams of the robe, which are devoid of any plasticity, appear as clearly defined lines and blend into the general rhythm of the figure. Thus in this figure we have a melodious play of forms not found in other types, which does not, however, detract from the sense of tranquillity and majesty that it evokes. Despite their aristocratic features, the finest works are distinguished by a powerful tension sustained from within in which much still survives of the Dvāravatī

APPX. PL. 12

Buddha. Certain Siamese figures also resemble this type in their less slender and elegant form, and more rounded heads. During the late period, however, this naturally often degenerates into a dull bare glibness; the expression becomes hard and cold.

At that time — from the 16th century onwards — a final type of the Buddha comes to the fore in Siam, as in Cambodia: 'Buddha in princely attire' (Buddha paré). This figure already appears earlier in Khmer art, and also in Indian Late Mahāyāna art, during the Pāla period, whence it spread to Burma, Nepal and Tibet. In eastern Asia, where it is particularly popular, the figure usually represented is Vairocana as the Ādi-Buddha, wearing a crown and jewellery of the kind worn by Bodhisattvas. Early examples are the colossal Buddhas from Bāmiyān, which were originally covered with jewellery and ornamental chains. The Musée Guimet in Paris has a fragmentary clay figure from Fondukistan, from the 7th century, with a jewel-studded shoulder cape worn over the monk's habit. The 'Buddha paré' does not appear in Indochina until a relatively late date. Curiously enough it is to be found both in Hīnayāna as well as Vajrayāna areas — i.e. in completely different religious systems — although it apparently stands in contradiction to the nature of the Buddha, who is otherwise invariably shown without any adornment.

PLATE P. 141

PLATE P. 142

Any attempt at interpretation raises complex problems; at the risk of some simplification, we can put forward a number of ideas that may help towards an explanation. In the first place, from the standpoint of the doctrine of the Three Bodies (cf. p. 172), the Buddha appears richly bejewelled, in the glory and brilliance of a transcendental being, when he manifests himself as Sambhoga-kāya to the Bodhisattvas in a supernatural realm. Another concept relevant in this connection is that of the Buddha as world ruler *(cakravartin)* or cosmocrator, embracing within himself the entire world, and indeed the entire universe, and making them manifest; this role entitles him to wear princely jewellery. This older concept was apparently linked to the later one of the Sambhoga-kāya. The idea of the *cakravartin* later merged with that of the Ādi-Buddha, the Absolute, Original, or All-embracing Buddha, whose true self is invisible, but who manifests himself as ruler of the universe to those who meditate upon him, or to Bodhisattvas. It is in this form that the bejewelled Buddha appears in Vajrayāna — notably as Vairocana, the central figure of the Two Mandalas (cf. Ch. IV, sec. 1). His absolute nature, whence all other Buddhas emanate or are made manifest, is also indicated in another way: by the presence of figures of the 'Five Buddhas of Wisdom' (cf. Ch. IV, sec. 1) on his crown. Elsewhere, however, he is sometimes manifested in the guise of a Bodhisattva, as Vajrasattva, whose crown likewise bears images of the Five Buddhas. In Indochina the idea of embellishing the Buddha with princely adornment was connected with the ideology of sacral kingship, according to which the ruler was an incarnate god (Shiva)

FIG. 58

FIG. 62

or the Buddha. In Siam, too, the Buddha shared with the ruler the function of protecting the kingdom. The Siamese type of figure is distinguished by a note of cool nobility and by an increasingly schematized treatment of the body and garments. A characteristic trait is the upper garment standing out stiffly away from the body, like a thin sheet.

From a historical point of view the types of the Buddha figure in the Hīnayāna lands of Indochina are by and large based on the metaphysical idea of the Buddha developed by Mahāyāna, and in the first place on the conviction that his representation is possible at all.

Yet the followers of Hīnayāna do not fall back on the aniconic principle, as one might expect; nor do they represent the Buddha only as a historical person, in the empirical situations he encountered during his earthly existence. This is due, not only to the development of religious thought in Hīnayāna itself, but also to the fact that the Indian models (produced between the Gupta and Pāla periods) that were taken as authoritative by Indochinese artists belonged to the advanced Mahāyāna. But in the Dvāravatī Buddha, as in that of Ceylon, there is still much more of the historical Shākyamuni's human simplicity and spiritual energy than is present in the Siamese Buddha. From the latter there emanates a certain coldness, an aura of noble sublimity; the Buddha seems to be holding himself aloof from men's mundane problems. This figure becomes to an increasing extent a hieratic cult symbol, which can hardly be distinguished from the figures found in Mahāyāna.

In none of the types of Buddha figure in Indochina or Indonesia can one detect any influence of the Gandhāran style — not even in the modified form that this obtained at Mathurā, where it developed into one of the classical Gupta types. For the specific Gupta style which was adopted in southern Asia was that of Sārnāth, Ajantā, Elūrā, etc., which had no trace whatsoever of Gandhāra about it — to say nothing of Pāla art, which exhibited strong Hindu influences. Thus, although there are considerable variants in India and southern Asia, this area has an underlying unity in the assumptions on which its art is built. On the other hand, the basis of the second vast sphere of Buddhist art, that of Central and eastern Asia, was in the main provided by Gandhāran art, and only secondarily by other models from India itself (effective for a time in China). But in the course of development this art became ever further removed from its starting-point, so that the result was once again something completely alien to Gandhāran art. We shall now outline briefly the development of the Buddha image from Gandhāra to Japan, without going into details about individual works. Some information is to be found in the plates and captions about the standard iconographic types in eastern Asia, so that we can limit our survey to the changes in style that took place.

The development of the Gandhāran style proper has already been discussed, at least in general outline: it was the late phase in particular which exerted an influence outside Gandhāra, with its highly abstract schematization of form. Among the most important monuments which adopted and carried on this trend are the two colossal Buddha figures at Bāmiyān. The smaller one apparently originates from the 3rd or 4th century, whereas the larger one is at least one hundred years later. The former belongs to a phase of Gandhāran style that still has relatively supple and voluminous modelling of the body, and of the flowing garment draped over it. But in the one illustrated here the hard, almost stereometric body PLATE P. 142 is covered by a system of schematic ridges like cords — and they were indeed modelled with the aid of cords. From accounts by Chinese pilgrims we know of another colossus — a figure of Maitreya in gilded wood, said to have measured 80 feet in height. It stood at Darel, on the upper reaches of the Indus, and may have been erected as early as the 3rd century. It is unfortunate that it has not survived, for it would have been an important link in the chain of colossi that reaches as far as China (Yünkang, Lungmên). Hsüan-tsang saw two statues of approximately the same height at Kuchā. The first works of this kind may have been based on the colossal statues of Late Antiquity, for the idea of cosmocrator was common to them both.

The Gandhāran type spread fairly rapidly eastwards by way of such important centres as Khotan (where the sculpture on the stūpa at Rawak is an outstanding example), Kuchā and Khocho. This applies not only to Buddha figures but also to those of Bodhisattvas and other categories, such as deities and men. In Central Asia these models were of course often PLATE P. 143 copied long after China had gone over to completely different styles, and even after Central Asian art had itself been responsible, in many wall-paintings, for a quite singular stylization of the Buddha image, which APPX. PL. 3 effected a great transformation in the Gandhāran prototype and the other models. This frequently led to a disproportion in the relative and absolute chronology. Plates 16 to 18 in the appendix show the close affinity which exists between a Gandhāran Buddha that still has fairly 'classical' features, a clay figure from the Khocho area (from the 5th cent. or later, but nevertheless a fitting illustration of this intermediary type of style), and a Chinese Buddha in bronze, produced at the latest in or about 475 (another figure which bears a strong resemblance to it dates from 443). The standing posture, the treatment of the garment, the relation between body and garment, the linear schematization of the folds and the way in which they run, the leitmotif of the hems jutting out like fins at the bottom that can be traced back to neo-Attic classicism — all these features are similar in these figures, and yet there is unmistakably an increasing tendency towards abstraction and ornamentalization, and a transformation of the spiritual content and expression. Thus in these Chinese works, which are still influenced by Gandhāra, one can note a definite tendency to move away from the influences of Antiquity. Yet from a stylistic point of view this Buddha figure is a hybrid. It lasts for no more than a short period during the latter half of the 5th century. It may be seen to particular advantage in the colossal statue of the Buddha in Cave XX at Yünkang (460—480), as well as in a number of other rock-cut sculptures and small bronzes — among which, incidentally, there are a whole range of different styles dating from the early period. The earliest caves at Tun-huang also have figures executed in this soft, rather expressionless style; the folds are draped round the body in supple curves, but at the same time give the impression of an abstract design. Influences of this kind presumably reached Yünkang directly from Tun-huang, since in 439 tens of thousands of the local inhabitants were moved from the Tun-huang area by the Wei conquerors to the region of their capital, Ta-t'ung — i.e. to the neighbourhood of Yünkang. But whatever was done in the way of art in northern China was almost completely destroyed during the persecution of the Buddhists in or about 450.

PLATE 42 — PRAJNĀPĀRAMITĀ. Andesite. From one of the Singhasāri temples, eastern Java. Approx. 1300. Height 126 cm. *Rijksmuseum voor Volkenkunde, Leyden.*
Prajnāpāramitā probably appeared in Mahāyāna Buddhism at the beginning of the Christian era. She personifies the highest form of transcendental wisdom, interpreted not only as spiritual virtue, but given a mythological form. She is described — as 'mothe of all Buddhas' — in the *sūtras,* which dealt with her: these southern Indian texts constitute a most important section of Buddhist literature. In them greater emphasis is given to the female concept of the universal principle than is the case in the north: it is identified with wisdom and maternity, but at the same time is seen as unapproachable and chaste. In many respects an affinity exist between Prajnāpāramitā and the Sophia of the Gnostics. In Tantrism she becomes the shakti of the Absolute (Ādi-) Buddha.
This statue is one of the finest masterpieces of Buddhist art. It follows the classification of Prajnāpāramitā's appearance given in one of the *sādhanas* (manuals of ritual and iconography), and represents the 'yellow Prajnāpāramitā', who is distinguished by the following features: both her hands are in the gesture of teaching; she is seated in the posture of meditation; she wears costly jewellery; and she has, resting on a lotus to her left, a book containing the text of the *Prajnāpāramitā.* On her forehead she wears the *ūrnā,* denoting the highest level of Enlightenment. This statue is probably also a 'portrait' of a queen of the Singhasāri Dynsty, namely Dedes (first half of 13th cent.) — not, of course, a portrait in the modern sense, but an attempt to identify her with the mystica body of the sacred personage concerned, in the same way as the supreme Buddha or Hindu deity becomes incarnate in the ruler. This perhaps explains why this figure combines withdrawal from the world to a sanctified sphere with a note of noble charm and humanity. This relationship is, generally speaking, characteristic of classical Javanese art. It distinguishes this figure from other esoteric Buddhist works. (Detail: cf. Plate on p. 208.)

Detail: PLATE 42 cf. Plate on p. 207.

Fig. 55 — Buddha. Rubbing from relief at Ma-hao, Szechuan province, China. 3rd cent. A.D.

Fig. 56 — Buddhist figures on Chinese bronze mirrors (rubbings). Right: found near Nara, Japan, first half of 3rd cent. Top left: Museum of Fine Arts, Boston, 270—350; bottom left: Ostasiatisches Museum, Berlin, 270—350

During the 5th century southern China was also affected by influences from Central Asia — especially from Khotan — but there were other influences at work as well, from the direction of South-east Asia. Proof of the rapidity with which this development took place is afforded by a small Chinese Bodhisattva figure in bronze, which can without doubt be ascribed to the period about the year 300, but which copies the Gandhāran prototype in a manner that is still rather clumsy. Today several very early Buddha images are known to exist in China. The oldest is a rather crudely executed relief in a sepulchral chamber at Ma-hao, Szechuan province,

APPX. PL. 22
APPX. PL. 21

FIG. 55

The scroll, which measures 18.81 m. in length (cf. Plate on p. 169), includes a series of sixteen individual portraits of Lohans (in H. Chapin's enumeration, Nos. 14—). Although the names of these Indian disciples of the Buddha are throughout given in Chinese characters, the identification and iconography of Lohan figures are in many cases difficult to ascertain. The Lohan is clad as a Chinese priest, but has non-Chinese facial features. He is shown sitting in a cave, which is illumined by his aureole. In front of him, on the left, there stands a Chinese monk worshipping him, and on the right a boy of exotic appearance holding up before him a mirror (?): this is probably intended to denote the Lohan's magic powers. On the right is a dragon pedestal, on which stands a vase containing a peony — both typical Chinese symbols of good fortune. On the rock to the right is a censer, suspended by a chain.

dating from the 3rd century — i.e. not long after the rule of the Han Dynasty came to an end. At approximately the same time small ceramic figures in relief of the Yüeh-yao type were made in Chekiang. Round about the year 300 Buddhist figures — including a triad — occurred in the ornamentation of some Chinese bronze mirrors (now in Boston and Berlin); and from the 3rd and 4th centuries we also have mirrors featuring Buddha figures, and groups of such figures which, it is worth noting, were found in Japanese graves: they thus furnish early evidence of the contact that existed between Japan and China. All these are quite primitive works, and even the oldest known dated Buddha statue (338, Brundage, formerly Loo Collection), although quite massive in proportions, still has some very ancient features. These earliest specimens are, however, no doubt but a faint echo of a form of Buddhist art which played quite an important part, especially in southern China, already during the 3rd and 4th centuries; they substantiate everything we know from other sources about the spread of Buddhism in China (cf. pp. 81 ff.).

In the north, of course, it is much easier to trace the course of development, for we have a large number of magnificent monuments (Yünkang, Lungmên, etc.); in this region the Chinese genius soon shook off all dependence upon foreign influences. The schematized Gandhāran Buddha — itself a derived, not really an original, form — was a rather rigid figure, of insipid spiritual content, little suited to development; and it survived so tenaciously for the sole reason that it could profit by the difference in cultural level between Gandhāra and Central Asia. But as soon as it had performed its function of inspiring the creative powers of a highly cultured people such as the Chinese, the latter energetically set about transforming these alien forms — in much the same way as was happening simultaneously in Mathurā. Even adopted elements, such as the hems of garments folded in zigzag form, or spreading out like fish-fins, are given a totally different style and character. The Buddha image in the so-called Wei style, which developed under the fresh impulse afforded by an ardent religious movement, deserves to be called archaic, so long as we bear in mind that a style of this kind possesses great spiritual force and a high degree of formal potency, that in a way it even has a certain finesse and mannerism, and cannot by any means be regarded as naive — still less as primitive. In these figures, produced in the main during the first half of the 6th century, the body, simplified in order to achieve monumentality, is virtually devoid of any plastic quality; it is no more than a block-shaped base on which to drape the garment, and it is the latter that actually conveys the formal expression. The head is stereometric, and the features are carved into it

FIG. 56

APPX. PL. 23

APPX. PL. 14, 24

PLATE P. 144

APPX. PL. 14

Fig. 57 — Development of seated Buddha figure in Chinese sculpture, 460—750

with vigorous, clearly defined lines; yet, despite the hardness of the body, the expression is one of spirituality and withdrawal, frequently blossoming out into an 'archaic smile' (which the reader may compare with the entirely different, 'over-ripe smile' of the later Khmer figures). The outline of the figure is angular; there is a rhythmic movement to and fro; the folds of the garment, which are pressed down flat, make an ornamental abstract pattern of lines that is frequently very elegant; and in some cases all forms seem to flicker like flames. All this makes for vigour and tension, despite the hardness and rigidity; and for a sublimity that is remote from the life of men; it seems to be reaching out beyond the world of natural and organic life to the loftiest domains of the spirit.

PLATE P. 191

This style was complete in itself. It had reached the ultimate stage of development, and could only continue by taking a totally different direction — by making, not a radical break, but a gradual, yet decisive transformation. As a result of this — and in part, it seems probable, under influences from southern Asia, which in the ultimate resort derived from Amarāvatī — hard and angular lines of the body take on a rounded form; garments are no longer shown pressed down flat, with angular folds, but are indicated by softer curved lines; planes are modelled with greater suppleness; volumes begin to swell slightly from within, giving the effect of plasticity and faintly suggesting movement. Although the figure still retains its column-like character, has considerable tension in its surface, and shows curves of the folds that are cut in graphically, all the forms are now rounded, instead of being flat and angular. The expression, too, becomes more kindly, warm-hearted and human. We know from Buddhist history that at this time — during the latter half of the 6th century, under the Northern Ch'i and Northern Chou Dynasties — there flourished a cult of merciful redeemers, inspired by an attitude of pious devotion *(bhakti).*

FIG. 57

APPX. PL. 26, 30

PLATE P. 145

APPX. PL. 19

During the Sui and early T'ang periods development proceeded along the same lines. The soft plasticity, swelling up from within, was further intensified. It affected all the bodily forms, and the garments as well; there was greater feeling for the organic structure and living function of the fully-developed body; the garment came to play an independent role, equal to that of the body; and there was greater freedom and assurance in treatment. This resulted in an inner unity between the natural structure and its artistic representation. This unity was combined with perfect beauty and a sense of harmony and balance, which made this art truly classical, a model for the whole of eastern Asia. It was a style that fitted China's position as a great centre of civilization. The finest Buddha figures of this phase succeed in combining majesty, spiritual power, and warm humanity. In the Bodhisattvas the trend towards organic representation

APPX. PL. 31
PLATE P. 212

PLATE P. 193

and flowing movement of forms sometimes results in a splendid dance-like rhythm. In the powerful warrior-deities the body is energetic and active, the expression forceful. The apogee of this style in China itself is reached in the sculpted figures in the caves of T'ien-lung-shan. These were presumably carved under strong Gupta influence, but these latter elements no longer seem alien; instead they help to perfect an endogenous development that is proceeding along lines of its own. Many other outstanding works were produced in China that have not come down to us. Here Japan can help to fill the gap.

In Korea, and especially in Japan, the course of development runs parallel to that in China, since for both countries China was the source of inspiration. The Buddha figures in Korea have a characteristic calm and

PLATE P. 146

restraint. Only to a limited extent do they reflect the various changes of style. The finer details which distinguish them from Chinese or Japanese works cannot be considered here, partly owing to limitations of space, and partly because as yet it is not really possible to analyse these features, except in regard to a few points — such as the proportions, or the style of the folds, of some of the small bronzes (cf. p. 93).

The same applies to the Japanese art of the corresponding periods, i.e. the Asuka and Nara periods (approx. 600—800). No doubt some of the progress made may be accredited to original work by the Japanese themselves; but to ascertain this with certainty would be a comprehensive and difficult task. Generally speaking, stylistic development follows that of China stage by stage. This may be seen clearly by comparing the following Plates: 24,

CF. APPX.
PLATES

25 and 14; 15, 26 and 27; 19 and 20 (in this order) — remembering, however, that one has to take into account the different kinds of material used. Masterpieces of large bronze sculpture are only to be found in the ancient

temples in and around Nara (Hōryūji, Yakushiji, Tōshōdaiji, Tōdaiji, Kōfukuji and others). As we have just pointed out, they have to serve as a substitute for their Chinese models, which have not survived, whereas stone sculptures and small bronzes are better represented in China. Japan is likewise able to serve as a perfect substitute in regard to works executed in dry-lacquer technique, a very limited number of which have also survived in China. In this technique the figure is built up out of layers of coarse cloth soaked in lacquer, upon which the finer details are then modelled.

In so far as Chinese and Japanese paintings have survived from these periods, their style changes correspondingly, but with a greater wealth of forms and colours. In this connection particular mention must be made of two treasures. In the first place, the wall-paintings in the Golden Hall in the Hōryūji Temple (near Nara, Japan; early 8th cent.), now unfortunately destroyed. These represented the mature T'ang style, with its imposing majesty, lyrical delicacy and perfect elegance of form. Secondly,   PLATE P. 194
the exceptionally large collection of paintings at Tun-huang, from which we can follow the whole development from the Wei to the T'ang style.

In China the Sung period, so far as we know, produced little that was new in the Buddha image. The classical type evolved in the T'ang period was   PLATE P. 166
continued in a more or less imitative form, and remained standard, with but relatively minor modifications, far into the Ming and Ch'ing periods. The spiritual content steadily declined, especially in the case of Lamaist mass-produced objects. A different situation prevailed with regard to the Bodhisattva image, which was far less subject to the limitations imposed by solemn austerity and the hieratic attitude of meditation. Here Sung artists continued to develop the first beginnings, clearly evident already   APPX. PL. 31
in T'ang sculpture, of a tendency towards loosening and movement in the body, and towards a picturesque 'baroque' resolution of form. This   PLATE P. 196
led to the production of some novel and important works. The representation of Arhats, enlightened disciples of the Buddha, also reached a climax and remained at a fairly high level right up to the Ming period. Generally speaking, it must be admitted that later the figures degenerate into mere routine products.

Up to the end of the Nara period (approx. 800) the course of development in Japan followed that in China. Subsequently contact between the two countries became more intermittent. This was partly due to cultural and partly to political reasons: in the middle of the 8th century the power of the T'ang Dynasty was seriously undermined. The result was that steps were taken to seek out new ways. The soft modelling of the T'ang and

APPX. PL. 28 Nara styles gave way in the Jōgan period (9th cent.) to a block-like style of carving. The rather plump figures were draped in garments, the heavily curved folds of which show an extremely lively play of lines, rendered most expressive by an abstract and dynamic rhythm; this is indicative of the artists' superb feeling for the form suggested by the material. Where previously preference was given to such soft materials as bronze, lacquer and clay, now wood was favoured almost exclusively. This was due, not only to technical and economic reasons, but also to the fact that it was best suited to the Japanese sense of form. But the hard expressive style of carving fairly soon disappeared, and in a process of gradual transition gave way to a softer style, plastically less expansive, but at the same time delicate, noble and restrained. In its perfection of form, harmony and tranquillity it was a truly classical style — a pure expression of the aristocratic culture of the Fujiwara period. In the hands of the great master APPX. PL. 29 Jōchō (approx. 990—1057) this type of the Buddha became one of the most splendid of all realizations of the Buddha idea as such, and of the Amitābha figure in particular. It was imbued with vitality, majesty and gracious charm. In the painting of this period many masterpieces have survived which exhibit the utmost perfection of technique. Here, too, this PLATE P. 163 aristocratic Buddha ideal is expressed in an effective and captivating manner: remoteness and withdrawal from the finite world are combined with a truly supernatural beauty.

In sculpture the Fujiwara style soon became rigid and turned into a stereotyped imitative art — for the very reason that it had provided the classical model, which was so convenient to copy. But in or about 1200 a movement of opposition arose, when the courtly Fujiwara culture was ousted from its leading position by the knightly culture of the Kamakura period. In the hands of artists such as Unkei and members of his school the Buddha once again appeared as a noble majestic figure, with a forceful expression. Each fold of his garment was given more vigour and plasticity, more inner tension — despite the calm grandeur; this was made possible PLATE P. 164 by careful preparatory study of the subject-matter in nature, and of the way in which it functioned. This ability to produce vigorous and expressive works, which stemmed from an intimate feeling for organic forms and spiritual life, also yielded magnificent images of religious personages, and APPX. PL. 33 led to a flowering of the art of portraiture. Yet, a few exceptions apart, this style was in the last resort unable to prevail over the flat Late Fujiwara style, which held on stubbornly to its position of predominance. Just as in China, so also in Japan Buddhist sculpture of real significance did not develop after 1300; and the traditional cult painting, in which outstanding works were still produced during the same period as Kamakura sculpture, likewise underwent a very rapid decline.

However, Ch'an (Zen) Budhism provided new impulses for art, especially in the case of the Buddha image — in China during the late Sung period (13th cent.), and in Japan during the Ashikaga period (14th—16th cents.). Although Ch'an temples contain cult statues — in most cases of a very conventional kind — the rites performed before them do not form the focal-point of religious life; indeed, a thorough-going Ch'an Buddhist may even, as a well-known story informs us, use a Buddha statue for firewood, and do so with a clear conscience. The Buddha is not primarily conceived as a superhuman and even 'supra-mundane' figure, symbolizing the Absolute, but as a historical personage, as the monk Shākyamuni, who strove for Enlightenment, attained it through meditation, and then transmitted to his disciples the road by which it could be achieved — less by sermons than by direct 'transmission from spirit to spirit', for which no oral communication was necessary. To a certain extent this interpretation of the Buddha as a historical person indicates a return to Buddhism in its original form.

Artists — and here this means painters, especially the great ink-painters of the Sung period, such as Liang K'ai — represented the Buddha as a   APPX. PL. 34
man engaged in a spiritual struggle, dressed in a simple everyday garment, devoid of any traditional symbols other than the *ushnīsha,* the sign of Enlightenment; but their finest works show a magnificent ability to penetrate into the inner nature of this figure, into its spiritual power and solemn majesty. This concept is not endangered, but rather aided, by a courageous realism which shows no concern about the ancient requirement that a representation of the Buddha should possess a lofty idealized form. In the well-known and most impressive painting by Liang K'ai he is shown in an almost merciless fashion as an ascetic. This probably does not refer to the time when Shākyamuni left the mountain wilderness in despair after his fruitless ascetic experiences, but rather his return to this world after attaining Enlightenment. The interpretation of this painting may be debatable — its very depth may perhaps lie in its ambiguity — but here the spirit of Ch'an speaks to the beholder with unequivocal and arresting force, through one of the most moving works portraying a great religious figure known to world art.

Possibly we have an older version of the same theme in a painting of the early 11th century representing the Buddha under a blossoming tree, in a standing or a striding posture. This may be a copy of an original by the Central Asian painter Wei-ch'ih I-sêng (7th cent.). In any case, here,   PLATE P. 165

too, the Buddha is represented as a human being; indeed, he is depicted distinctly as an Indian. His Enlightenment is indicated, not so much by the slight suggestion of an *ushnīsha*, but rather by his attitude and expression, by the solemn colour of his red and golden robe, and by the atmosphere of nature all abloom — in other words, by psychological and lyrical means such as are unknown to hieratic cult painting. These late formulations of the Buddha image, created by presenting the person and life of Shākyamuni in its historicity, return to the original concept of Buddhism — or at least approximate to it closely. This completes the cycle of religious and artistic development begun more than a thousand years earlier — in which, despite all the strong ties of tradition, the main theme of Buddhism was given a vast number of very different, and even totally contradictory, interpretations.

IV. THE HIERARCHY OF SACRED FIGURES

1. Configurations

A Buddha figure is generally not found alone, in isolation; at the very least it is incorporated into the building of which it forms the sacral centre. From a functional point of view this is achieved by positioning it in the centre, or along the medial axis, of the building, in an apse or niche, or upon an altar, so that the *via sacra* of the entire temple complex leads up to it; it is the focal point of the iconographic programme and of the liturgy. From an aesthetic point of view this incorporation is achieved by the proportions of the figure in relation to the shrine in which it is situated, to the altar or throne-base on which it stands, as well as to the surrounding halo and the canopy suspended above it (frequently in the form of a decorated ceiling or cupola). All these elements are often combined in such a way as to form a composite whole. It is only when we perceive the functional, iconographic and formal unity between a Buddha figure and the sanctuary that we can comprehend its meaning. The same applies to any other cult image. Furthermore, the Buddha figure is very frequently incorporated into a group, either large or small, of sculpted or painted figures; these configurations are related to the building where they are situated in much the same way. The presence of sacred figures makes the consecrated area or shrine a 'Land of Buddha', which it is the artist's task to convey to the believer, who sees it, as it were, in a vision. From this point of view it is immaterial whether this divine sphere is represented by a cult chamber with statues, or by the imaginary sacred sphere of a cult painting.

FIGS. 29, 31, 38, 39, 41, 46

PLATE P. 38

FIG. 41

The religious and artistic premises underlying such extensive compositions did not, of course, exist from the very beginning of Buddhist history. At first there was but the one and only Buddha: the historical Shākyamuni, the human founder of the doctrine, and of the community of monks and laymen. This group of persons, occasionally supplemented by worshipping deities, is depicted in the early statuary at Mathurā and also in some reliefs from Gandhāra. But already in Hīnayāna we have 'Buddhas' in the plural, and they increase in number very rapidly with the spread of Mahāyāna. Buddhist thought led to various types of this plurality which at first sight seem most perplexing; these types were then represented by painters and sculptors in their works.

The first concept to appear — probably at a very early stage of development — was that of a number of 'historical' predecessors of Shākyamuni, continued in the person of his successor Maitreya. This series of figures (either with Maitreya or without) also appears on Gandhāran reliefs, as well as in aniconic form on Stūpa I at Sānchī, and time and time again in later Buddhist art. The logical development of this idea led to the production of a great number of 'Buddhas of all Worlds and all Ages' — theoretically, as many as there are grains of sand in the Ganges. They are not susceptible to measurement by criteria of time or space. In many cases they appear on temple walls and ceilings, in infinite rows of tiny figures, as the Thousand, Three Thousand, or Ten Thousand Buddhas. A pair of

Fig. 58 — Central section of the Garbhadhātu mandala (Japanese: Taizōkai mandara), Japan

Buddhas is described as having been seen in a vision in the *Lotus Sūtra,* dating from the 2nd century A.D. at the latest, and is represented very frequently in art: this pair consists of Shākyamuni and Prabhūtaratna, one of his legendary predecessors. The doctrine of the Three Bodies (cf. p. 172) led to a 'trinity' of the various forms assumed by one and the same Buddha. An idea that is in some ways similar gave rise to the concept of the Five Buddhas, consisting of the central and supreme Ādi-Buddha Vairocana and the four Dhyāni Buddhas (a common but incorrect term), who sprang from him through the power of his meditation. The latter are oriented towards the four points of the compass and are distinguished from another by their *mudrās.* Such a group of five Buddhas forms the centre-piece of one of the two huge Vajrayāna mandalas. We have already Fig. 58 come across an architectonic and plastic mandala of this type in the Borobudur (cf. pp. 133 f.).

These Buddha groups comprise units of the same type, which are in some cases graded according to their rank in the metaphysical hierarchy, and are also distinguished from one another by their iconography, although they remain within the same category of figures. The vast majority of configurations, however, are based on a different structural principle, that of the religious hierarchy, with its multiplicity of ranks. (We are not concerned here with narrative and illustrative representations: on these, see Ch. V.) The simplest one, and historically the oldest, is a triad consisting of the Buddha and two attendants: he is flanked either by gods or *yakshas,* who offer him protection and veneration, or by other worshippers, and in particular by monks and Bodhisattvas. The former hold a privileged position as listeners and disciples, the latter as manifestations and emanations of the Buddha concerned, and of his power of wisdom and mercy. This position they retained in all the regions where Buddhist works of art were produced, and in all periods. The monks and Arhats, struggling with their own spiritual and moral strength to attain self-realization and 'the emancipation of self', are prototypes of the followers of Hīnayāna. The Bodhisattvas, on the other hand, with their infinite wisdom, their compassion and readiness for self-sacrifice, and their redeeming grace, are prototypes of the followers of Mahāyāna, who put their trust in the power of others. It remains uncertain whether, as has recently been maintained, the strictly axial and symmetrical triadic group may be derived, historically and typologically, from western Asia (and in particular from the ancient Near East and Persia). We find it both in rudimentary and in fully developed form already in the art of Mathurā and Gandhāra. Preliminary stages are to be found even earlier in Indian art (Bhārhut,

PLATES PP. 35,
77
APPX. PL. 25

PLATE P. 166

PLATE P. 166

PLATE P. 169

PLATE P. 170

APPX. PL. 4

Sānchī), in the form of worshippers flanking a cult object (Fig 50).

The triad consisting of a Buddha and two Bodhisattvas, the archetype of the hierarchic group, constitutes the nucleus of virtually every larger configuration. It may be enlarged to a group of five by the addition of two monks — usually Ānanda and Kāshyapa, the two principal disciples of Shākyamuni, who represent the original monastic community; such groups of five were likewise extremely popular. The number of monks or Bodhisattvas may, however, be considerably increased. On the periphery of such large configurations a place is given to the four celestial kings or protectors of the world *(Lokapālas)* and the two 'gate guardians' *(Dvārapālas)*. These afford protection to the central group of most sacred figures, and indeed to the whole sanctuary in the temple hall and at the temple gate — and perform the same function in paintings as well. Their purpose is to ward off evil powers from the sacral sphere of the 'land of Buddha'. Above the heads of the group of Buddhas one frequently finds celestial beings known as *apsarases,* or once again Bodhisattvas. These express veneration for the Buddha, his teaching and his community, by bringing sacrificial offerings in the form of flowers and incense, as well as by music and dancing. All these attendant figures are called the Buddha's 'family' or retinue *(parivāra)*. In the painting and sculpture of India and southern Asia compositions of many figures are less frequently arranged in the hieratic symmetry and systematic gradation so popular in the art of Central and eastern Asia. In the latter areas they hold a privileged position as an iconographic theme and as a formal type, especially in groups of large statues in temples, and also in scrolls and paintings. The centre need not always be occupied by a Buddha: in principle any sacred figure — a Bodhisattva, a Vidyārāja, or a deity — may be the principal figure of a group, according to the requirements of the cult concerned. Around them are arranged symmetrically all kinds of creatures, as a sort of 'family'; their rank in the pantheon varies, but they are always subordinate to the main figure.

Chinese Buddhist sculpture produced a configuration of a special kind: the stone votive stele erected in front of temple halls or by graves. On the front — but frequently on the rear and the narrow sides as well — are several relief panels with detailed representations: groups of Buddhas in niches, often with worshippers and donors; individual images of Buddhas and Bodhisattvas in separate registers; and compositions or scenes illustrating the life of Shākyamuni or a *sūtra* text. In the example shown we can see, at the bottom, a lotus pond, lions and tutelary deities; above this is a configuration, the main group, consisting of one Buddha, two Bod-

*Fig. 59 — Diagram of a wall-
painting in the Golden Hall
of the Hōryūji, Japan*

hisattvas, and four monks; over this group is a scene taken from the
Vimalakīrti Sūtra; and right on top Maitreya meditating under a tree
(or else Shākyamuni as a youthful prince). The stele is crowned by typical
Chinese celestial dragons — a re-interpretation of the Indian snake kings
(nāgarāja) which also occur frequently in Buddhist legend. These stelae,
which were popular between the 6th century and the T'ang period, often
bear votive inscriptions with exact dates, and are therefore extremely
valuable to the art historian. They are derived from the stelae with inscriptions and the commemorative stelae which were common from the
Han period onwards; but the pictorial representations on them were
probably inspired by reliefs on the walls of cave-temples. Possibly the
first stimulus to produce such reliefs may have been given by the sculptures
on monuments at Gandhāra; these furnish many examples of panels
placed vertically over one another, featuring ritual and ceremonial compositions as well as narrative scenes. Since there was no place for stone reliefs
in the wooden temple architecture of China, the indigenous type of stele
was used.

Fig. 60 — Wood-cut representing the so-called Taima Mandara (Sukhāvatī of Buddha Amitābha). Tapestry, much restored by painting. 8th cent. Taima-dera, Japan

Plate p. 169

Plate p. 252

The configurations are usually based upon *sūtra* texts, which describe with boundless poetic imagination the Buddha's sermons before a vast assembly of Bodhisattvas, monks and other people, in the splendour of an imaginary supernatural realm: in a manner of speaking, therefore, these ceremonial and hieratic groups are 'illustrations'. Another source of such groups of different figures are the biographical and legendary tales about Shākyamuni's spiritual career, some of which have similarly given rise to symmetrical compositions in which the Buddha is the focal point. In certain circumstances the tale recorded in the text then leads to the establishment of a hieratic configuration (for further details, see Ch. V).

Many texts describe in the most vivid detail the visionary realm or 'Pure Land' of a Buddha; and most of these typical configurations are in essence concise representations of this theme. They are thus frequently found on the walls of temples facing the four points of the compass, the location of the 'pure Lands' of the most popular Buddhas (in most cases Shākyamuni, Maitreya, Bhaishajyaguru — the healing Buddha — and Amitābha). An example of this is the 'Golden Hall' at Hōryūji in Japan. Special emphasis was given to 'Sukhāvatī', the 'Pure Land' of the Buddha Amitābha, situated in the western quarter. It was represented most effectively at Tun-huang and all over eastern Asia, in wall-paintings and scrolls that were frequently of monumental size; these give a literal illustration of the texts, but at the same time have as their central group a large configuration serving as a cult image. It is set within an architectonic framework, is divided into several sub-groups, and also shows the faithful blissfully reincarnated as little children in lotus-blossoms. The central panel is bordered on the right and left by series of pictorial compositions illustrating the relevant legend — i.e. the chain of 'causes' of which, according to the doctrine of karma, reincarnation in glory is the consequence or 'fruit'. In contrast to the usual type of configurations, which appear devoid of three-dimensional space, and have a neutral and empty ground, here the picture seems to be built up from a central perspective-point; but in fact (except in the case of some small marginal buildings) this is the usual eastern Asian construction of space with lines of depth (orthogonals) running parallel, the only difference being that here these parallels converge towards a medial axis. But this fact is in itself remarkable, since it is not common elsewhere in eastern Asian three-dimensional representations. This means that the strict hieratic composition of the picture was intended to convey a non-empirical other-worldly ideal realm. This type of image is mainly met with in eastern Asia (including Tun-huang). The origin of its iconography and form is as yet unclear — possibly, as in the case of the Buddha Amitābha himself, it is derived from the Near East.

The small panels with pictures which sometimes occur on the lower border of the Sukhāvatī panorama represent — in accordance with the texts — nine variations of the story how Amitābha, accompanied by a host of his Bodhisattvas, soars down from his realm to the death-bed of a believer, to receive him and lead him to his glorious reincarnation. This special theme was also treated in independent paintings and was particularly popular in Japan (under the name of Amida-Raigō). Amitābha and his companions gradually cease to be so strictly bound by the symmetry of the configuration; their movements become more dynamic; and eventually

FIG. 59

FIG. 60

PLATE P. 179

they are to be seen soaring swiftly across the picture at an oblique angle. This is an interesting illustration of the transition from a hieratic cult image, worshipped by devout believers, to the portrayal of an event taking place in time and space: the finite and the infinite worlds come to be shown, not as mutually opposed, but as approximating to one another and linked.

FIG. 58 A configuration of a very different kind from that discussed hitherto is the mandala. This is not an illustration to a text, a visionary image of a future state of redemption — a living realization, as it were, of the holy personages depicted. Instead, it is a far more theoretical and speculative construction, an abstract and schematic diagram of the world. It is primarily a geometric system of lines, circles and panels — indeed, this is its purest form, and the highest from the ontological standpoint, since it is least blurred by images drawn from the phenomenal world. A mere secondary role is played by the figures of holy personages with which it is filled in, or the symbols that represent them (e.g. the wheel, *vajra,* etc.),

FIG. 70 or even the mystical characters *(siddham)*. A mandala may also be formed by the layout of architectural members (e.g. pillars) of a sanctuary, as we saw when considering stūpas, pagodas and the Borobudur. The mandala probably entered Buddhism from Hinduism, in which it played an outstanding part in cult and meditation from very ancient times right up to the present. The original meaning of the Sanskrit term mandala was 'circle', especially a magic circle in which deities were invoked and represented — and also an altar. In Mahāyāna, and especially in Vajrayāna, it means a tablet, divided into circles and rectangular panels representing the metaphysical structure of the world (shown in its development outwards from the centre), which is designed to serve the believer as an aid to meditation on the way to perfect Enlightenment, i.e. on the means of re-incorporating himself into the original unity. For this reason the mandala has been appropriately called a 'diagram for meditation' (von Glasenapp) or a 'psycho-cosmogram' (Tucci), since no essential difference exists between the mind of the onlooker and the real essence of the world. Almost every Buddha, Bodhisattva or other sacred being may be the centre of a mandala. The most fully developed form is that of a pair, the 'mandalas of the Two Worlds' — an all-embracing cosmic diagram comprising hundreds of figures or symbols. The centre of each of its constituent mandalas is — in accordance with the doctrine of non-duality — the Ādi-Buddha Vairocana, representing the Absolute and at the same time all individual phenomena. On one hand, in the 'Diamond World' *(vajradhātu),* it represents the potential undisclosed aspect of the world

PLATE 49 – ARHAT (LOHAN). Hanging scroll: ink and pigments on silk. 12th cent. Japan. Height 96 cm. *National Museum, Tokyo* (formerly in Raigō-ji Temple, Shiga province).
The Arhat (Chinese: Lohan; Japanese: Rakan) is feeding a mythological animal from his begging-bowl, thus exercising the Buddhist virtues of charity and sympathy for all living creatures.

PLATE 50 – THE PATRIARCH SHUBHĀKARASIMHA. Hanging scroll: ink and colours on silk. Ichijō-ji, Kyōto, Japan. 12th cent., based on an earlier model. Height 162 cm., probably somewhat shortened.

Shubhākarasimha (Chinese: Shan-wu-wei; Japanese: Ze(n)-mu-i; roughly equivalent to 'Sublime Lion') was a prince from Central Asia who lived from 636 to 735. He became a priest of an esoteric Buddhist sect and worked in China, *inter alia* as translator of the principal *sūtras*, such as the *Vairocana Sūtra;* he is holding a sacred scroll of this kind reverently before his brow. Shubhākarasimha is one of the patriarchs of the T'ien-t'ai school. Beside him is the Lokapāla (Guardian of the World) Vaishravana (Japanese: Bishamon), whom the patriarch is apparently evoking into existence by means of a *mantra* (magic formula). As 'Guardian of the North' the Lokapāla is regarded as protector of the T'ien-t'ai (Japanese: Ten-dai) monastery on Mount Hiei, north of Kyōto.

PLATE 51 – MYŌE-SHŌNIN. Detail from a hanging scroll: light ink and colours on paper. Kōzan-ji, Kyōto, Japan. Beginning of 13th cent. Height of scroll 1.46 m., of detail shown approx. 90 cm.

This portrait of the venerable (Shōnin) Myōe, 1173–1232, was probably done by one of his disciples who was a painter as well as a monk. He is depicted in a very lifelike way and with magnificent brushwork, at his daily meditation in a tree on the slope behind his monastery. Beside him, on a branch to the right, are his rosary and censer, and on the ground his wooden sandals. This is one of the most impressive renderings of the simple Buddhist monastic way of life, with its practice of meditation and intimacy with nature.

which is to be realized by insight — Absolute Wisdom, as pure idea that is unchangeable and indestructible. On the other hand, it represents the 'World of the Womb' *(garbha[kosha]dhātu)*, the actual aspect of the world, as it develops dynamically in its innumerable manifestations — as the principle of reason in the world, the 'womb' which yields the 'fruit', the ability to perceive the Absolute and to realize its ultimate identity with the phenomenal aspect — in other words, redemption itself.

The artistic form of a mandala can vary, since it is only a general means of bringing about system and order. Whole works of architecture, or parts of them, may constitute a mandala; so may groups of sculptured figures, drawings of geometric symbols or figures, inscribed tablets, paintings (wall-paintings or scrolls, painted in rich colours or even in gold), and finally even impermanent figures produced from coloured sand or fragrant powder. (This is not the place to go into the interpretation of the mandala given in the depth psychology of C. G. Jung and others.)

All configurations have in common certain principles of form inherent in their character as hieratic cult images, divorced from space and time. These are: symmetry, axiality, centrality and frontality. Centrality implies the preponderance of the central figure, attained by its dominating size and the hieratic scaling of the other figures according to their importance. Frontality implies an arrangement in the two-dimensional plane; the work is situated *vis-à-vis* the beholder, and at the same time beyond the empirical, three-dimensional, phenomenal world. For most sacred figures are divorced from the sphere of *samsāra*. In art all means must be brought into play in order to give them the requisite transcendental character, and to define the area in which they are situated as ideal — in other words, as a symbolic sphere. From an iconographic and formal point of view, as well as from the standpoint of ritual function, this type of configuration, in all its manifold forms, is the antithesis of the representation of narrative: the latter is inherently limited in space and time; it is located in the empirical world, in the sphere of human action and suffering. This is a type of representation which we shall come back to later.

2. *Individual Types*

Below the supreme central figure of the Buddha (cf. Ch. III) there is a numerous pantheon, the members of which are graded in strict sequence according to rank. Corresponding to this is a sequence of types of figure — infinitely richer in Mahāyāna than in Hīnayāna, where it is limited to a small number of sacred personages grouped around the Buddha Shākya-

Fig. 61 — Torsos of Bodhisattva: a) from Sānchī, India. Pāla style, 7th—9th cents. Victoria and Albert Museum, London. b) From Lung-yen-shan, Hopei province, China. Approx. 700. Mrs. Rockefeller Collection, New York

muni. We have already traced the main phases in the stylistic development of the Buddha image. Owing to limitations of space, we shall now only point out some of the principal differences in the artistic formulation of the most important types of figure, going through the hierarchy from the top downwards.

Closest to the Buddha is the Bodhisattva, 'One whose nature is Understanding (or Enlightenment)', who in innumerable incarnations has attained the supreme wisdom and virtue necessary for Buddhahood and entrance into the perfect state of nirvāna, but who for the time being voluntarily and magnanimously renounces his personal redemption to help redeem all other living beings. To this end he applies all possible expedients *(upāya)*, especially by adopting many different incarnations. His compassion *(karunā)* finds a response in the pious devotion *(bhakti)* of the believer; with the non-believer it brings about his conversion. Bodhisattvas are seen as emanations of the essence of Buddhas, and wisdom and mercy on their part are seen as manifestations of the wisdom and mercy of Buddhas. Bodhisattvas are intermediaries between the Buddha, who has entered nirvāna, and the *samsāra* sphere of suffering — i.e. they are concerned with what is above as well as with what is below them. On one hand they no longer belong to the world of *samsāra;* but on the other hand they have only entered nirvāna potentially, not in actual fact. The Bodhisattva is a specifically Mahāyāna concept: partly because he mediates between the realms of *samsāra* and nirvāna (which in Hīnayāna are sharply opposed), and partly because of his altruism, his readiness to sacrifice himself in order to redeem others and save the world. In this way the Bodhisattva, representing the religious ideal of Mahāyāna, stands in contrast to the Arhat, the ideal figure of original Buddhism, who strives to attain salvation through his own power. The monastic severity of early Buddhism is thus supplemented by an emotional element of loving devotion, of enthusiasm, of belief in the miraculous. This gives Buddhist art a lyrical charm which it originally lacked.

The difficult task of comprising in one image the intermediate and dual nature of the Bodhisattva was from the start solved in a brilliant fashion; the result was the creation of a large number of masterpieces. The Bodhisattva appears as a sublime, superhuman, blessed being, elevated above the finite world yet not entirely divorced from it, as is the case with the Buddha. For this reason he is depicted in a more human, terrestrial and less abstract form. His figure has vitality, suppleness and mobility, kindliness and beauty. His turns of the body and gestures enable him to penetrate into the third dimension of empirical existence to a much greater extent than the Buddha ever can. Characteristic is the pose of the body known as *tribhanga* ('thrice bent'), which superficially appears to be related to the PLATE P. 193 Greek *contrapposto*. This affords it a quality of charming suppleness, calling to mind the grace of a dancer.

Bodhisattvas are depicted wearing a richly folded garment covering the APPX. PL. lower part of the body, leaving the upper part bare, a long 'shawl', and 30, 31 the costly jewellery appropriate to a prince: a towering coiffure, with strings of beads threaded into the hair, pendants and pectorals, armlets and anklets. Most of them are shown holding one or more attributes: a lotus flower, a bottle of nectar, a sword, a scroll, or other objects too varied to enumerate here. Many of them have on their foreheads the sign of Enlightenment, the *ūrnā*, and an aureole behind the head or the whole body. In appearance a Bodhisattva is partly mundane and partly spiritual; this serves to distinguish him from a Buddha. On the other hand, the two figures are related: the Bodhisattva is shown turning in veneration towards the Buddha, of whom he is deemed to be a mystical descendant; by the *tribhanga* posture he helps to bring about the compact group of the triad. Yet he also exhibits the attitude of a mediator, by turning at the FIG. 59 same time towards the world, and by his more mundane appearance generally. From its origins in Gandhāran art the Bodhisattva figure is represented as a young Indian prince; but attempts were increasingly made to soften the typically masculine features and to give the figure a APPX. PL. 21 character at once more engaging and more majestic, both in the bodily form and in the posture. For this reason the Westerner is inclined to PLATE P. 180 regard the Indian type, rather portly and voluptuous, as somewhat femi- APPX. PL. 31 nine in character. But the artists attempted with ever greater success to reproduce in this way one of the most important features of a Bodhisattva: his asexual (or 'supra-sexual') character, a natural consequence of the fact that he had overcome all the determinatives and dualities of the empirical domain, the world of *samsāra*.

This basic type is to be met with in the Buddhist art of all countries where Bodhisattvas were worshipped — from Gandhāra in the west to Java in the south and Japan in the east — i.e., mainly in Mahāyāna areas, but also in some others. In Gandhāra it apparently evolved in close association with the development of Mahāyāna, at first as a figure accompanying the

Buddha, but from the 3rd century onwards as an independent cult figure as well. The Bodhisattvas of Mathurā bear a closer resemblance to the ancient figures of *yakshas*. On the other hand, the graceful princely type, with its rich adornment, is continued in a modified form in Gupta art, as well as in the Mahāyāna art of central Java. The latter is derived from the former, and like that of Shrīvijaya, produced some magnificent Bodhisattva figures.[18] The Gupta type, and its later variant the Pāla type, seem to have had a fairly immediate effect upon T'ang sculpture in China. In the Hīnayāna regions, especially in Ceylon and Thailand, this type of Bodhisattva plays no significant part; even Lokeshvara, who is of such importance in Cambodia, is not so much a Bodhisattva in the Mahāyāna sense as 'Lord of the World' in the sense of Hindu mythology, on the pattern of Brahmā and Shiva.

Originally there was only *one* Bodhisattva in Buddhism and in the texts associated with it: Shākyamuni himself, in the Jātaka tales of his earlier lives, in which he appears in all kinds of incarnations, ranging from king down to animal, and notably in his last existence, during the period prior to his Enlightenment (i.e. his becoming Buddha) — in other words, when he was already designated for Buddhahood. This was in accordance with the initial belief in one single Buddha, to which reference has been made above, and it was not until the doctrine of the existence of several (and, indeed, innumerable) Buddhas arose that there came to be a large number of Bodhisattvas as well. To them were added, in the course of time, many purely imaginary figures; and great saintly monks and teachers were regarded as Bodhisattvas as well. They were seen either as incarnations of them or as potential Buddhas; often this title was conferred upon them as a mark of honour. Shākyamuni is naturally most frequently portrayed as a Bodhisattva in representations that have some bearing on the story of his life, i.e. in narrative works as opposed to cult images. Since he was a prince, his appearance was noble and he was embellished with the rich jewellery appropriate to his princely rank. This may be one of the sources for the standard Bodhisattva figure. The other source may be sought in the regal appearance of deities such as Indra and Brahmā, and possibly also in the idea of a world ruler *(cakravartin)*, which was transferred to the Bodhisattva type. But, as we shall see, these two types are also sharply distinguished from one another. Shākyamuni is frequently represented in a posture of meditation — the first such meditation in his life, when he was still in the royal park belonging to his father. The right foot rests

PLATE P. 180

PLATES PP. 37, 191

PLATE P. 192

18 B. P. Groslier, op. cit., p. 88.

238

upon the left knee; the right knee supports the right arm, and the right hand touches the cheek. The pose is one of charming nonchalant pensiveness — not yet the unshakable attitude found in the later, final meditation under the Bodhi Tree, when the Buddha seems to be engrossed in contemplation of eternity, divorced from space and time.

The princely posture is also used for Maitreya, the Buddha of the future cosmic age, who still tarries as a Bodhisattva in the Tushita heaven, waiting the hour of his last incarnation, whereupon he will spend a lifetime on earth like Shākyamuni, but in a world that is happier and in some sense closer to salvation. Maitreya, in other words, is a kind of Messiah figure. (We shall not discuss the possibility of Maitreya and other Bodhisattvas having originated from the Near East, and whether they may be connected with Iranian concepts of a saviour and of gods of light. Recent research suggests that these hypotheses deserve to be given consideration, but at the same time one must beware of underestimating the differences between the concepts and figures of Zoroastrianism and Buddhism.)

Maitreya was probably the first new Bodhisattva figure to develop. It was the logical consequence of the idea that there were consecutive Buddhas in the past, present and future. He first appeared in Gandhāran art, and then became the most popular Bodhisattva, especially during the early period APPX. PL. 24 of Buddhism in eastern Asia — in China during the Six Dynasties period, in Korea at the time of the Three States, and in Japan during the Asuka APPX. PL. 15 period, from which several images have survived to the present day. He is not only represented in the seated posture described, but also in another one resembling the European seated posture, with the ankles crossed — an attitude of expectancy and preparedness. In the finest works his expression also conveys a consciousness of his exalted mission: it is an indescribable mixture of shy restraint, as of a budding flower, and a sense of promise and ultimate perfection in the distant future. But this type soon disappeared again: from 500 onwards Maitreya came to be regarded ever more frequently as a Buddha who has attained perfection and as lord of a 'Pure Land'. He is represented in cult statues and paintings, often in the PLATE P. 169 usual large configurations.

Of the vast number of Mahāyāna Bodhisattvas only the most important ones can be mentioned here. Pride of place is taken by Avalokiteshvara, the greatest and most famous of all Bodhisattvas. His name denotes either 'the lord who looks down mercifully [upon the suffering of the world]' or 'lord of resplendent brilliance'. In China he is called Kuan-shih-yin, or Kuanyin for short; according to the etymology advanced by ancient translators, Avalokiteshvara means 'he that looks upon the world's cries of distress', ready to help the suffering. The Koreans pronounce the Chinese name as K(w)anseum, the Japanese as K(w)an-ze-on, or usually as Kannon. Avalokiteshvara is the compassionate succourer in distress *par excellence*. He enjoyed immense popularity all over Asia, in various phases of the development of Buddhism and at different levels of spirituality; thus also in art he is the Bodhisattva who is represented more frequently than any other. He may perhaps originate from the Iranian religion of light, like the Buddha Amitābha, as whose attendant he first appears in the triadic groups of Gandhāran art — in conjunction with his less important partner, Mahāsthāmaprāpta. Religious speculation and popular piety invest him with immense wisdom and the power to work miracles, as a result of which, as Buddhism becomes hinduized and popularized, he becomes cosmic ruler of the world, resembling Brahmā, and finally, in Tantrism, is assimilated to Shiva. He thus also came to be associated with the

PLATES PP. 37, 191

ideology of sacral kingship *(devarāja)*, especially in Indochina, in the guise of Lokeshvara ('Lord of the World') . Like Shiva, Avalokiteshvara possesses various magic powers, symbolized in many of his guises by his having

PLATE P. 198

several heads and arms. Like Shiva again, he could also take on a fearsome guise, and could put his arms around a *shakti* in mystical union. But these

PLATE P. 210

manifestations of Bodhisattva are restricted to Vajrayāna, and even in many Vajrayāna areas are of limited importance — they play their most significant role in Tibet, which is outside the scope of this volume.

From the Gandhāran period onwards Avalokiteshvara appears as a typical

APPX. PL. 21

Bodhisattva figure, as a young prince wearing costly attire and jewellery, and this remains his basic form throughout almost the whole of Asia. The sign by which he may be recognized, but which only gradually acquired a strictly obligatory character, is a small seated or standing

PLATES PP. 182, 191

Buddha figure on the front of his head-dress: Amitābha, whose manifestation he is believed to be. Further attributes, which are of course also worn by other Bodhisattvas, are the lotus flower (thus he is called Padmapāni, 'the one holding a lotus') and a bottle of nectar. In his function as attendant on, and 'ambassador' of, Amitābha he may be seen

PLATE P. 195
PLATE P. 194

everywhere on Sukhāvatī and Raigō images, but in sculpture and painting he also appears as a separate cult image. In addition to this basic form Avalokiteshvara takes on innumerable other guises, for his ability to transform himself knows no limits; it springs from his infinite readiness to help others and from his magic powers.

In the late Tantric forms of the middle of the 1st millennium A.D. these ideas are brought out in a striking manner. Consider, for example,

Cintāmani-cakra-Avalokiteshvara (rendered with 'wishing jewel' and PLATE P. 198 Wheel of the Doctrine), whose six arms fulfil all wishes. A similar significance is ascribed to the Thousand-armed Avalokiteshvara. The Eleven-faced Avalokiteshvara carries on his head nine further Bodhisattva heads and is crowned by a Buddha head. According to one explanation three of these nine faces express sympathy with the suffering, three anger about evil, and three joy about goodness; the Buddha head (of Amitābha, of course) signifies the wisdom of Enlightenment as the source and goal of Avalokiteshvara's activity. According to another explanation the large head and the nine small Bodhisattva heads symbolize the ten stages of the Bodhisattva's endeavours, and the eleventh crowning head their 'fruit', i.e. Buddhahood. Also met with is a series of six manifestations of Avalokiteshvara, as helpers of those living creatures who suffer in the six realms of the *samsāra* cycle (i.e. the realms of purgatory, of the ravenous spirits of the dead *(preta)*, of animals, of pugnacious demons *(asura)*, of human beings and of deities).

All too often, even in specialist literature (and for this reason it is necessary to go into this problem here), the view is expressed that Avalokiteshvara appears in eastern Asia as a female figure, that Kuanyin is a 'goddess of mercy', or 'the Madonna of the East', since the Bodhisattva is often portrayed carrying a child in his arms. Put in these terms, this view is completely erroneous. Never is it possible for a Bodhisattva to be a 'god' or a 'goddess'. (We shall come back to this point later.) Moreover, in eastern Asian thinking a divine mother is found only at what, from the standpoint of the Bodhisattva idea, is a low level of myth-making. Apart from this, the idea that Kuanyin is feminine contradicts the notion that any Bodhisattva has overcome the difference between the sexes, as well as any other dualities found in the sphere of *samsāra*. Moreover, it also contradicts the visual evidence, in most of the sculpted and painted figures, including those from more recent epochs after the Sung period, which shows that the figures are not female. On the contrary, many of them have a small PLATES PP. 195, 196 moustache and correspond in other respects as well to the princely Bodhisattva type. Originally, indeed, it was masculine — for according to Buddhist thought only reincarnation as a man may lead to Buddhahood — but it does display some traits that can easily be mistaken for feminine ones. They are designed to suggest the absence of characteristics of either sex. This is indeed brought out in most representations: for example, the attire, coiffure, jewellery, the soft contours of the body, and the *tribhanga* pose all contribute to this effect. In addition to this there are renderings of Kuanyin in which he is shown clad in wide flowing garments, with the head covered, and occasionally even carrying a child in his arms, or alternatively which depict a maiden carrying a basket of fish.

These representations stem from a period not earlier than the latter half of the Sung period, which is a very late era for Buddhist art; in most cases they are of much more recent date. With regard to the former type, we may say that already in the 'Lotus Sūtra' (200 A.D. at the latest) Avalokiteshvara is said to grant women their desire to bear children, and to fulfil innumerable other wishes as well as easing any distress. But Avalokiteshvara himself can on no account be regarded as a mother; and if in China Kuanyin is depicted holding a child this is not a child of his own. (One other point: it would also be virtually impossible to speak of 'her' child because the Chinese and Japanese languages have no genders.) The other type may be explained by reference to a legend — one that is not uncommon in Buddhism: the tale of Ma-lang-fu, which tells of Avalokiteshvara's deliberate and helpful incarnation as a girl, as a result of which the inhabitants of a certain part of China were converted to Buddhism. The Bodhisattva here uses a 'skilful expedient' (upāya), but remains what he is and does not really change into a woman. There are even paintings of Ma-lang-fu, alias Kuanyin, with the Fish-Basket in which he is shown wearing a moustache! Two other motifs may have played a more important part here. In the first place, Avalokiteshvara the succourer in distress may now and then have been merged with popular tutelary goddesses, especially those of mariners — a process that occurs frequently as a religion becomes popularized. Secondly, the later image of Kuanyin may possibly have been influenced by the concept of a female partner of Avalokiteshvara, Tārā — particularly in the mild and kindly form of the 'white Tārā'. But even 'Kuanyin clad in a white robe' is never represented in the form of a female figure as distinctly as a tārā normally would be. Myth-making, popular syncretism, reinterpretation of ancient concepts in a new sense, native legendary motifs: all this shows that we are dealing here with a secondary form of development, a more recent phase superimposed on the original concept and irrelevant to Buddhist teaching and art during the crucial main epochs (i.e. to approximately 1100–1200). This syncretic popularization is directly connected with the social and intellectual decline of Buddhism from the Sung period onwards; and it is one of the clearest testimonies to its fusion with Chinese legends, with their strong tinge of Taoism, and with the popular religion of the country. In so far as the late images of Kuanyin really imply a trend towards femininity, and this is not just a misinterpretation, they may be seen as a phenomenon of folkloristic popularization. They have little to do with the true and sublime concept of the Bodhisattva — one of the most noble in all Buddhist thought, which led to some of the most magnificent works in the whole of Buddhist art. There is no denying that a certain amiability and charm emanates from these popular but not very significant figures.

We are faced with an altogether different problem in the case of the figure of Prajnāpāramitā, Supreme Wisdom, which in some points corresponds to the Sophia of the Gnostics. This figure originated in Tantrism, and developed from an abstract religious-philosophical concept into a sacred being, from a *nomen* to a *numen*. Partly in conformity with the grammatical gender of the Sanskrit concept, but probably for deeper psychological reasons as well, this figure is represented in female guise, as the counterpart of the supreme Buddha (strictly speaking, she is not a Bodhisattva). According to the testimony of Fa-hsien she appeared in India about 400 A.D. at the latest. She was popular in southern Asia, where the queen was regarded as her incarnation, just as the king was thought to be an incarnation of Lokeshvara or Shiva. She also found a place in the Vajrayāna mandala of eastern Asia; but in this case she was furnished with six arms, to symbolize the six perfections of the highest form of wisdom; elsewhere the number of arms was even greater. Prajnāpāramitā is also referred to as 'the Mother of all Buddhas' — which is of course to be taken in a metaphorical and metaphysical sense. Another hypostasis of a religious-philosophical concept occurs with the Bodhisattva Akāshagarbha. As his name (= 'womb of the void') denotes, he embodies one of the principal ideas of Mahāyāna: understanding that the true nature of the world is emptiness *(shūnyatā)*.

PLATES PP. 207, 208

The Absolute Buddha Vairocana also appears in Vajrayāna art in the guise of a Bodhisattva: as Vajrasattva, who under Hindu influence is occasionally represented with four faces. He is also depicted with five bodies. The latter form represents the five Buddhas which form a group in the centre of the mandala (cf. p. 225), and these in turn are manifested in the crowns of the five Bodhisattva heads. This shows the interrelationship, indeed the ultimate unity, between appearance and essence, between 'cause' and 'fruit', conveyed by the reciprocal representation of all these symbolic figures.

PLATE P. 198 FIG. 62

Of the large number of Bodhisattvas we shall select only three more that play an important role in art, especially in eastern Asia. Samantabhadra and Manjushrī are also manifestations of supreme wisdom and ethical perfection. They appear in triadic groups as attendants of Shākyamuni, who has now long since become a 'trans-historical' Buddha. One of them

Fig. 62 — Vajrasattva: form of Buddha Vairocana. Iconographic ink-drawing. 13th cent. Japan. Seattle Art Museum. Cf. p. 243

is seated on a white elephant with six tusks, the other on a golden lion. Both animals symbolize the mighty power of insight that can conquer all obstacles. In Tantrism Samantabhadra is regarded as a manifestation of Vajrasattva (Vairocana). Manjushrī is provided with two attributes which symbolize this understanding in different ways: the book of Prajnāpāramitā, which contains the all-enlightening truth, and the sword that cuts through all the darkness of delusion and error. In Mahāyāna art, especially in eastern Asia, these two Bodhisattvas are rendered with all the majesty and charm of which the artist's poetic imagination is capable. A special

PLATE P. 209 case is Kshitigarbha ('Womb of Earth'), the only Bodhisattva who appears in the guise of a monk, but distinguished from ordinary monks by the *ūrnā* on his brow, by his nimbus, and by his attribute of a wish-jewel *(cintāmani)*. He is one of the most amiable figures in the whole pantheon, and was widely worshipped and represented in works of art, especially in Japan, from the 11th century onwards; he is still popular there today.

Vajrayāna, already mentioned several times as the source of a large number of figures, also includes the category of Vidyārājas, the 'kings of wisdom *(vidyā)*', most prominent among whom are a group of five dominating FIG. 63 figures. Like Prajñāpāramitā, these represent the hypostasis of various aspects of the absolute wisdom manifest in the Buddha Vairocana; they are related both to him and to the four Buddhas that sprang forth from him; like the latter, they are oriented towards the four cardinal directions; and they thus hold a very high rank in the hierarchy. Whereas the Bodhisattva represents the gentle and calm *(shānta)* aspect of the supreme sacred essence, the Vidyārāja represents the wrathful *(krodha)* one. In both these types of figure a primeval religious experience has assumed a Buddhist form — that 'harmony in contrast' of the *numinosum* which Rudolf Otto has called the *fascinans* and the *tremendum*. In Vajrayāna even the Bodhisattva may manifest himself either in a mild or in a wrathful guise; the PLATE P. 210 latter is illustrated by the horse-headed Avalokiteshvara.

In this case of course we are dealing with an alient element, which penetrated into Buddhism from Hindu mythology — or to be exact, from Shivaist mythology. According to this view the god, who comprises the entire world, with all its polarities, wears a dual aspect: graceful and creative, yet at the same time fearful and destructive. It is from Shivaist mythology and iconography that most of these terrifying Buddhist figures originate, as do many of their attributes and symbols — among them the 'third eye', an eye of natural shape placed vertically in the middle of the forehead. In Buddhist art it only occurs among these figures, and testifies to their religious and historical origin; it must not be confused with the *ūrnā* of the Buddhas and most Bodhisattvas. According to Buddhist teaching the wrath of the Vidyārājas, the weapons they carry, and the blazing flames of their aureoles are directed against the darkness of igno- PLATE P. 211 rance and illusion *(a-vidyā)*, which hinders men from understanding the true nature of all things, and thus from attaining emancipation and redemption; it is thus the source of all evil. As incarnations of the Buddha's wisdom, the Vidyārājas exert a beneficent effect. The most important of them, Acala ('the unmovable, unshakable one') is an 'emissary' of the Ādi-Buddha Vairocana, and is known by one of the many names of Shiva. His figure, like most of these fearsome Tantric beings, is derived ultimately from India, but was adopted in definitive form in China from the T'ang period onwards. It was particularly widely diffused in Japan after the late 9th century. From an artistic point of view it was embodied most impressively in works of sculpture and painting which convey the nature of this figure, and those of the other Vidyārājas, in an extremely con-

Fig. 63 — Rāgarāja (Japanese: Aizen-Myōō), one of the 'kings of wisdom' of Vajrayāna Buddhism. Iconographic drawing. Japan

vincing manner by vigorous, dynamic and expressive treatment of form and by sombre glowing colours.

Tantrism developed on an extensive scale in India, Nepal and Tibet as well as in China (where only a few ancient works have survived), and also in Japan (where they are to be found in abundance). In all these countries, from the middle of the 1st millennium A.D. onwards, a vast number of sacred figures appeared which belonged to the category of Bodhisattvas and Vidyārājas. Some of them are derived from Hindu deities; others owe their existence to the Tantric tendency to differentiate and classify the mystical and scholastic pantheon, to systematize it, and to make it ever more perfect and complete. It was arranged in the form of an ordered diagram in large mandalas, and described in detail in such comprehensive texts as the *Sādhanamālā*. Many of these figures have a multiplication of heads, arms and legs, as well as their attributes and colours, which symbolizes omniscience, omnipresence and omnipotence. Only a few general remarks on this point are possible here; we shall refrain (quite gladly!) from considering in detail the extremely complicated iconography of these figures, let alone their history, about which little is as yet known.

Deities *(deva)* are one rank below the categories discussed so far. The latter rank very high in the hierarchy since they belong to the sphere of nirvāna and in one way or another are closely related to the Buddha (or to the Buddhas in the plural). But with the *deva* an important border-line has been crossed: for they already form part of the *samsāra* cycle of re-birth, of the six realms of existence *(gati,* cf. pp. 241 f.). These deities reside in celestial spheres *(devaloka)*, situated one above the other. They vary in character and rank: they rise above the 'world of desire' *(kāmadhātu)* first of all to the 'world of pure form' *(rūpadhātu)* and then to the 'world without form' *(arūpadhātu)*. They may be visualized in various stages of meditation. Although the *devas* are far superior to men as regards their life-span, their state of bliss, and their freedom from 'earthly remains', they are not immortal and do not rule the world; still less have they entered nirvāna. Some exceptions apart, all of them are subject to karma; in order to be redeemed, they have to be re-born on the human plane — because, as it is put so well, in their blissful state, free from any desires, they are too far removed from the experience of suffering to be able to comprehend the nature of life; for life as such means to adhere blindly to deceptive appearances, and this leads to the growth of desires, and ultimately to suffering; yet it is necessary to transcend this if one is to take the first step towards emancipation, towards Buddhahood. (This shows how wrong it is to call Buddhas or Bodhisattvas 'gods' or 'deities': it is true that there was often something that resembled theism in popular religious beliefs; yet this belief was not actually the same thing as theism, and never attained the level of authentic doctrine. In art, too, the type of Buddha and Bodhisattva figure was always distinguished from that of the *deva*.) Ancient Indian deities were taken over by Buddhists, who entrusted them with various functions: to bring good fortune and aid in times of distress, to promote good and ward off evil, to ensure due order in the natural and moral world, and above all to protect and worship the Buddha, his doctrine and the Buddhist community. The cult of gods was regarded by the earliest Buddhists as something tinged with a low form of popular religiosity; it was not, however, on that account despised or combated.

Already in early works of art at Bhārhut, Bhāja, Mathurā, Gandhāra and elsewhere we find a number of deities, either performing a tutelary function or distributing their blessing. In the Gandhāran reliefs the main gods are Indra and Brahmā, who appear in scenes taken from the legend of the Buddha, or as his attendants or worshippers. But in the course of development the mythological substratum once more came to the fore, and the gods soon acquired a respected position, as can be observed in a large number of iconographically differentiated Mahāyāna works.

PLATES PP. 35, 77

The following categories of divine beings are of particular importance in the history of art — especially in eastern Asia, where Japan once again has the best preserved works to offer.

(*i*). The Twelve Gods: Brahmā, Indra and ten others, some of whom are of Vedic origin. These are associated with the elements of nature, the points of the compass, heaven and earth, the sun and the moon; they thus have a cosmological significance as well. In art they appear predominantly as noble figures, wearing costly robes and jewellery (in China and Japan, even the fashions of the T'ang period are often followed). This type also includes Shrī or Lakshmī, the very popular goddess of good fortune and beauty, frequently represented as an elegant Chinese lady. Some gods are rendered mounted on symbolic animals. The garments and jewellery worn by these figures are expressly distinguished from those of Bodhisattvas by their greater 'worldliness', by features denoting a particular ethnic region or historical period.

(ii). The Four Guardians of the World *(Lokapāla)* or Celestial Kings *(Devarāja),* who protect the parts of the world situated in the four cardinal directions; since each sanctuary represents a 'realm of the Buddha', they also serve to protect the temple in which they are situated, and especially the central group of Buddhas in the main hall, against inimical forces. These are probably derived ultimately from the category of *yakshas;* it is as such, at any rate, that they appear on the railings of the stūpas at Bhārhut (1st century B.C.). Related to these in their function and appearance are 'the Twelve Divine Generals', the retinue of the Buddha Bhaishajyaguru. The latter and the Four Guardians of the World were represented in some magnificent works of eastern Asian art. Particular mention should be made of the medieval Japanese sculptures (7th—13th cents.) in which the gods were portrayed with vigorous dynamism and frequently with demonic features — the very reverse of the tranquil detachment of the Buddhas and the spiritual grace of the Bodhisattvas.

PLATE P. 212 *(iii).* The two Gate Guardians *(Dvārapāla)* of the temple are distinguished from the Guardians of the World; the latter are equipped and armed like knights, whereas the former appear as fearsome muscular athletes,[19] half-naked and usually carrying a thunderbolt *(vajra);* they ward off enemies, keeping them away from the sacred area. Thus despite their terrifying appearance they act entirely in a beneficent manner, as aides of the Buddha. This type of figure is also derived from the *yaksha* — one of the categories of low-ranking local genii and gods of nature that are widespread in Indian popular mythology, and which are also represented as female figures *(yakshī).*[20] They became amazingly prolific as the iconographic source of several types of figure — even including that of the standing Buddha at Mathurā (cf. p. 176), as well as of the Bodhisattva there. A *yaksha* may be seen on many reliefs from Gandhāra, as a protector of the Buddha. Already here he is depicted armed with a thunderbolt or bundle of arrows (denoting lightning), which is at the same time an attribute of Indra. Under the influence of Tantrism the two gate guardians, who were derived from a single *yaksha* figure, came to express an esoteric

19 W. Speiser, op. cit., p. 163.
20 H. Goetz, op. cit., p. 50.

symbolism based on the polarity of the world — the same polarity that underlay the mandalas of the Two Worlds (cf. p. 230). So far as the history of religious thought is concerned, the *Dvārapālas* already take us down to the level of the inferior deities.

(iv). The latter include a large number of divine, semi-divine or demonic PLATE P. 213 beings who are likewise protectors and worshippers of the realm of the Buddha. Some of them are primordial deities, like the dragon kings derived from Indian *nāgas;* others are inhabitants of the heavens, similar to angels; others again are monsters who, under the benign and ennobling influence of Buddhism, turn into charitable succourers of suffering mankind. Thus for example the demoness Hāritī, who before she was converted by Buddha used to devour children, becomes the protector of children and enables women to bear offspring. From Gandhāra onwards this motherly figure is represented again and again in a most attractive manner, either with one or with several children about her. In contrast to Kuanyin we here encounter a real mother goddess, but on the lower level of the deities committed to *samsāra*.

(v). So far as this last group is concerned, at least in Japanese art mention must be made of the Shintō gods *(kami:* cf. p. 104); in art, however, there are only a few representations of them, since in the Shintō religion the deities are actually regarded as too mysterious to portray; by and large there are only some sculptures of none too great importance. There is, however, a kind of mandala which correlates the *kami* of a temple, often rendered in a delightful manner amidst a landscape, with the Buddhist figures whose *avatāras* they are.

In the hierarchy of Buddhist figures the next rank below that of the gods is occupied by human beings — but only so long as they have not as yet attained Enlightenment, and thus are ready to enter nirvāna; once this has been attained, through the monastic life, they stand far above the gods, who are bound by *samsāra*. In configurations they also occupy a superior place, immediately next to the Buddha. According to Mahāyāna PLATES PP. 166, 169, 170 doctrine, however, the most enlightened human beings, the Arhats, only come after the Bodhisattvas, since they seek to attain redemption solely for themselves, without trying to bring about salvation for others or sacrificing themselves for their sake. Within the group of human figures, and especially those of monks, we also find a strict hierarchy. Buddhist artists produced magnificent images of the *homo religiosus* in all the various gradations of his spiritual rank and achievement.

From the standpoint of the history of religion and art, the origins of this type are of course rooted in the Buddha himself, who was a monk and became a model for all his disciples. Even where Buddha is elevated to a symbol of the Absolute, he always retains his character as a monk. (The only exception is the Buddha clad in princely attire: cf. p. 203.) He is attended by his personal disciples, who may be seen already in early works of art constituting his audience when he delivers sermons, and in other scenes that have a bearing on the story of his life. They are especially numerous on reliefs at Gandhāra, where the heads are highly expressive of character and frequently recall Roman portraits. The figures, clad in monkish garb, bear a resemblance to statues of philosophers in Antiquity. From the very start these figures are distinguished from those of the Buddha himself by the fact that they are less idealized. In Indian, Ceylonese and Indonesian art numerous figures of monks are to be found which express with great beauty and an air of wise detachment a certain renunciation of worldly life. In the Mahāyāna art of eastern Asia they are combined to form a firmly established group, the Ten Great Disciples. Protagonists of the latter (who may represent the group as a whole, as well as the order of monks itself) are Kāshyapa and Ānanda, the old man and the young man; in configurations they frequently appear next to the Buddha. In the Kōfukuji temple at Nara in Japan there is a magnificent group of these Ten Disciples, dating from the 8th century, which — like so many other Japanese works in various fields of artistic endeavour from the 7th and 8th centuries — can serve as a substitute for Chinese works that have unfortunately been lost.

Arhats ('Worthy of Adoration')[21] are monks who have attained an almost superhuman character and who, on account of their advanced Enlightenment, may enter nirvāna on their death without having to undergo another re-birth. This type of figure flourished especially in Chinese art, and also in Japanese art under the influence of China. This is probably due to the vigorous 'humanist' interest in man felt in eastern Asia, which extended to portrait-like representation of individual personages. It finds

[21] W. Speiser, op. cit., p. 160.

PLATE 52 — BODHIDHARMA (DARUMA). Hanging scroll: ink and light colours on paper (the red of the garment has faded). Japan. 16th cent. Height approx. 1.54 m. *Dept. of Far Eastern Art, Ehemals Staatliche Museen, Berlin.*
Bodhidharma was an Indian monk who is said to have transmitted meditative Buddhism (Ch'an; Japanese: Zen) to China in approx. 500. He is highly venerated by adherents of Zen as their first patriarch. In Zen art he is always represented as a man of almost demonic spiritual power. His fixed, almost savage, glaring expression may be explained by reference to a legend. Once when the master was plunged in

meditation his eyes closed in sleep; thereupon he angrily cut off his eyelids and threw them to the ground; from them there sprouted the tea-shrub, the leaves of which are used by monks as a remedy against sleepiness. This painting is an example of the monochrome (or near-monochrome) ink-paintings done in Zen monasteries.

PLATE 53 – THE BUDDHA BATHING BEFORE HIS FIRST SERMON. Relief on the interior wall of the 1st gallery of the Borobudur, Java (detail). Stone, originally with a finish. Approx. 750–800. Height approx. 100 cm. This cycle of reliefs represents the legendary life of the Buddha Shākyamuni from his pre-existence as a Bodhisattva in the Tushita heaven up to his First Sermon, in the Deer Park at Benares. It is based on the *Lalita Vistara,* which ends with this sermon. The detail shown is the last but one of the 120 scenes. It depicts five disciples reverently giving the Buddha a ceremonial bath in a lotus-pond: two of them are pouring water over him, while a third holds his clothes in readiness on a tray (the Buddha is nevertheless wearing his usual monk's habit); two other disciples are holding bowls of flowers. On the right stands a *nāga* (water spirit, probably that of the pond) holding a honorific umbrella. The lotus-pond is indicated by the lotus leaves and blossoms that can be seen sprouting forth beneath the Buddha and between all the figures.

254

expression in some brilliant portraits of monks and priests. The representation of Arhats — called Lohan in China and Rakan in Japan — obtained a powerful impulse in China from the 7th century onwards, and in particular after the 9th and 10th centuries. In Japan it flourished from about the 12th to the 15th century. But in both countries preliminary stages in the development of these figures can be detected earlier. All manner of magical powers were ascribed to the Arhats as the fruit of their outstanding wisdom. In the course of their development some of them adopted a grotesque appearance, as demonic magicians who could burst asunder the limits imposed by their human existence. Taoist influences were also no doubt at work here. Around each Arhat figure a legend arose, and eventually men forgot that any relationship had existed between it and a particular historical figure. However, parallel with this tendency towards the superhuman, a different tradition survived, according to which Arhats were seen in a simpler and more human form — and thus also more conventionally. Groups came to be built up consisting of sixteen, eighteen, and even five hundred Arhats. In eastern Asian sculpture and painting they were represented in a number of ever-varying psychological types, remarkable for the imagination shown in their expressive facial features. From the Sung period onwards painters, influenced by Taoist nature mysticism, came to depict Arhats in the setting of a landscape, and added benign attendants in the shape of animals of every kind. Of these works those that possess the greatest religious and artistic merit are images of profound insight, depicting men from whom emanates great self-assurance and spirituality, men who are on the eve of attaining ulti-

PLATES PP.
214, 231

PLATE 54 — PRINCE MAHĀSATTVA SACRIFICING HIMSELF TO A STARVING TIGRESS. Detail from a wall-painting in Cave 428 (No. 135 Pelliot). Tun-huang. Tempera technique. Approx. 520—530.
Illustration of one of the best-known Jātakas, i.e. legends about earlier incarnations of Shākyamuni, in which (often in the form of an animal) he gradually earns himself such a good karma by his wisdom and boundless self-sacrifice that in his last incarnation he is able to reach Buddhahood. The Vyāghrī-Jātaka, which is illustrated scene by scene in three long registers, tells the story of three brothers, the sons of a prince, who go hunting and discover in a gorge a starving tigress with her cubs. The youngest brother, Mahāsattva ('The Great Being'), throws himself from the cliff in compassion; the tigress devours him; the two other brothers return and give an account of his fate to their father. They erect a stūpa in his memory, whereupon he appears to them as a perfect Buddha. The detail illustrated here, which only represents a small portion of this story, shows: (above) the brothers leaving for the hunt; (centre) the fall and death of the youngest brother; and (below) his elder brothers returning home. Although this painting is still archaic from a stylistic point of view, it is significant in the history of art on account of its lively, almost dramatic pictorial relation of a theme that was of importance in Buddhist ethics, and also on account of the way in which the scenes are inserted into a landscape which serves both to separate them and to link them together.

mate freedom. This is frequently brought home by stark realism, which nevertheless transcends empirical reality, the blind sphere of *samsāra*.

A more 'normal' kind of humanity is evident in the figures of monks which portray historical personages belonging to various schools of Buddhism. Among them are, first and foremost, the great patriarchs of Hīnayāna and Mahāyāna, such as Nāgārjuna, Asanga, Vasubhandu and many others,

PLATE P. 232

who are comparable to the Church Fathers of Christianity. Then there are heads of schools, teachers and abbots who attained prominence in the past; and finally certain contemporaries, of whom large numbers of authentic portraits have been handed down, particularly in Japan. All of these figures bear witness to the traditional link between teaching and cult within each school. They represent in a very personal way the continuity that all these schools possessed. The patriarchs are often depicted in groups of five, seven, eight and so on; they are either group portraits or series of individual portraits. In most cases, of course, they are ideal

APPX. PL. 33

portraits — as, for example, when the great sculptor Unkei attempted to visualize Asanga: this was during the early 13th century, at the height of a period when pious Buddhists were endeavouring to represent holy personages as effectively and as close to life as possible. The result is a typical Japanese face, with rather crudely-cut features, which expresses in a most ingenious way the profoundly spiritual character of this philosopher. Eastern Asian artists were also fond of depicting Indian patriarchs as 'exotic', non-Chinese or non-Japanese types; in actual fact they show Central and western Asian features. In many cases, however, they were taken without further ado from the artists' own immediate environment. Genuine portraits, either of contemporaries or based upon authentic tradition, appear only at a relatively late date. (The history of eastern Asian portraiture, incidentally, is still a relatively unexplored field.) But in Japan, from about 1200 onwards, if not earlier, we have a large number of authentic painted and sculpted portraits of priests conceived in this manner. Most of them are extraordinarily impressive. In almost every instance images of Arhats served cult purposes, as did portraits of patriarchs and priests: they either formed part of the retinue of a Buddha — i.e. belonged to his sacred configuration — or else served as the focal point of the rites performed to commemorate the foundation of the school or temple concerned. These ceremonies often used to take place in chapels erected especially for this purpose, as is still the case nowadays. In addition to these official cult portraits there are intimate and unconventional likenesses made on the basis of personal contact between the subject and

PLATE P. 234

the artist (occasionally one of his disciples). An example of the latter is the most attractive portrait of Myōe Shōnin.

The portraiture of Arhats, patriarchs and priests was promoted with great vigour by adherents of the Ch'an (Zen) school, which attached great importance to deeply religious personages, to contact between masters and pupils, and to the handing on of traditions 'from spirit to spirit'. In this case the chain of tradition plays an enhanced role, and is based entirely on personal relationships. The Ch'an sect to some extent fell back upon the original form of Buddhism: i.e. it went back beyond the Mahāyāna tradition in matters of dogma and cult, by demanding that each individual should seek Enlightenment independently, by way of meditation. Hence adherents of this school of thought took as their model the Buddha's early disciples and the way of the Arhat. The main figure of this school, Bodhidharma, the first of its patriarchs, occupies pride of place in Ch'an PLATE P. 251 art as well. In ink-paintings he was depicted with the greatest virtuosity, as an almost demonic figure, by the use of forceful, concentrated and expressive brushwork. The element of the grotesque, which plays no small part in the Ch'an school, serves to symbolize the immediacy of religious phenomena that are remote from everything 'normal', conventional, and sanctified by tradition. Ch'an art led to fresh interpretations of traditional iconography, in a way that was sometimes outrageously novel. Whenever an opportunity presented itself, attempts were made to introduce a new concept that was simple, to the point, and which implied a rejection of all kinds of ritual symbolism — as in representations of Bodhisattvas, for example. (The most notable illustration of this tendency is 'Kuanyin clad in a white robe', by Mu-ch'i, dating from the latter half of the 13th century.) It even led to the introduction of new types of figure, such as that of the pot-bellied mendicant friar Pu-tai, who wears an air of serene and superior indifference to the world, and the two scurrilous freaks Han-shan and Shih-tê, who do indeed possess superior wisdom of a kind. Japanese Zen painters of the late period in particular, such as Hakuin and others, cast off all restraint in their unconventional brushwork, in order to destroy once again the traditions and usages that had grown up over the centuries within Zen itself, and so to manifest visually the creative act involved in gaining experience of self and of the world about one. The Ch'an attitude to life was most clearly expressed in representations of nature — in landscapes, but also in very simple, prosaic and material objects of everyday use. The most striking example of this is again a work by Mu-ch'i: a small ink-painting, executed in black and white, showing six *kaki* fruit. It appears to be just a still life, but in fact is an ontological statement on the profoundest level. Therefore it is one of the greatest works of Buddhist art. If we go one step further, this form of art leads to a non-representational symbol, such as an empty circle, or a character — for example, the word NOT or NOUGHT. Both of these imply the highest positive form of true reality: something that can no longer be expressed in words, but may be experienced in every object encountered and at every moment of time.

Ch'an art thus breaks away from the fixed conventions of earlier hieratic cult art. In its themes and forms it contributes a number of new ideas, enlivening a tradition that by this time (during the Sung and Ashikaga periods) had begun to decline into sheer imitation. Yet Ch'an art was itself only a late offshoot of an astonishingly vigorous tradition. For all the figures in its hierarchy, quite irrespective of their age or origin, may be traced far back into the history of Buddhism and Buddhist art: in some cases even to its remotest beginnings. This, too, demonstrates the basic continuity and oecumenical unity of Buddhist art, which extended over an immense area and a lengthy period of time.

The hierarchy of sacred figures is manifest not only in iconography, in the types of figure depicted, but also in the style in which they are executed. In other words, there is a hierarchy of styles which conforms exactly to that of the figures, with their various levels of spirituality, and to some extent remains independent of the changes that took place in the historical development of art styles. In accordance with his nature a Buddha is almost invariably depicted in a more rigid, idealized and 'abstract' style than a Bodhisattva, whose importance in the Buddhist religion necessitates a stronger infusion of mundane elements, and thus also of certain styles that will make its form more readily perceptible to the senses, without, however, dragging it too far down into the world of empirical reality. This step into the sphere of *samsāra* is taken by the figures of deities. From a stylistic point of view this is denoted by a marked accentuation of realism in the physical appearance, by increased dynamism in the bodily movements, and also by the expression of psychological qualities. All this is evident from every detail in the formal treatment. In spite of the similarities that appear to exist between a Bodhisattva and a deity, exact stylistic analysis reveals a very subtle difference, which can be detected even in the finest details: for example, in the concept of the body, in its movements, in its plastic quality, in the treatment of the garment or of the lines of the figure, and finally in the colour-scheme. A Bodhisattva is shown in an ideal state, remote from the temporal plane; in the case of a god or goddess, on the other hand, everything is definitely more 'terrestrial', more tangible, heavier, and closer to the sphere of man. Their appearance is also more firmly related to a particular region (e.g., China) or epoch (e.g., the T'ang period). Again, within the category of deities there are further gradations according to the spiritual rank possessed by each figure in mythology. Indra, for example, is idealized to a greater extent than the four Guardians of the World.

Figures of human beings are invariably in the empirical sphere and are often represented with a realism reminiscent of portraiture. Here again there is a gradation of form according to spiritual rank. It is amazing to see what fine stylistic nuances are used to distinguish an Arhat from an ordinary monk; paradoxically, realistic treatment here becomes spiritualized and idealized — without, however, attaining the absolute ideal expressed in a figure of the Buddha.

This fine differentiation between various styles could be demonstrated feature by feature in a series of examples, produced at the same time and in the same area: we have in mind representations comprising a Buddha, the Bodhisattva Kshitigarbha in the guise of a monk, an Arhat, a patriarch and an abbot of that period. The large configurations in sculpture and painting illustrate this phenomenon in an impressive way, although the viewer brought up on European art may well be inordinately confused by the juxtaposition of different styles, which have to be interpreted as different *levels of style,* based upon the religious hierarchy. Used to a chronological sequence of largely homogeneous stylistic phases, he may be misled into assuming that these figures, so obviously divergent in form, must have been produced at very different epochs. Such a broad spectrum of possible styles did not, however, exist from the start: in the history of Buddhist art it was necessary first to formulate a repertoire of iconographic and formal types extensive enough to make such differentiation possible. But already in Gandhāran art, with its varied background of styles, we can see a juxtaposition of different styles serving different artistic purposes and types. These should not be taken simply as indicative of various stylistic phases, or used for the purpose of dating (cf. p. 32). In this case, too, the figures of human beings or even of gods stand out distinctly, so far as their style is concerned, from those of superior categories of beings. In the fully-fledged Mahāyāna art of eastern Asia this principle operates even more forcibly; but in this case, too, it comes into play only once the complete repertoire of styles had developed, ranging from virtually abstract idealized forms to palpably realistic ones. Thus it did not yet apply during the early Six Dynasties period, when all types of figure were characterized (not exclusively, but in the main) by an archaic rigid uniformity of style, and were distinguished from one another by iconographic and symbolic features rather than by their stylistic formulation. It was only after the T'ang period, with its spiritual universality and cultural maturity, had provided a more diversified range of media for formal expression that fine nuances of style could make themselves felt — as they had to do if all the various types of figure were to be represented. This system of forms then became the model throughout eastern Asia, although it was modified on independent lines in Korea and especially in Japan. Let us take one

APPX. PL. 25

example: the style of the Bodhisattva figure during the Six Dynasties period still bears a great resemblance to that of the Buddha figure, but gradually the difference between the two becomes more accentuated. The Buddha remains more conservative in character (i.e. the style is modified

PLATE P. 145

to a lesser extent) because the style of this type is determined by religious considerations. Only in the case of the Bodhisattva, not in that of the

APPX. PL.
30, 31
PLATE P. 196

Buddha, did a style develop during a late phase that could be called 'baroque'; this may be understood only in the light of the fact that styles appropriate to the various types represented and styles appropriate to the various periods were continually being superimposed upon one another.

T'ang art, and that of succeeding schools in China and Japan, call to mind a further consideration: if, as in this case, we are dealing with works of a mature and late phase, which are the product of a long process of development and of various foreign influences, these works frequently reflect a number of different *layers of style* which developed historically and are determined by traditional factors; and analysis of these strata is essential if we are to explain the structure of a work satisfactorily (on this point, cf. p. 107). But it would be erroneous to maintain that in Buddhist art, which was so powerfully limited by respect for tradition, and where iconographic types were fixed with such precision, there only existed styles graded according to a hierarchial system, and that there was little or no modification of style with the passage of time. The latter *did* occur, just as it did in any other kind of art. Any figure can be dated fairly accurately, on the basis of the stylistic phase to which it belongs (within, of course, the historical sphere in which it appears and develops). But this can and should only be attempted once one has ascertained the type of style involved, its level, and possibly also the stylistic stratification of the work in question. Only with the aid of such a system of co-ordinates is it possible to determine accurately the place of a work in the history of stylistic development.

V. NARRATIVE WORKS

The works of Buddhist art which we have examined so far have been cult images, representing sacred figures either individually or in groups, as metaphysical symbols of beings not susceptible to measurement in terms of time or space (except in so far as they portray historical personages, but even these in the main serve a ritual purpose). Only occasionally does a 'historical' element come into play in the case of cult images — as, for example, in representations of Maitreya as the Buddha of the Future; but here we are dealing with a story of spiritual salvation, not a mundane empirical tale. On the other hand, some cult images, such as those of Buddha meditating or preaching, or the one in which he invokes the earth as a witness, are rooted in his biography — that is to say, in the spiritual career of a particular historical personage, whose life on earth took place at a certain time, although at the same time it also forms part of the history of salvation. The same applies to the dimension of space: the events upon which the Buddha images discussed above are based occurred at certain places which can be physically determined, but the *sūtras* elevate the Buddha's preaching to a supernatural sphere, or alternatively the historical and geographical location of the event concerned may acquire a mythical character, e.g. the Vulture Peak (Gridhrakūta, near Rājagriha in Magadha) where Shākyamuni is said to have preached the 'Lotus Sūtra'. If a legendary and divine place such as the 'Pure Land of Amitābha' is said to be situated in the west, this area is deemed to lie outside the finite world. As is clearly shown by its formal structure when represented in works of art, it is located in an ideal realm that has no existence other than in visionary imagination (cf. p. 229). The same applies to the 'history' of Amitābha and his promise of redemption, which goes back to the earliest aeons, the ultimate result (in Buddhist terminology, its 'fruit') of which is the 'Pure Land'. This, too, is a story of salvation that claims to possess a universal validity transcending time.
Generally speaking, however, the cult images lack any kind of 'historical' element — especially when, as in the mandala, they describe the absolute character and metaphysical structure of the world according to a highly scholastic system, and seek to convey a spiritual vision by means of geometric symbolism. Bodhisattvas, Vidyārājas and many other figures in the pantheon cannot boast of a complete 'history', as the Buddha can; they

are, as it were, figurative symbols of certain religious ideas, pure creations of the human mind. (Their origin, which is of interest only to the historian of religion, is irrelevant here.)

It is a different matter when we are dealing with representations of the historical and legendary biography of Shākyamuni, or events from his earlier incarnations described in the Jātakas, although these are in a sense also (to some extent, at least) part of the history of salvation. For such works exist *to tell a tale:* the event itself forms the actual theme, and moreover in almost all cases we have a text that is illustrated more or less literally. The same applies to representations — either as individual pictures or as a sequence of them — of tales from the *sūtras,* such as the experiences of the devout boy Sudhāna, who sought ultimate truth (in the *Avatamsaka Sūtra*), or the scenes that occur in the *Vimalakīrti Sūtra.* We have mentioned here the three most important themes that occur in narrative works: scenes from the biography of the Buddha, from the Jātakas, and from the *sūtras.* We have now to indicate some examples and describe the typical ways of representation.

The illustration of the life of Shākyamuni and its antecedents in the Jātakas was always one of the great themes of Buddhist art. Already during the very early period, when the Buddha was not yet depicted *in persona,* there was a tendency to take as subjects scenes from his last incarnation on earth, and from his earlier lives. We may find them in the reliefs at PLATE P. 76 Bhārhut, Sānchī and even in those at Amarāvatī.[22] In all these scenes the main figure, who is suggested merely by a symbol, is surrounded by a number of persons depicted in vigorous activity. In such cases archaic conventions of style do not inhibit at all the visual immediacy of the representation. In this way many delightful motifs were borrowed, especially from the Jātaka stories, in which the future Buddha becomes in- APPX. PL. 2 carnate as an animal. Here various ancient animal legends attain, as it were, a higher, sacred meaning. A characteristic feature is the fondness for representation of life in all its tumultuous variety: a number of dynamic figures force their way forwards, as though emerging into the light out of the shadowy depths. The illustrative paintings in the Ajantā caves show a similar rich variety, unrestrained by rational principles of composition.

Of a very different character are the extremely numerous reliefs at Gandhāra. These are based on models taken from Antiquity, especially from the reliefs on sarcophagi. They provide an opportunity for the representation, on a smooth ground, of a number of figures either conceived in-

[22] H. Goetz, op. cit., pp. 54, 58.

dividually and shown in statuary poses or alternatively depicted in movements of 'classical' rhythm. Only occasionally in such works do we
find the clear disposition of forms overshadowed by a typically Indian
wealth of figures. In general the Gandhāran reliefs bear a great resemblance to those of early Christian times, which is not surprising in view
of the fact that they share a common stylistic basis, a similar attitude of
mind, and a similar subject-matter. Owing to the tendency towards biography that is a peculiar feature of early Buddhism, and possibly owing
to the fact that Gandhāran art may have been influenced by the reliefs of
Late Antiquity in which mythological scenes are represented, the latter
occur in large numbers in Gandhāran art. From these scenes it is not
difficult to piece together a complete history of the Buddha's life, including many episodes which ceased to attract much interest in later
periods.

Artists carved reliefs on panels which without exception were situated on
monuments in the places mentioned above. Some of these panels were
long and narrow, and bore friezes; others were rectangular or square;
others again were round, and were used for medallions and the like.
Depending on the shape of the panel, the representation either moved on
from one phase of the event described to the other, in an epic form
(exemplified by the reliefs on the *toranas* of Stūpa I at Sānchī), or alternatively the theme was concentrated into a single climactic event, and the
number of persons involved in it was reduced. Frequently the iconographic programme and the architectonic plan (e.g., of the stūpa which
featured the reliefs) made it necessary to restrict the biographical scenes
to the main events in the Buddha's life — those that were of cardinal
significance in the history of salvation. These include the following: his
Birth, Enlightenment, First Sermon, Entry into Nirvāna, i.e. his incarnation on earth in preparation for his final and crucial journey to his
goal of becoming Buddha, his acquisition of the necessary wisdom for this
achievement, the announcement of this fact, and finally the 'fruit' — i.e.
ultimate liberation. These chronological events are thus interpreted in
a non-temporal sense. This is shown particularly clearly in renderings of FIG. 64
his birth. These frequently depict, not the child Siddhārta, but the
Buddha in a state of perfection, complete with *ushnīsha,* aureole, and
other signs. In other cases he is shown in the posture of meditation, in
which according to legend he spent the time between his miraculous conception and his birth in his mother's womb. Mahāyāna teaching always
tends to attach more importance to the propagation of the doctrine than
to the narration of a historical tale. Thus, since Mahāyāna influence made

itself felt strongly at Gandhāra, there was an inclination here, despite all the fondness for illustration, to concentrate the event depicted as much as possible, by restricting the scope of the theme. From a formal point of view, too, interest centered upon the main figure in the group. As a result one particular moment was singled out of the historical pattern of events, and was then intensified until it obtained an eternal validity. To put the point differently: instead of an event being represented spatially, in the form of a continuous relief, the principles adopted were those of non-spatial hieratic frontality, axiality and symmetry. This means that narrative pictures gradually took on the character of cult images. Such scenic compositions, divorced from the series of illustrations, occur with particular frequency in Central and eastern Asian painting. In Japan the story of Buddha's entry into nirvāna, recounted with a mass of realistic detail, used to serve, and still serves nowadays, as a cult image during the annual ceremony commemorating the Buddha's death. Here we have a narrative image used *as* a cult image; but there are also cases where a narrative image is found *in* a cult image: for example, where historical scenes relating to and resulting in his salvation appear on the socle of a Buddha figure, or on the base of a cult symbol such as a stūpa. In contrast to the cult image, which always signifies the absolute world, that of nirvāna, the narrative image in most cases depicts the world of *samsāra* — but in such a way as to make it clear that it can be overcome: it can thus be said to pursue a transcendent goal beyond itself. Nevertheless, in treating these themes Buddhist artists make ample use of the phenomena found on the empirical plane of existence. That is to say, they are fond of setting the sacred legends in their own actual cultural environment; they relate them as though they had observed them directly themselves, with an abundance of realistic detail and local colour — except in so far as they are based upon a foreign ideal prototype, as is the case with the works of Gandhāran artists, which draw little vitality from their local setting. For this reason narrative images are usually of very great interest to the historian of culture. They afford an insight into the problems which the artist faced in giving shape to the world of phenomena, in interpreting reality: in portraying man, human society, other living creatures, landscapes, and three-dimensional space — phenomena which in cult images either play no part at all or are elevated to a 'supra-empirical' idealized and symbolic form.

PLATE P. 273

PLATE P. 56

Within the Indian cultural sphere classical Buddhist art reached its peak in the Borobudur in Java; this also represents the acme of achievement in regard to the pictorial epic narrative and its translation into a solemn

Fig. 64 — Scenes from the life of Shākyamuni. Detail of wall-painting showing the legend of King Ajatashatru (birth, attack of Māra, first sermon, death). From Kyzyl. 7th cent. Formerly in Berlin

Fig. 65 — Self-sacrifice to a tiger: detail of wall-painting, based on a Jātaka. From Kyzyl. Cf. Plate 54 and text on p. 267

configuration. The former preponderates in the reliefs of the Jātakas and the life of the Buddha; these are several hundred metres in length, and lend themselves to the representation of a detailed narrative made up of a long series of scenes. Some of the biographical images, it is true, are raised to a slightly more exalted plane; the wealth of detail is limited, and the composition given a stricter sense of order, since it deals with sacred truths. The higher the spheres to which the *sūtra* illustrations lead the beholder (cf. pp. 134 f.), the more hieratic their style becomes, and the greater their resemblance to cult images; the style is thus related directly to the spiritual plane of the theme depicted. Javanese artists have clearly registered outstanding achievements in the way in which they have narrated these stories. It is a testimony to their excellence that they were also able to produce the sublime cult image of the Buddha, and indeed to build the entire Borobudur, right up to the symbol of nirvāna in the uppermost stūpa, as a comprehensive image of the world inspired by profound religious feeling.

PLATE P. 252

In the field of Buddhist narrative images Indochinese art can boast of no such singular achievements that merit detailed discussion. The stucco reliefs of the Sukhothai period in Siam, for example, do not surpass those in India or Indonesia. The late Siamese paintings produced between the 17th and 19th centuries — splendid gay wall-paintings, banners, panel-paintings, and paintings in gold lacquer of biographical and legendary themes — are charming in their way, but are not really anything more than mechanical products; everything more ancient, and possibly more significant, seems to have been lost. There are, however, a few exceptions. They include the wall-paintings recently discovered in the closed crypt of the tower-like temple of the Khmer type called Wat Rājapūrana at Ayuthia (1424). These wall-paintings depict series of hieratic figures of the Buddha and monks as well as illustrations of the Jātakas. The magnificent narrative relief friezes at Angkor in Cambodia are in the main on Hindu themes.

In Central Asia special interest was taken in representing historical narratives in places that were greatly influenced by Hīnayāna, notably in the region of Kuchā. At Turfan this interest is much less extensive. Here we find narrative images of Pranidhi scenes, which took place during previous incarnations of the Buddha (cf. pp. 70 f.). They already have something of the formal character appropriate to a cult image. The transitoriness of a temporal event finds expression only in the fact that the Buddha is represented in a striding posture and making a three-quarter turn. The Jātaka scenes in wall-paintings in the chapels at Kyzyl (near Kuchā, approx. 500?) are worthy of note because in many instances the setting is a mountainous landscape, represented not as a single large uniform area, but divided into a number of rhomb-shaped compartments, separated by schematized small cells, as it were, each of which contains a separate scene. The flat hills, which call to mind paintings on stage scenery, cover the entire surface with a decorative pattern suggestive of scales. In this scheme of representation one can detect a strong Near Eastern influence, deriving ultimately from Mesopotamia, but transmitted by way of Iran. Here narrative images are set in the landscape in an archaic manner and not really incorporated into it.

Quite different are the wall-paintings in Cave 428 at Tun-huang (approx. 520—530). They also follow an archaic scheme of composition, in which there is no continuous uniform space, and here, too, the mountains are stylyzed and coloured in a decorative way; but between them there are narrow strips on which the artist can depict some connected narrative — e.g. the Jātaka that tells of the Bodhisattva (i.e. the future Shākyamuni) who sacrificed himself to a starving mother-tiger and her young. In these friezes landscape serves to separate the various phases of the narrative from one another, but at the same time helps to join them together. They are in fact nothing other than Chinese horizontal painted scrolls (hand-scrolls, as they are called) transferred to the surface of the wall. This is a very ancient type of picture, especially characteristic of eastern Asian painting, which developed in an ingenious way both in narrative and in landscape painting between the 5th and 13th centuries, and was still popular later as well. In it lengthy stories and entire panoramic landscapes unfold (in the literal sense of the word) before the viewer in consecutive stages. In representing the biography of the Buddha, and in Jātaka stories, the hand-scroll was apparently seldom used in China and Japan, to judge by those

APPX. PL. 3

FIG. 65

PLATE P. 254

that have survived or are documented. The only important work we have is the 'Sūtra of Cause and Fruit in the Past and Present' (Japanese: *Kako-Genzai-Inga-Kyō*). It is an illustration of the Buddha's life in which the narrative picture is placed over the continuous text. By comparison with the friezes at Tun-huang it bears witness to a tendency towards slightly more realistic representation, but is nevertheless essentially archaic. It developed in Japan between 730 and 770 but is based, not upon contemporary Chinese models of the advanced T'ang style, but upon those of a slightly earlier period.

In eastern Asia biographical and legendary narratives are of course also represented in the normal way, with individual scenes represented in relief panels that form part of the shrine where they are sited. Examples of these may be found in the caves at Yünkang (5th–6th centuries). In painting these panels were often arranged vertically, one above the other, as was already the practice in Indian art (at Gandhāra, in Gupta reliefs and elsewhere). This applied particularly to scenes taken from the life of the Buddha — we have quite delightful scrolls or 'banners' of this kind from Tun-huang which concentrate mainly upon four or eight principal events in the Buddha's career. In Japan a similar treatment was given to the life of Crown Prince Shōtoku (574–622), since many mystical parallels were thought to exist between his life and that of the Buddha. With the development of landscape painting these sequences of pictures become increasingly embedded in elaborate natural scenery, so that in 'reading' the story one takes a journey, as it were, through scenery abounding in natural life.

PLATE P. 252

For the pictorial representation of biographical events, however, especially in the case of historical Buddhist personages, the hand-scroll was of course far more popular in eastern Asia. This pictorial form was also frequently used for other stories, such as legends — dealing, for example, with Bodhisattvas and other holy beings, with saintly men and miracle-working images — as well as for chronicles that recorded the history of major temples, important events in religious history, and the like. The first group of narrative pictures mentioned — the Buddha legend, Jātakas and illustrations of *sūtras* — treat themes common to all the Buddhist lands, based upon canonical texts. The second group is clearly distinguished from the first by the historical and biographical character of the subjects portrayed, which are frequently confined to the region or even the locality concerned. These are not based upon texts, or at least only upon those relevant only to a certain region, such as Japan. Finally, in view of these limitations, it is not possible for these narrative pictures to develop into cult images. Another result was a greater influx of elements taken from real life, and consequently greater realism in style. Last but not least, the deeply rooted humanistic interest taken in man that was to be found in the cultures of eastern Asia may have played a part in developing this branch of art, the narrative scroll, by introducing subjects taken from history and biography, chronicles and legends: the development of portraiture in eastern Asia is also relevant in this connection. This attitude did not, as one might perhaps have expected, lead to intense attention being given to the biography of the Buddha, treated as realistically as possible, among artists and those who commissioned their work. This may be due to the relatively slight interest taken by the Mahāyāna countries in such themes, which are more Hīnayānist in character.

From China there have survived only a few relics of this illustrative form of painting on Buddhist themes. Most of the Chinese hand-scrolls either deal with historical, courtly or literary subjects, or alternatively are splendid landscapes. On the other hand, we have a number of highly important scroll paintings from Japan, especially from the era when this type of picture flourished, in the Fujiwara and Kamakura periods (approx. 1100—1350). In Japan the hand-scroll is called an *emaki* (or *emaki-mono*); it is frequently several metres in length, but only 25—50 cm. in width, and occasionally a complete work consists of three, ten or even nearly fifty scrolls. It is the usual practice to produce the pictures on paper with ink and paint. Many of them are actually books, since they also contain a written text, in fine calligraphy, and with a fair amount of detail; the illustrated parts usually alternate with sections of the text. The pictorial parts are, however, not simply short illustrations interspersed in the text. In many cases they continue for some way without a break, extensive areas being covered at a time, so that the representation can only be viewed by gradually unrolling it from right to left — whereupon one scene unfolds after another. This is therefore in fact an epic picture, which lends itself remarkably well to the illustration of lengthy stories, and is probably the most perfect form of narrative picture known to world art.

Within the comprehensive sphere of profane themes we find on one hand historical subjects — including events taken from Japanese history, such as the rebellion that broke out during the Heiji era (1156—9), or the failure of the attempts by the Mongols to conquer Japan (1274 and 1281), one important internally and the other internationally — and on the other hand illustrations drawn from classical Japanese literature, e.g. from the *Tales of Prince Genji*. We are solely concerned here with the religious, i.e. predominantly Buddhist, *emaki;* they occasionally deal with the legend of the Buddha or one of the *sūtras,* but such themes are not prominent. Two different themes which occur more frequently are biographies of priests and temple chronicles, the latter being partly historical and partly legendary in character. (We cannot go into detail about individual works, since this would mean relating the whole story in each case.) Often the chronicle of a temple and the cult image erected in it are intermingled with all kinds of wondrous events — as, for example, in the *Shigisan-Engi-Emaki* (approx. 1170—80) or the *Taima-Mandara-Engi* (latter half of 13th cent.). The latter describes the legendary execution of the well-known tapestry showing the Paradise of Amitābha. These miracles are said to be due to the ardent zeal of the donors, to the spiritual virtue of the priests, and the mercy shown by a Buddha, a Bodhisattva or a god. This deity can also be a Shintō *kami* in which a Buddhist being is incarnate. This results from the syncretism that occurred between Buddhism and the Japanese national cult during the medieval period (cf. p. 104). Pictures of this kind are supposed, not only to narrate, but also to preach. Since these stories usually demonstrate, following the doctrine of karma, how all good or evil actions obtain their due recompense, and how in all events there is a universal, often latent, connection between cause and effect, this type of narrative picture is called *engi-emaki. Engi* is the Sino-Japanese translation of the central Buddhist concept of *pratītya-samut-pāda* ('origin in dependence'). Biographies of priests also in effect serve the purpose of spiritual edification. Among these heroes are such famous personalities as Hsüan-tsang, whose pilgrimage from China to India by way of Central Asia is related in a colourful presentation set in a quasi-Chinese environment. Another is Hōnen Shōnin (1133—1212; pictorial biography from the first half of the 14th century), the founder of the religious reform movement in Japan, which propagated with success the simple belief in the Buddha of redemption Amida (Amitābha), and preached that by invoking his name re-birth could be attained in his 'Pure Land'. Of even greater artistic charm is the pictorial biography, painted

FIG. 60

PLATE 55 — THE FIRST BATH AND FIRST STEPS OF SHĀKYAMUNI. Detail of a narrow hanging scroll. Ink, colours and gold on silk. T'ang period. From Tun-huang. Approx. 34 × 19 cm. *British Museum.*
The scene on top shows the child being bathed in a golden bowl by some women, while above him nine dragons appear in a thunder-cloud to afford him protection (or, according to another version, to give him water). The scene below represents the first seven steps which the new-born babe took in all directions whereupon, raising one arm to the heavens and stretching the other down towards the earth, he uttered the following words: 'I am the greatest in the world. I have been born for the last time. I shall put an end to all suffering of birth, old age, and death.' With every step he took a lotus sprang up from the ground. The cartouches for inscriptions at the sides remained empty.

in 1299, of one of his successors: Ippen Shōnin (1239—1289), a wandering preacher who travelled through the whole of the country.

All these themes are represented with a wealth of local colour, with keen feeling for the life of the people, whether city-dwellers, villagers, or members of other social groups; they are set within an extensive framework of landscape, depicted with loving care, in a manner that has no equal elsewhere in all Buddhist art. For this reason we can say that in Japan the narrative picture reached its ultimate climax. This was its final peak of achievement — the earlier ones being the series of reliefs at Sānchī, Amarāvatī, Gandhāra and in the Borobudur.

With this type of picture eastern Asian artists had moved a long way from the traditional basis of their art, from familiar subjects ultimately derived from India — namely, the legend of the Buddha, the Jātakas and the *sūtras*. They opened up new fields of subject-matter, drawing upon their own history and environment and upon their personal religious experience. To a similar extent and with equal success the Ch'an (Zen) school also embarked upon entirely new paths in narrative pictures, as it did in regard to other artistic problems as well (cf. Ch. III and IV). The historical tradition of this school concentrated upon the personalities of the great Ch'an masters. It manifested itself in the continuous direct contact between master and disciple, transmitted without the aid of texts, and indeed without any words whatever, but simply by being passed on 'from spirit to spirit'. Meditation, which for adherents of Ch'an is the essence of spiritual life, is based on the so-called *kung-an* (Japanese: *kō-an*): the tasks for meditation which pupils were set by their masters, which in most cases were deliberately devised to demolish rational thought and to awaken, by their harsh impact, the capacity for superior insight *(satori)*. Frequently these problems took the form of some paradoxical dictum, or a short and at first sight apparently senseless dialogue between some master of the past and his pupil. All these dialogues or pronouncements actually took place at some particular moment in time; they belong to a tradition rooted in certain personages; they thus to a great extent possess a historical, biographical and topical character — and even a scenic one, in view of the dramatic circumstances in which they frequently originated. Though based entirely upon Mahāyāna thought, Ch'an approximates to the original form of Buddhism in so far as it performs a kind of refor-

PLATE 57 — CEILING ORNAMENT. In Cave 320, Tun-huang. Painting in tempera technique on plaster. T'ang period (8th cent.?).

Cf. Plate on p. 38. The pattern in the centre is based upon the lotus motif. Characteristic of T'ang ornamentation is the rainbow-like gradation of colour values within one and the same pattern. The entire ceiling painting represents a canopy suspended over the Buddha chapel, symbolizing the 'Dome of Heaven'.

mation: it dispenses with myth, magic and miracle, with superhuman merciful powers, dogmas, written words of wisdom, pious works and ritual of every kind; and instead goes back to the spiritual struggle that takes place among men all the time in everyday life. The historical or biographical events, as well as anecdotal ones, that crystallized out of these personal contacts between master and pupil, and from these *kung-an*, yielded new subjects for narrative pictures. Among the ink-paintings of eastern Asia, which are closely connected with Ch'an Buddhism, were a large number of magnificent works of this kind. In China they were produced mainly during the Southern Sung Dynasty (12th–13th cents.), and in Japan during the Ashikaga period (14th–16th cents.), but occasionally even as late as the 18th and 19th centuries (e.g. the works of Hakuin, Sengai and others).

Two groups stand out. One comprises representations of certain personal contacts that were of crucial importance in Ch'an tradition. They are exemplified by the story of Hui-k'o, depicted with due solemnity and vigour by the Japanese artist-monk Sesshū (1420–1506). In this story Hui-k'o cuts off his own arm to prove the seriousness of his aspirations to the patriarch Bodhidharma, meditating with his face to the wall. The other group comprises illustrations of the innumerable *kung-an* anecdotes. These also in effect tell of encounters between certain powerful unique personalities and are accordingly represented emphatically — frequently in a drastic or grotesque manner. Ch'an images of the Buddha, Bodhisattvas and especially Arhats, patriarchs and masters are likewise unconventional, drawn from original visual experience; together with the narrative pictures we have been discussing, they form the vast corpus of Ch'an art.

This was the last flowering of Buddhist art. It was a completely fresh and original development, which drew its inspiration from the depths of the Buddhist religion. It was produced at a time when traditional cult art was already on the decline virtually everywhere. The Ch'an genius expressed itself above all in fascinating ink-paintings, which revealed the actual truth about the object portrayed and also the true nature of the artist himself; they were convincing vehicles for the spiritual dynamism unleashed by Ch'an teachings. Yet in its innermost nature Ch'an art, as has been pointed out at the end of Chapter IV, no longer seeks to produce a representational, didactic picture, one that embodies a certain doctrine, still less a ritual or miracle-working image. Its objective is to transcend all manner of imagery. So long as it still remains within the visual sphere it finds purest expression in an abstract symbol or in a written character; but taken to ultimate conclusions it culminates in an empty picture, in a 'formless form', in the 'thundering silence'.

VI. SYMBOLISM AND ORNAMENTATION

Buddhist art thus describes a circle, from the non-pictorial symbol at its beginning to the non-pictorial symbol at its close, from the image that is *not yet* an image to the image that is *no longer* one. The history of Buddhist art has led us through a rich world of imagery; during the journey we even came across a belief in the power of imagery that is in many cases not far removed from a belief in magic. The finest works, however, are those that actually aim at some goal beyond themselves. Thereby the picture acquires a form so sublime, and at times so abstract, that the viewer is transported to a sphere beyond all limits of imagery and form. In Buddhist art, and especially in Mahāyāna art, there is in principle nothing that is not a symbol; strictly speaking, even the Buddha himself is a symbol — for in spite of being richly endowed with meaning, he also displays all the provisional qualities of a symbol, and can be termed 'just' a symbol. This applies equally to every other sacred figure and to every detail in its image. This is why we have already referred on several occasions to symbols. We shall not repeat here what we have said above; but to call to mind the omnipresence of symbolic meaning we shall list the most important categories by their key words. Virtually all these symbols are common to the entire Buddhist *oikoumene,* or at least to its Mahāyāna areas; and it is precisely in this very impressive concentrated form that the Buddhist message was carried to so many peoples in so many widely separated lands.

Every Buddhist figure, in so far as it is not a portrait and does not occur in a subordinate role in narrative pictures, embodies a certain religious idea, and is thus a symbol capable of precise definition. Certain characteristic features serve as distinguishing marks: in the case of the Buddha, the 32 *lakshanas,* including the *ushnīsha* and *ūrnā,* various forms of aureole and throne, as well as numerous gestures of the hands *(mudrās).* Especially during the early period, some symbols may at first represent the person of the Buddha; they can be related to certain major events in his life or legendary career, and later develop into separate, universally recognized symbols for Buddhist doctrine — for example, the Tree of Enlightenment, the Wheel of Doctrine (also in the form of a swastika), FIGS. 66, 67 the stūpa and some others. Most of them originate in pre-Buddhist times and occur in other cultures as well. The Bodhisattvas and Vidyārājas

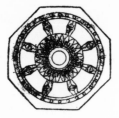

Fig. 66 — *Wheel of the Doctrine (Dharmacakra). Japanese drawing*

Fig. 67 — *Frieze with leaves of pipal-tree (ficus religiosa), the Tree of Enlightenment. From Gandhāra. Peshāwar Museum*

also have certain characteristic bodily features, as well as items of clothing and jewellery, attributes, *mudrās,* attitudes, seated postures, and throne socles, all of which define not only the figure as such, but also its various forms, manifestations or aspects of being (as, for instance, in the case of Avalokiteshvara); alternatively, they may denote a certain moment or PLATES PP. 198, 210 event that occurred in the course of their history (as, for instance, the pensive and expectant attitude of Maitreya). The attributes may include PLATE P. 192 specifically Buddhist symbols or generally current signs of good luck and even weapons: in Buddhist teaching these have the purpose of directing their destructive power against enemies of the doctrine — i.e. against the arch-enemy Delusion, the antithesis of and impediment to Enlightenment. Some figures have specific animals added to them which make some statement about their nature or the religious function they fulfil; alternatively they may be present during important events, as the gazelles were when the Buddha delivered his First Sermon. Such symbols may by themselves represent the entire figure or scene: for instance, the wheel with gazelles PLATE P. 98 kneeling to the left and right of it, which stands for the First Sermon, or PLATE P. 211 the sword encircled by a dragon, which denotes the Vidyārāja Acala. Among symbols of plants pride of place is taken by the lotus flower, which symbolizes the essential nature of all human beings and all things, in principle unpolluted by the mud of the *samsāra* sphere, or by Delusion, and realized by attaining Enlightenment. At the same time it forms a cosmic symbol which unfolds in all directions: the stalk represents the *axis mundi,* and thus the lotus also serves as the throne of the Buddha FIGS. 58, 59 and the centre of the mandala.

Each figure has its symbolic colours, which vary according to the specific form in which it appears. We can be certain that in Buddhist art a colour was hardly ever chosen for fortuitous reasons, or on purely aesthetic grounds. All colours and other signs were strictly regulated, and were

278

Fig. 68 — Five-pointed vajra

recorded in books of iconographic rules. The same holds good for numbers, which not only play a part in the composition of groups or in figures with multiple heads and arms, but are particularly important in iconometry (i.e. the proportions given to sacred figures in accordance with religious, as distinct from aesthetic, considerations): the measurements vary with the rank held by the sacred figure in the religious hierarchy. In all this there was of course plenty of scope for mystical speculation. Vajrayāna in particular developed a highly complex system of symbols, and also produced some types that were peculiar to it alone. It further enriched the extensive treasury of symbols by drawing upon Hindu sources, as was done elsewhere — a fact which reminds us that the entire repertoire of Buddhist symbolism is composed of various historical strata, of which some, and possibly most, overlap with pre-Buddhist or non-Buddhist cultural spheres. The central position in Vajrayāna is held by the *vajra* symbol, which gave this school of thought its name. Originally *vajra* probably meant the thunderbolt, trident, or bundle of arrows (= lightning) of the celestial deity, as it is found in many other mythologies. It also signified a club, as a weapon wielded by the gods. Later it was interpreted as a 'diamond' and symbolized the Absolute, or true reality, which is as indestructible and pure as a diamond; as the latter overcomes all other substances by virtue of its hardness, so also the power of the Absolute and of Supreme Wisdom overcomes all obstacles in its path.

FIG. 68

The dialectical antithesis is the bell: whereas the *vajra* represents the 'Diamond World' (cf. p. 230), the bell suggests the 'World of the Maternal Womb', i.e. the phenomenal world. In shaktism it also represents the female principle in contrast to the male, represented by the *vajra*, here conceived as a phallus. The fact that the sound of a bell dies away quickly makes it especially suitable as a simile for the phenomenal world. In Vajrayāna these symbols play a part both as attributes of sacred figures and also as cult implements used in the complex and mysterious liturgy. In addition to symbolic figures and cult symbols of this kind, Vajrayāna also has mystical characters (*siddham*), which are derived from an Indian script and represent the mystical syllables (*mantra*), or seeds (*bīja*), which embody the innermost nature, the sacral substance and magical power of the innumerable figures. They may also represent these figures in art and

FIG. 69

Fig. 69 — Vajra bell

279

Fig. 70 — Symbolic character (siddham) A, representing Ādi-Buddha Vairocana as the archetypal principle of all things. Japanese drawing

ritual — thus we find *siddham* signs encircled by an aureole on a lotus throne which serve as cult images — in which case they are by no means inferior in value to these figures themselves: rather the reverse, for they can boast a more exalted degree of spirituality and purity. Since cult symbols (or attributes) as well as *siddham* characters may take the place of pictures of sacred personages, we find both in mandalas, in lieu of figures.

The mandala itself is likewise a central symbol, of an abstract and geometric character, representing the metaphysical structure of the world. We have already noted that buildings may also constitute such an image of the world, both in their plan and in their structure: they may either form an abstract diagram resembling a mandala, or depict it visually — as, for example, when a temple and all the furnishings within it represent the 'Pure Land' of Amitābha. The basic motifs of such sacred buildings likewise have the character of conspicuous and impressive symbols: for example, the polarity between the sacred monument and the sacred avenue leading up to it, which we can see in temple complexes that have such a *via sacra* and a shrine or tower in the centre, or again in the connection between mountain and cave (cf. p. 147), which is a characteristic feature of many sanctuaries.

In religious art every detail is a symbol of one kind or another: the choice of a linear or plastic style to represent different categories in the hierarchy, the choice of colours, and especially the principles of composition. We have noted above that frontality, axiality and symmetry are religious symbols and that even a certain composition of a painting may have some specific significance (cf. p. 229). Artistic media that seem only decorative, such as gold, possess an ontological meaning, indicating the nature of the subject: gold is especially frequently used to denote the 'absolute' colour of the Buddha. Alternatively, it forms part of the rich sacral splendour which makes manifest the supra-empirical brilliance of 'the realm of the

Buddha', and at the same time serves the devout believer as a votive gift and a 'spiritual ornament'.

Whereas Vajrayāna Buddhism developed its symbolism into a rich scholastic and mystical system, Hīnayāna Buddhism was by and large content with the small group of symbols originally connected with the person and life of the Buddha, and made little use of the mass of symbols mostly of Hindu origin, that had been taken over by Mahāyāna. On the other hand, Ch'an (Zen) Buddhists also renounce any fully-formed or binding system of symbols; in their view each insignificant object, each flower and each animal — indeed, each stone in the garden or implement used in everyday life can tell us something about true reality, and can express it with far more immediacy than is possible through a mass of symbols, which are necessarily fettered by tradition. The new symbols which Ch'an Buddhists produced themselves are few in number and are of an entirely different character (cf. p. 258).

In Buddhist art many symbols also have a decorative function and may be components of a highly developed system of ornamentation. They are encountered on a great variety of works of art: on buildings; on carved or painted figures, whose details (e.g. garments, jewellery, aureole, throne socle, etc.) frequently bear ornamental decoration; on cult implements of every kind, executed in different techniques; and last but not least on textiles. Some motifs are repeated in all the Buddhist lands, or in many of them, and form a common link between them. The less representational they are, and the more suited to abstract decoration, the easier it is to use them as ornaments. Plant motifs predominate over animal ones, and geometric motifs over those consisting of figures. In many cases the repertoire of ornamental motifs found in Buddhist art extends into a far broader sphere: Buddhist art even fulfilled an important func- FIGS. 71 a-d tion by transmitting motifs that originally had nothing at all to do with Buddhist thought or design. We can only touch upon the complex problems which this raises, since the history of ornamentation in the Buddhist lands, and in Asia generally, still remains to be written. It is one of the most important tasks awaiting future scholars.

Some of the main symbolic motifs, such as the lotus and the Wheel of Doctrine, appear in practically all the Buddhist countries. Others, on the other hand, are linked to certain Buddhist schools by their subject-matter and geographical location. This applies in particular to Tantric symbols, which are associated with Vajrayāna. But most motifs form an integral part of a comprehensive system of ornamentation that is characteristic of a certain Asian culture — e.g. that of India or Indochina, which to some

Fig. 71a — Ornament showing
vine-scrolls. 1st—2nd cent. B.C.
From Palmyra, Syria

Fig. 71b — Ornament showing vine-
scrolls. 4th cent. (?). From Gandhāra

Fig. 71c — Ornament showing
vine-scrolls. Approx. 500. From
Yünkang, northern China

Fig. 71d — Ornament showing vine-
scrolls. Approx. 720. From the Yakushiji Temple, Nara, Japan

extent is common ground for Buddhist works as well as Hindu ones; alternatively, they may form part of the Chinese system of ornamentation,
which reached its climax during the T'ang period and served as a model

PLATE P. 274 for other peoples in eastern Asia until the latter (especially the Japanese,
who displayed a great talent for ornamental art) gave these adopted motifs
a character of their own and developed them further. It is by no means
possible as yet to say definitely whence the extremely variegated T'ang
ornamental repertoire was derived. We know for certain that much was
taken over from India and western Asia, to no small extent through the
medium of Buddhism.

Here we touch upon the particularly interesting question of the processes
of transmission involved, which affected not only the vast cultures of
southern and eastern Asia, but the whole Buddhist sphere. These may be
traced especially clearly in the case of ornamentation. For example, the

FIGS. 71, 72 vine-scroll, the palmette or other motifs originally had no connection with
eastern Asia or with Buddhism, but were derived ultimately from the
Near East and from Antiquity. However, just as they penetrated into some
other cultures, such as that of Islam or the early medieval West, so they
also penetrated into Buddhism, and (not exclusively, but to a great extent)

Assyrian

Greek

Greek

Japanese

Byzantine

Sassanid

Chinese

Chinese

Byzantine

Arabic

Chinese

Chinese

Fig. 72 — Diffusion of ornamental motifs across Asia. (After Chūta Itō)

283

were carried along by Buddhist art as it spread across Asia. For this reason there is a surprising affinity between, for example, the friezes comprising leaves and scrolls to be found in the Romanesque churches of Central Europe and those in the cave-temples of China (Yünkang). These extensive links can probably be indicated most graphically by Figures 71 and 72, and by the diagram overleaf, rather than by a lengthy verbal description. In addition to motifs of Antique origin, an important part is played in Central and eastern Asian art by Sassanid motifs (and some that derive ultimately from Mesopotamia); the same motifs, as a result of the syncretizing, mediating and radiating function performed by Sassanid culture, also penetrated into medieval European art.

In the secular, but still more the Buddhist, art of the Six Dynasties and T'ang periods in China and her dependent areas we can see the complete repertoire of these motifs combined. The international character of this ornamentation, which was either Buddhist from the start or else became an auxiliary of Buddhist art, may be studied to best advantage in the numerous masterpieces and works of craftsmanship that have survived: for example, in the Hōryūji Temple or the treasure-house Shōsōin at Nara (Japan). Not only did different motifs and styles co-exist with one another simultaneously, but there was also a certain amount of historical

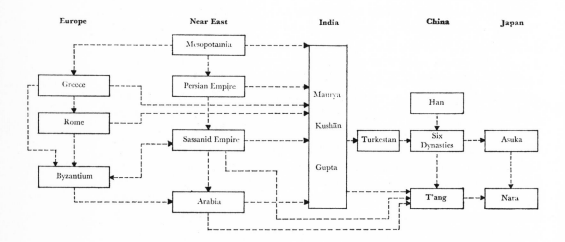

Fig. 73 — Diffusion of ornamental motifs across Asia. (After Chūta Itō)

stratification in the ornamentation of the mature cultures: as we know, this was also the case with regard to sculpture and painting (cf. p. 260). The analysis of this stratification shows that the various levels have their roots in earlier epochs, and sometimes in remote regions. That they were combined to form a unit was due, not only to the powers of synthesis possessed by the great civilizations, but in particular totthe fact that Buddhism played a major role in world history as a medium of cultural contact and exchange.

In spite of the oecumenical unity of Buddhist art, of the fact that it is everywhere based on much the same foundations, and of the surprising affinity between its various forms of expression, we should not overlook the unique characteristics of works produced in different regions and periods. The cultures involved were for the most part highly independent and richly endowed with creative imagination: they each had their own way of expressing their own particular view of Buddhism and the figures associated with that religion. The illustrations in this volume offer ample evidence of this. Take, for example, the large number of different Buddha images, produced in various countries and phases of stylistic development, which we discussed in Ch. III. These bear witness to the fact that the peoples of India, southern Asia, China and Japan not only have a different spiritual approach, but also a different feeling for the plastic quality of form, for the rhythmic treatment of line, and for proportion. Or consider the great distance that separates the Padmapāni Bodhisattva of Ajantā and a corresponding figure, only slightly later in date, in the Hōryūji Temple; or again, the contrast between the typical Chinese pagoda and the typical Japanese one. The various Buddhist lands each have their own distinct individual style. It is based on the survival, along with Buddhist concepts, of non-Buddhist ideas that it was impossible to suppress, and which came to exercise a certain modifying influence upon religion and philosophy, and thus also upon art. We have noted this most clearly in the relationship between Buddhism and Hinduism, but in principle the same holds good for all areas. The specifically Chinese element in Chinese Buddhist art has roots that go back to the 2nd millennium B.C. In the same way the specifically Japanese element in Japanese Buddhist art goes back to pre-Buddhist 'Shintōist' origins. As is usually the case in the history of culture, however, this individual and specific element in turn only developed fully and made itself felt effectively under the impact of external stimuli.

Having said this one must emphasize that, in spite of all the differences due to geographical and historical circumstances, the essential basic ideas, types of figure, formal principles and symbols form a common basis valid for all Buddhist areas. This is also true of the religious purpose and function of a work of Buddhist art. We have already had more than one occasion to mention these factors, and may conclude by enumerating them in a brief survey.

A work of Buddhist art may narrate the sacred story or illustrate sacred texts, thereby performing the function of recording or instructing. It may be (and generally is) a cult image, containing the sacral substance of the figure portrayed, which makes the latter 'present': it thereby serves as an 'instrument' *(yantra)* for the attainment of salvation. Or it may be an image designed to inspire a sense of piety in the believer, who turns to it with fond devotion *(bhakti);* or the basis for meditation and visionary experience; or a medium used in initiation. Frequently the work takes on the form of an orderly scheme, representing the structure of the material and spiritual world — in other words, a picture of the cosmos. Occasionally this cosmological and ontological function is combined with an ideology of sacral kingship, whereby the political power is incorporated into the world order and acts as its agent. Thus a Buddhist work of art, or rather the religious power contained within it, can radiate benediction — either upon the world at large or a single kingdom, upon a small community or an individual believer. In order to evoke this effect Buddhist works are offered as votive gifts; alternatively, they themselves (statues of the Buddha or the sanctuaries where they are kept) may be the recipients of such gifts, which serve to improve the donor's karma and bring him closer to the goal of salvation. Such gifts may consist, not only of buildings or images, but also of costly jewellery or other offerings, such as flowers, incense, music and dancing, so producing an earthly likeness of the heavenly 'realm of Buddha' in all its glory. This need for votive offerings *(pūjā)* and for a large number of sacral ornaments *(alamkāra, vyūha;* Japanese: *shōgon)* was at all times and places, even during the early period, one of the most fruitful stimuli to creative activity among Buddhist artists.

These various functions were only developed fully, of course, with Mahāyāna, and especially with Vajrayāna. In a reaction against the latter Ch'an (Zen) renounced most of the functional purposes served by works of Buddhist art. Adherents of this school regarded a work of art primarily as a spontaneous personal testimony on the artist's part, indicating the deeper understanding he had attained of the essence of things. But each Buddhist work is in one way or another symbolic. It has a meaning that transcends its appearance and immediate purpose. It stands for the Absolute, or the Nought (or Void) — that for which all images are only provisional signs. The real intention of a Buddhist work is to suggest the transcendence of all phenomena and all imagery that is a prerequisite for ultimate understanding and salvation. Although a work of art may have precisely definable purposes on various spiritual planes, ranging from sheer ritual magic to the highest and most sublime mystical speculation, any image will only fulfil its supreme function if it becomes a *mere* image, if it loses *all* its specific functional qualities. This is achieved by infinitely transcending its own limitations and by ever-increasing insight and Enlightenment on the part of the Buddhist believer.

APPENDICES

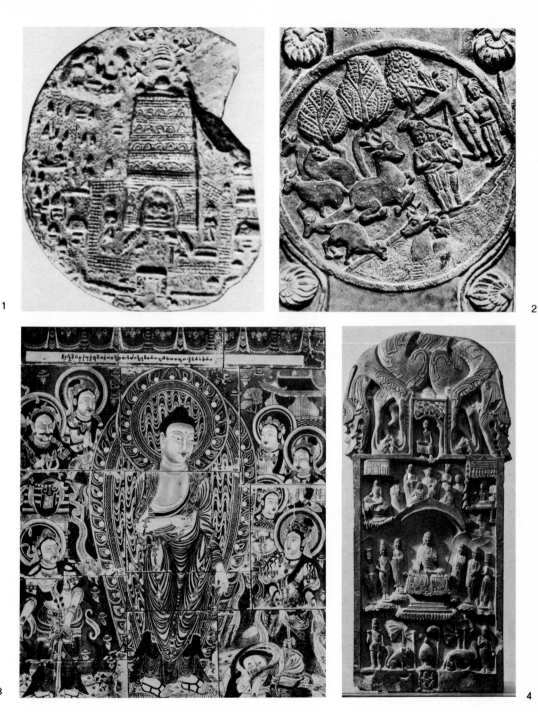

5

6

7

8

292

9

10

11

12

13

14

15

16, 17

18

19

20

21

22,23

24

25

26

27

28

29

30

31

32

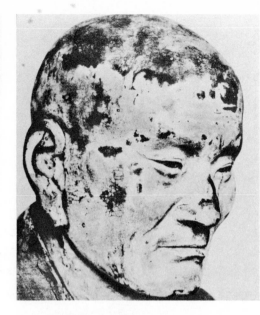

33

34

35

CAPTIONS TO APPENDIX OF PLATES

Note – This appendix is designed to fill some of the gaps not covered by the plates accompanying the text. If studied in connection with the latter, it is possible to trace relatively unbroken series of styles, particularly in regard to the image of the Buddha and Bodhisattva (cf. Part II, Chapters III and IV). Readers are invited to note that the plates are grouped as follows:

The top row (Plates 5, 6, 9, 10, 14, 15, 19 and 20) contains typical examples of stylistic modifications in representing the Buddha and Bodhisattva.

Plates 7, 8, 11, 12 and 13 are supplementary to the plates relating to India, Indonesia and Indochina.

Plates 16, 17, 18, 21 and 22 illustrate the link between Chinese early Buddhist sculpture and that of Gandhāra. Plates 24–31 afford examples of the most important stylistic phases of Chinese and Japanese Buddha and Bodhisattva figures between approx. 500 and 900 A.D.; cf. plates on pp. 144, 146, 164, 192, 193 and 196.

PLATE 1 – *Terracotta plaque from Kumrahar* near Patna, representing a tower shrine. 1st or 2nd cent. A.D. Diameter approx. 12 cm. Patna Museum. (After Coomaraswamy, *History of Indian and Indonesian Art*, Pl. 62.)

PLATE 2 – *Roundel in relief from the stone railing of a stūpa at Bhārhut*. Mriga Jātaka, in which the Buddha of the Future appears (twice) as a golden stag. Early 1st cent. B.C. Diameter 49 cm. Indian Museum, Calcutta. (After Kramrisch, *The Art of India*, Pl. 18.)

PLATE 3 – *Wall-painting from Turfan*, showing the Dīpamkara Jātaka. Dīpamkara, the Buddha of a distant epoch in the past, is being worshipped by a young Brahman, who is destined to become the Buddha of the Future. (So-called *pranidhi* scene; cf. text, p. 70.) Tempera. 8th/9th cents. Height 375 cm. Ehemalige Staatliche Museen, Berlin. (After Le Coq, *Chotscho*.)

PLATE 4 – *Votive stele from China*. Dated 557. Height 150 cm. Rietberg Museum, Zurich. (From a photograph by the Rietberg Museum.) Cf. text, p. 226.

PLATE 5 – *Head of the Buddha, presumably from the Rawak Stūpa (Khotan)*. Sun-baked mud coated with stucco plaster. Approx. 5th cent. Height 18.5 cm. Metropolitan Museum, New York. (After Priest, *Chinese Sculpture in the Metropolitan Museum of Art*, New York, 1944, Pl. 81.)

PLATE 6 – *Head of the Buddha from Sārnāth*. Sandstone. Early 6th cent. Height 20 cm. Archaeological Museum, Sārnāth. (After Rau, *Die Kunst Indiens*, Pl. 42.)

PLATE 7 – *Preaching Buddha from Sārnāth*. Sandstone. On the nimbus are two floating celestial beings worshipping the Buddha; the socle shows men worshipping the Wheel of the Doctrine. 5th cent. Height 158 cm. Archaeological Museum, Sārnāth. (After Rau, *op cit.*, Pl. 43.)

PLATE 8 – *Statue of Lokeshvara* in the cella of Tjandi Mendut Java. Stone. Approx. 800. Height approx. 250 cm. (After Bernet Kempers, *Ancient Indonesian Art*, Pl. 58.) Cf. text, p. 49.

PLATE 9 – *Head of the Buddha from Borobudur, Java*. Stone. 750/800. Height approx. 30 cm. (After Cohn, *Buddha in der Kunst des Ostens*, Pl. 49.)

PLATE 10 – *Head of the Buddha from Dvāravatī, Thailand*. Stone. 8th cent (?). Height 17 cm. Museum van Aziatische Kunst, Amsterdam (on loan; Lechner Collection). (After Rowland, *The Art and Architecture of India*, Pl. 164.)

PLATE 11 – *Standing Buddha from Dvāravatī*. Bronze. Between 6th and 12th cents. Height 68 cm. Metropolitan Museum, New York. (Courtesy of Metropolitan Museum of Art, Fletcher Fund, 1959.)

PLATE 12 – *Seated Buddha in bhūmisparsha-mudrā, Thailand*. Bronze. Dated 1481. Height 67 cm. Wat Pencamapabitra, Bangkok. (After Griswold, *Dated Buddha Images of Northern Siam*, frontispiece.)

PLATE 13 – *Seated Buddha in bhūmisparsha-mudrā, Thailand*. Bronze 14th cent. Height 94 cm. Prince Chalermbol Yugala Collection. (After Griswold, *op. cit.*, Fig. 2.)

PLATE 14 – *Head of a Bodhisattva from Lungmên (Pin-yang-tung), China*. Early 6th cent. Height 94 cm. (After Mizuno, *Bronze and Stone Sculpture of China*, Pl. 16.)

PLATE 15 – *Head of a seated Maitreya (Japanese: Miroku), Japan*. 7th cent. Height of whole figure 138 cm. Chūgūji monastery near Nara. (After original photograph.) Type of figure as in Plate on p. 192.

PLATE 16 – *Standing Buddha from Gandhāra*. Stone. It lacks the right hand, which is in the abhaya-mudrā. 2nd-5th cents. Museum, Lahore. (After original photograph.)

PLATE 17 – *Torso of a standing Buddha from Khocho*. Clay with reed and straw; originally painted and gilded. 5th cent. or later. Height 150 cm. (After Le Coq, *op. cit.*, Pl. 53.)

PLATE 18 – *Standing Maitreya (?) Buddha*. Bronze. China. Dated 477 (inscription probably not genuine, but materially correct). Height 53.3 cm. Metropolitan Museum, New York. (After Mizuno, *op. cit.*, Pl. 101.)

PLATE 19 – *Head of the Buddha from Lungmên (Fêng-hsien-sse), China*. Stone. 672–675. Height 46 cm. (After Mizuno, *op. cit.*, Pl. 18.)

PLATE 20 – *Head of a Bodhisattva from the Bhaishajyaguru triad*. Bronze; originally gilded. Approx. 725. Height of whole figure 312 cm. Yakushi-ji Temple, Nara. (After *Catalogue of Art Treasures of Ten Great Temples of Nara*, Vol. 13.)

PLATE 21 – *Standing Bodhisattva from Gandhāra*. Stone. 2nd-5th cents. Height 109 cm. Museum of Fine Arts, Boston. (After Rowland, *op. cit.*, Pl. 35.)

PLATE 22 – *Standing Bodhisattva, China*. Bronze. Approx. 300. Height 33.3 cm. Fujii-Yūrinkan, Kyōto. (After Mizuno, *op. cit.*, Pl. 6.)

PLATE 23 – *Seated Buddha, China*. Bronze. Dated 338. Height 39.4 cm. Avery Brundage Collection, San Francisco. (After Mizuno, *op. cit.*, Pl. 88.)

PLATE 24 – *Seated Maitreya Bodhisattva from Yünkang (Cave 15), North China*, Stone. Early 6th cent. Height 156 cm. Metropolitan Museum, New York. (After Priest, *op. cit.*, Pl. 21.)

PLATE 25 – *Shākyamuni Buddha with two Bodhisattvas*. Main cult image in the Golden Hall of the Hōryūji near Nara, Japan. Bronze sculpture by Tori. 623. Height of the main figure, excluding socle and nimbus, 85 cm. (After *Catalogue of Art Treasures…*, Vol. 1.)

PLATE 26 – *Standing Buddha, China*. Marble. Hands originally in abhaya- and varada-mudrā, as in Plates 24 and 25. Northern Ch'i Dynasty (550–577). Height of whole figure 260 cm. Nezu Museum, Tokyo. (After Mizuno, *op. cit.*, Pl. 61.)

PLATE 27 – *Standing Bhaishajyaguru Buddha (Japanese: Yakushi), Japan*. Bronze. Attribute: medicine-jar. Hakuhō period (latter half of 7th cent. – early 8th cent.). Shin Yakushiji Temple, Nara. Height 73 cm. (After an original photograph.)

PLATE 28 – *Seated Shākyamuni Buddha (Japanese: Shaka), shown preaching*. Japan. Wood. Jōgan period (9th cent.). Height 110 cm. Murōji Temple, Nara province. (After *Pageant of Japanese Art*, Vol. 3, Tokyo, 1952.)

PLATE 29 – *Seated Amitābha (Japanese: Amida) Buddha, Japan*. Shown in *mudrā* of meditation. Gilded wood carving by Jōchō. 1053. Phoenix Hall (Hōōdō) of the Byōdō-in Temple, Uji near Kyōto. (After *Pageant of Japanese Art*, Vol. 3 Tokyo, 1952.)

PLATE 30 – *Standing Avalokiteshvara (Chinese: Kuanyin) Bodhisattva, China*. Stone. Padmapāni: 'holding a lotus-bud'. From Ch'ang-an. Approx. 570. Height 249 cm. Museum of Fine Arts, Boston. (Courtesy of Museum of Fine Arts.)

PLATE 31 – *Standing Avalokiteshvara (Chinese: Kuanyin) Bodhisattva, China*. Gilded bronze. T'ang Dynasty, probably 8th cent. Height 35 cm. Fogg Museum of Art, Cambridge, Mass. (Courtesy of Fogg Museum.)

PLATE 32 – *Head of a Brahman from Hadda, Afghanistan*. From a Buddhist scene on a relief in stucco. 5th cent., Height 17 cm. Museum für Völkerkunde, Berlin. (After Rau, *op. cit.*, Pl. 26.)

PLATE 33 – *Head of Asanga (Japanese: Muchaku)*. Japan. Wood. Carved by Unkei. Approx. 1208. Height of whole figure 186 cm. Temple of Kōfukuji, Nara. (After *Catalogue of Art Treasures…*, Vol. 15.)

PLATE 34 – *Shākyamuni returning from the mountains*. Detail from a painting by Liang K'ai (China, approx. 1140–1210). Ink and light colours on silk. Height of painting 118 cm., of detail approx. 50 cm. Shima Eiichi Collection, Tokyo. (After Tanaka Ichimatsu, *Ryōkai* = Liang K'ai, Tokyo, 1957.) Cf. text on p. 221.

PLATE 35 – *Bodhidharma and Hui K'o*. Painting by Sesshū. (Japan, 1420–1506). Ink and light colours on paper. Height 200 cm. (here slightly cut down). (After Sesshū, ed. Tokyo National Museum, Kyōto, 1956, Plate 22.) Cf. text on p. 276 f.

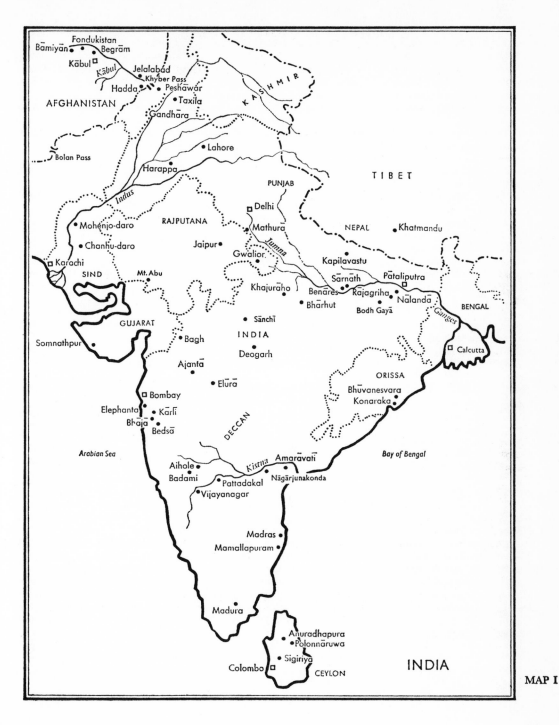

Bāmiyān • •Begrām
• Fondukistan
Kābul □ Kābul
Jelalabād
• Khyber Pass
Hadda • •Peshāwar
AFGHANISTAN
• Taxila
• Gandhāra

KASHMIR

• Lahore

Bolan Pass

Harappa •

Indus

TIBET

PUNJAB

□ Delhi

Mohénjo-daro •
RAJPUTANA
• Mathura

Chanhu-daro •
Jaipur •
• Gwalior
Jumna
NEPAL
• Khatmandu

□ Karachi
SIND

Mt. Abu •

Khajuraho •
• Kapilavastu
• Sarnath
Benares • □ Pātaliputra
• Rajagriha
• Nālanda
BENGAL

GUJARAT

Bhārhut • • Bodh Gayā

Ganges

Somnathpur •
• Bagh
INDIA
• Deogarh

• Sānchī

□ Calcutta

• Ajantā
ORISSA

• Elūrā
• Bhuvanesvara
Konaraka •

□ Bombay
Elephanta •
Bhāja • Kārlī
• Bedsā
DECCAN

Arabian Sea

Aihole •
Badami •
Kistna
• Amarāvatī
Bay of Bengal

• Pattadakal
Nāgārjunakonda •
• Vijayanagar

Madras •
Mamallapuram •

Madura •

• Anuradhapura
• Polonnāruwa
Colombo □ • Sigiriya
CEYLON

INDIA

MAP I

CHRONOLOGICAL TABLE

	INDIA	CEYLON	INDONESIA	INDOCHINA
B.C.				
500	563?—483?: Shākyamuni, the Buddha	5th c. B.C.—8th c. A.D.: ANURĀDHAPURA PERIOD		(Cf. detailed tables in B. Ph. Groslier, *Indochina*)
400	approx. 324—187: MAURYA DYNASTY			
300	approx. 273—232: Ashoka *Sānchī, Stūpa I (core)*	latter half of 3rd c.: introduction of Buddhism		
200				
100	*Bhārhut; Sānchī, enlargement of Stūpa I; Ajantā IX—X* approx. 50: *Caitya hall at Bhājā*			
0	From 1st c. A.D.: Mahāyāna fully developed *Sānchī, Stūpa I, torana reliefs; caitya hall at Bedsā* approx. 25 B.C.—320 A.D.: LATE ĀNDHRA			1st—6th c.: KINGDOM OF FUNAN
A.D.				
100	approx. 50—5th/7th c.: KUSHĀN DYNASTY 128? 144?: Kanishka 1st?/2nd c.: *earliest Buddha images in Mathurā and Gandhāra* approx. 120: *caitya hall at Kārlī* 2nd c.: Nāgārjuna (Mādhyamaka doctrine) 2nd/3rd c.: *Mathurā art (early phase); Amarāvatī, Nāgārjunakonda*		From 2nd c. or earlier: Indian colonization of Java 2nd—7th c.: *Early Indonesian art*	
200	2nd—5th c.: *Gandhāran art* 249: Sassanid invasion of Gandhāra	2nd/3rd c.: *sculpture influenced by Amarāvatī*	2nd—6th c.: gradual spread of Buddhism	2nd/3rd c.: Buddhist culture in Tongking

CHRONOLOGICAL TABLE

CENTRAL ASIA	CHINA	KOREA	JAPAN	
	481—221: WARRING STATES (Late Chou Period)			B.C. 500
				400
			to approx. 200 B.C.: JŌMON PERIOD	300
	221—206: CH'IN DYNASTY 206 B.C.—220 A.D.: HAN DYNASTY			
			approx. 200 B.C.— 550 A.D.: YAYOI (TUMULUS) PERIOD	200
		108 B.C.—313 A.D.: NANG-NANG (LOLANG, RAKURŌ): Han colony 1st c. B.C.?—668: KOGURYO 1st c. B.C.?—663: PAEKCHE 1st c. B.C.?—668: SILLA		100
				0
				A.D. 100
	65: first evidence of Buddhist communities			
	220—265: THREE EMPIRES 265—581: SIX DYNASTIES PERIOD 265—420: Western and Eastern Ch'in Dynasty			200

CHRONOLOGICAL TABLE

	INDIA	CEYLON	INDONESIA	INDOCHINA
300	320–approx. 550/650: GUPTA PERIOD *Mathurā; Sārnāth; Bodh Gayā*			approx. 300: *bronze Buddha from Dong-duong (Annam)*
	4th c.: Asanga and Vasubandhu (Yogācāra school)			
400	4th/5th c.: *Hadda sculpture* 455–500: White Huns invade Gandhāra approx. 450—8th c.: *Ajantā caves*			*Buddhist art in Funan under Gupta influence*
500	5th/6th c.: *classical Gupta style in Mathurā and Sārnāth Mahābodhi Temple at Bodh Gayā*			
	from approx. 6th c.: development of Vajrayāna			550—900: Cambodian kingdom of CHEN-LA 6th—8th c.: *Mahāyāna art linked to Hinduism (Shivaism) and ruler cult* 7th—12th c.: DVĀRAVATĪ *Hīnayāna art*
600	606—647: Harsha approx. 640: Hsüan-tsang at Nālandā		from 7th c.: SHRĪVIJAYA KINGDOM IN SUMATRA (Palembang) Mahāyāna (Vajrayāna) makes headway	
	approx. 650: Buddhism spreads to Tibet		approx. 650—930: *Central Javanese art (under Late Gupta and Pāla influence)*	
	7th/8th c.: *Late Gupta art; Elūrā, Ajantā, etc.*		685—: I-ching at Palembang	

CHRONOLOGICAL TABLE

CENTRAL ASIA	CHINA	KOREA	JAPAN	
3rd/4th c.: *paintings at Miran* 3rd/4th c.: *Gandhāran influences transmitted to China* 3rd—5th c.: *colossal Buddhas at Bāmiyān*	3rd/4th c.: spread of Buddhism in North and South China; *earliest surviving Buddha images, some under Gandhāran influence*		earliest cultural influences from Korea and China (including writing)	300
4th/5th c.?: *Khotan, sculpture on Rawak Stūpa* 366—700: *Tun-huang (latter half of 5th c.: earliest surviving paintings)*	386—535: NORTHERN WEI DYNASTY (T'o-pa) 399—414: Fa-hsien's pilgrimage	372: Koguryo Buddhist 384: Paekche Buddhist		
	402: Kumārajīva's journey to China 4th—7th c.: Maitreya cult From approx. 400: Amitābha cult 445/446: Buddhists persecuted 5th/6th c.: *Buddhist art in North China, cave temples (Yünkang, Lung-mên, etc.)*	424/524: Silla Buddhist	probable earliest sporadic contact with Buddhism	400
approx. 500—700: *paintings at Kyzyl (Kuchā area)* approx. 500: *1st Indo-Iranian style*	From approx. 500: Ch'an Buddhism brought to China (Bodhidharma)		closer contact with Buddhism 552 (official date): Buddhism adopted from Paekche 552—645: ASUKA (SUIKO) ERA 574—622: Crown Prince Shōtoku *Art under Korean influence*	500
	550—581: NORTHERN CH'I/NORTHERN CHOU DYNASTY *Caves of Hsiang-t'ang-shan* From late 6th c.: T'ien-tai school 581—618: SUI DYNASTY			
approx. 600/700: *2nd Indo-Iranian style* 7th c.?: *sculpture at Fondukistan* 640, 647: Turfan and Kuchā occupied by China	618—906: T'ANG DYNASTY capital at Ch'ang-an 629—645: Hsüan-tsang's pilgrimage	6th/7th c.: *Flowering of early Buddhist art in Koguryo, Paekche, Silla*	607: founding of Hōryūji	600
		668—935: Kingdoms united in GREATER SILLA EMPIRE (capital at Kyongju)	645—710: HAKUHŌ ERA *Art under Sui and Early T'ang influence*	
	671—695: I-ching's pilgrimage			

CHRONOLOGICAL TABLE

	INDIA	CEYLON	INDONESIA	INDOCHINA
700			*Hindu tjandis on Dieng plateau*	
	approx. 750—1200: PĀLA/SENA PERIOD Vajrayāna (centre in 9th c.: Nālandā); spread to Nepal and Tibet (8th/9th c.) *Late classical Buddhist art*		750/800 *Borobudur*	
		781—1290: POLONNĀRUWA PERIOD	778—: SHAILENDRA DYNASTY in Java (hegemony over Cambodia); *Mahāyāna art*	
800	8th—13th c.: Islam makes headway	8th/9th c.: *Mahāyānist sculpture*	approx. 800: *Tjandi Mendut Tjandi Kalasan Tjandi Sewu*	
	9th c.: *Mahābodhi Temple at Bodh Gayā restored*		9th c.: Shailendra hegemony over Shrīvijaya; from 10th c.: Shailendras in power there	9th c.—1177/1431: KHMER EMPIRE at Angkor
				9th/10th c.: *Buddhist art in Champa (Dong-duong)*
900			approx. 930—1530: *Eastern Javanese art*	
1000		from 11th c.: Theravāda (Hīnayāna) renaissance	Syncretism of Hinduism and Buddhism under MATARAM DYNASTY (King Airlangga)	10th/11th c.: *Mahāyānist Khmer art side by side with Hindu (and ruler cult)*

CHRONOLOGICAL TABLE

CENTRAL ASIA	CHINA	KOREA	JAPAN	
	7th/8th c.: *classical flowering period of Buddhist art. Painters: Wu Tao-tse (approx. 690-760) and others*	7th—9th c.: *classical Buddhist art under T'ang influence*	710—794: NARA PERIOD *Buddhist art on T'ang model*	700
751: Arab victory over T'ang army on the Talas; thereafter Islam makes headway	Until mid-8th c.: Late phase of caves at T'ien-lung-shan	7th/8th c.: *Pulkuk-sa* 8th c.: *Sokkul-am*	*Wall-paintings at Hōryūji Temples at Nara, the capital: Yakushiji, Tōdaiji, etc. (Colossal Buddha, 752)* 756: Shōsōin	
755—840: UIGHUR EMPIRE in eastern Turkestan (Manichaean and Buddhist)				
777—848: Tun-huang under Tibetan rule				
8th—9th c.: *monuments at Khocho (Turfan area) and Kumtura (near Kuchā) under T'ang influence*	8th/9th c.: *Vajrayāna art (Mi-tsung/Chên-yên school)*		794—897: JŌGAN PERIOD (capital: Heian = Kyōto) *Vajrayāna from China: Saichō, Kūkai (beginning of 9th c.)*	800
850—approx. 1300: *artistic work continued at Tun-huang*	843—845: persecution of Buddhists. Japanese monk Ennin in China		*Monasteries on Hiei-zan (Tendai school) and Kōyasan (Shingon school); syncretism of Buddhism and Shinto*	
868: *Diamond Sūtra print from Tun-huang*				
9th/10th c.: *paintings in Chinese style in southern Turkestan and Turfan (Bezeklik)*	906—960: FIVE DYNASTIES PERIOD	932—1392: KORYO PERIOD. Capital Kaesong	897—1185: FUJIWARA PERIOD. Capital (until 1868): Heian. Flowering period of courtly culture,	
Until 10th c. almost all eastern Turkestan Islamic	960—1278: SUNG DYNASTY 960—1127: Northern Sung	*Continuation of Silla art; some Sung influence*	largely independent of China and Korea *Architecture, sculpture and painting of Tendai and Shingon schools*	
	907—1125: Liao Dynasty			
	985: *Copy of Udayana Buddha produced for Chōnen (Seiryōji, Kyōto)*			
				1000
		1097: Ch'an (Son) Buddhism transmitted to Korea	1053: *Phoenix Hall of Byōdōin Temple near Uji (Amitābha statue by Jōchō)*	

CHRONOLOGICAL TABLE

	INDIA	CEYLON	INDONESIA	INDOCHINA
1100		12th c.: *Flowering of Polonnāruwa period* 12th c.: *Nirvāna group at Gal Vihāra; Wata-dage; Sat Mahal Pāsāda, etc.*		First half of 12th c.: *Angkor Vat* 1150—1220: *Buddhist monumental art under Dhāranīndravarman II and Jayavarman VII*
1200	End of Islamic conquests (Magadha, cradle of Buddhism, becomes Islamic)	13th c.: Tamil conquest ends; Theravāda until present day	1222—1292: SINGHASĀRI KINGDOM Latter half of 13th c.: *Tjandi Jago* towards 1300: *Prajnāpāramitā statue at Leyden*	12th c.: *Wat Kukut (Dvāravatī)* From approx. 1200: *Bayon (Angkor)* 12th/13th c.: *Lopburi style (Siam)* *Khmer influence (Mahāyānist)* From 13th c.: *Khmer art becomes Hīnayānist*
1300			Approx. 1300—1600: MOJOPAHIT KINGDOM 13th/14th c.: Islam makes headway	13th/14th c.: Rise of Thai kingdom (Hināyānist) 1292—1361: SUKHOTHAI 14th—16th c.: Chiengmai 1350—1767: AYUTHIA (Angkor reconquered in 1353) 14th/15th c.: *final stage in development of Siamese type of Buddha ('national style')* 1424: *wall-paintings at Wat Rājapūrana* 1431: final fall of Angkor
1400				
1500				
1600			1526: Islamic conversions come to an end	From 16th c.: *'Buddha in princely attire' occurs frequently in Siam*
1700				1782: Bangkok capital of Siam *'Bangkok style'*

CHRONOLOGICAL TABLE

CENTRAL ASIA	CHINA	KOREA	JAPAN	
	1127—1278: Southern Sung *Ch'an Buddhist ink-painting (esp. 13th c.)* Neo-Confucianism		*Flowering of belief in Amitābha (Hōnen and others) and art associated with it*	1100
			1185—1336: KAMAKURA PERIOD	
approx. 1215/20: eastern Turkestan conquered by Mongols		1206—36: Mongol invasions	Kamakura headquarters of the military rulers; feudal warrior culture; introduction of Zen Buddhism *(monasteries at Kyōto and Kamakura)* Fresh Chinese influence (Sung)	1200
	1278—1368: YÜAN (Mongol) DYNASTY Lamaism makes headway, esp. in Northern China		*Sculpture: Unkei and his school; colossal Buddha at Kamakura (1252)*	
			1336—1573: ASHIKAGA (MUROMACHI) PERIOD	1300
	1368—1644: MING DYNASTY *Late Buddhist art (imitative); predominance of literary men's non-Buddhist painting (wên-jên-hua)*	1392—1910: YI DYNASTY Confucianism. *Decline of Buddhism and Buddhist art*	15th/16th c.: *Flowering period of Zen art (ink-painting, tea cult, etc.) in Kyōto under strong Chinese influence* 1420—1506: *Sesshū (Zen monk, ink-painter); many followers*	1400
				1500
			1573—1603: MOMOYAMA PERIOD	
				1600
	1644—1912: CH'ING DYNASTY *Buddhist art chiefly Lamaist*		1603—1868: TOKUGAWA PERIOD. Residence of the rulers (shōguns) at Edo (= Tōkyō). Renaissance of Confucianism and Shintō; *late phase of Zen painting (Hakuin and others)*	1700

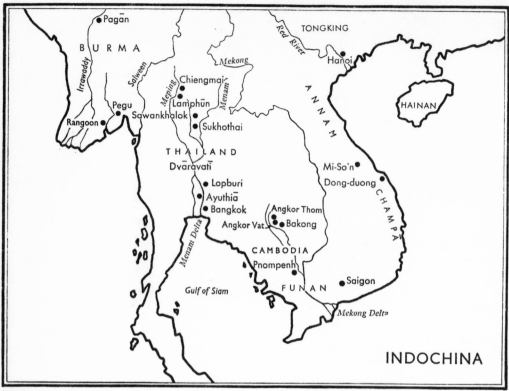

MAP II

MAP III

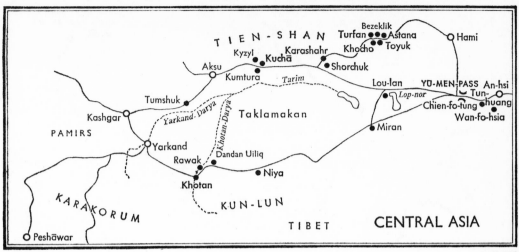

CENTRAL ASIA

MAP IV

CHINA

MAP V

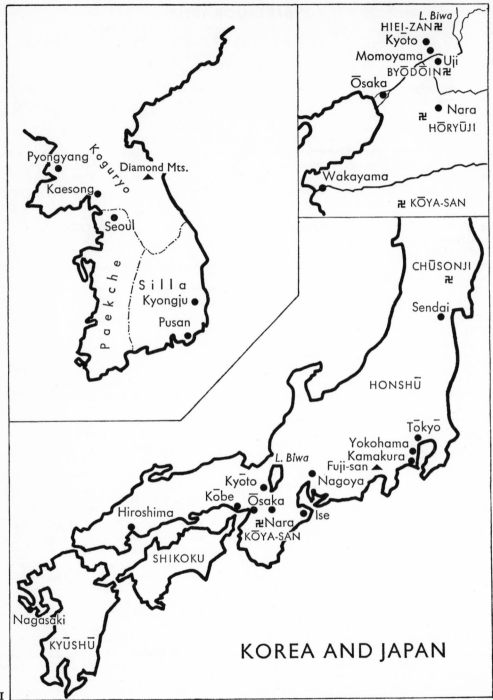

L. Biwa

HIEI-ZAN卍
Kyōto ●
Momoyama ●
●Uji
BYŌDŌIN卍
Ōsaka ●

卍 ● Nara
HŌRYŪJI

Wakayama
●

卍 KŌYA-SAN

Pyongyang
●
Kaesong
●

Koguryo

Diamond Mts.
▲

Seoul
●

Silla
Kyongju ●
Pusan
●

Paekche

CHŪSONJI
卍

Sendai
●

HONSHŪ

Tōkyō
●
Yokohama ●
Kamakura ●
Fuji-san ▲
Nagoya ●

L. Biwa

Kyōto
●
Kōbe
●
Ōsaka
●
卍 Nara
KŌYA-SAN

Ise
●

Hiroshima
●

SHIKOKU

Nagasaki
●

KYŪSHŪ

KOREA AND JAPAN

MAP VI

312

BIBLIOGRAPHY

This bibliography does not include general works on the history of culture and art which have appeared in earlier volumes in the ART OF THE WORLD series — on India, Indonesia, Indochina (particularly extensive) and China — or which will appear in subsequent volumes on Burma — Korea — Tibet and Japan, other than works that are important for the study of Buddhist art. This bibliography does, however, contain some introductory works on Buddhism by students of comparative religion. It is limited in the main to more recent publications which contain references to most of the earlier literature. Older works are accordingly only mentioned if they are basic standard texts, or if they contain particularly valuable or comprehensive illustrations. Some works which have extensive bibliographies are indicated by the letter (B). See the bibliography and notes to my *Buddhistische Kunst Ostasiens* (Stuttgart, 1957) for titles of numerous works on the history of the culture, religion and art of eastern Asia (including India and Central Asia). For reasons of space no mention is made here of general histories and encyclopaedias on the history of religion in which — especially if they were published recently — Buddhism and its role in Asian cultural and art history are treated in a satisfactory manner.

Literature on art history published only in Asian languages (in the main Chinese and Japanese) is omitted here since it is available only to the specialist; some works with résumés in European languages are, however, included.

DOCTRINE, TEXTS AND HISTORY OF BUDDHISM

Beck, H., Buddhism. 2 vols. (Sammlung Göschen, 174, 770). 2nd ed. Berlin-Leipzig, 1920, 1922. Re-edited by Heimo Rau, Stuttgart, 1958.

Bibliographie Bouddhique, vol. 1 (1928-9), Paris, 1930 — (current).

Conze, E., Buddhism. London, 1951; 2nd ed., Oxford, 1953.

Conze, E., Buddhist Texts Through the Ages. New York, 1954.

Cowell, E. B. (ed.), The Jātaka, or Stories of the Buddha's Former Births. 6 vols. and index vol. Cambridge, 1895—1907, 1913.

Dumoulin, H., Zen. Geschichte und Gestalt. Berne, 1959.

Dutoit, J. (tr.), Jātakam. Das Buch der Erzählungen aus früheren Existenzen Buddhas. 7 vols. Leipzig, 1908—21.

Foucaux, Ph. E. (tr.), Lalitavistara. Histoire du Bouddha Çakya-Mouni. 2 vols. Paris, 1884, 1892.

Frauwallner, E., Die Philosophie des Buddhismus. Berlin, 1956; 2nd ed., 1958.

Giles, H. A., The Travels of Fa-hsien, or Record of the Buddhistic Kingdoms, Re-translated. Cambridge, 1923; 3rd impression, London, 1959.

Glasenapp, H. von, Die nichtchristlichen Religionen. (Fischer-Lexikon.) Frankfurt, 1957.

Glasenapp, H. von, Die Religionen Indiens. (Kröners Taschenausgabe, 140.) Stuttgart, 1943. (B)

Glasenapp, H. von, Der Buddhismus in Indien und im Fernen Osten. Berlin-Zurich, 1936. (B)

Glasenapp, H. von, Buddhismus und Gottesidee. (Akad. d. Wiss. u. d. Lit., Abhandlungen d. geistes- u. sozialwiss. Klasse, Jg. 1954, Nr. 8.) Mainz, 1954.

Glasenapp, H. von, Buddhistische Mysterien. Die geheimen Lehren und Riten des Diamant-Fahrzeugs [Vajrayāna]. Stuttgart, 1940.

Grousset, R., Sur les traces du Bouddha. Paris, 1929. (English translation: In the Footsteps of the Buddha, 1932.)

Gundert, W. (tr. and comm.), Bi-yän-lu. Meister Yüan-wu's Niederschrift von der Smaragdenen Felswand. Chapters 1—33. Munich, 1960. [Basic text of Zen Buddhism.]

Herrmann, A., Historical and Commercial Atlas of China. Cambridge, Mass., 1935. [Contains maps of Asia, incl. some on history of religion.]

Hônen, the Buddhist Saint. Translated by H. H. Coates and R. Ishizuka. Tokyo, 1925; 2nd ed., 1930; re-edited Kyōto, 1949. [Also useful guide to Buddhism, esp. in eastern Asia.]

Kern, H. H. (tr.), The Saddharma-Pundarīka or the Lotus of the True Law. (Sacred Books of the East, 21.) Oxford, 1884.

Mensching, G., Buddhistische Geisteswelt. Texte ausgewählt und eingeleitet. Darmstadt, 1955.

Müller, F. M. (tr.), Buddhist Mahāyāna Texts. [Includes Sukhāvatī-Vyūha.] (Sacred Books of the East, 49.) Oxford, 1894, 1927.

Der Ochs und sein Hirte. Eine altchinesische Zengeschichte. Commentary by R. Ohtsu; translated by K. Tsujimura and H. Buchner. Pfullingen, 1958.

Suzuki, D. T., Essays in Zen Buddhism. 1st series: London, 1927, 1949, 1958; 2nd series: Kyōto, 1933, London, 1950; 3rd series: Kyōto, 1934, London, 1953.

Suzuki, D. T., Zen Buddhism and its Influence on Japanese Culture. Kyōto, 1938.

Suzuki, D. T., An Introduction to Zen Buddhism. Kyōto, 1934.

Thomas, E. J., The History of Buddhist Thought. London, 1933.

Thomas, E. J., The Life of Buddha as Legend and History. London, 1927; 2nd ed., 1930.

Tucci, G., The Theory and Practice of the Mandala. London, 1961.

2500 Years of Buddhism. Ed. by P. V. Bapat. Delhi, 1956.

Waley, A., The Real Tripitaka. London, 1952. [Hsüan-tsang's pilgrimage.]

Walleser, M. (tr.), Die Mittlere Lehre des Nāgārjuna. Translated from the Tibetan. Heidelberg, 1911. — (idem.), translated from the Chinese version. Heidelberg, 1912.

Warren, H. C. (tr.), Buddhism in Translations. Cambridge, Mass., 1896; 10th issue, 1953.

Zürcher, E., Buddhism. Its Origin and Spread in Words, Maps and Pictures. Amsterdam, 1962.

ICONOGRAPHY AND SYMBOLISM OF BUDDHIST ART

Behrsing, S., Der Heiligenschein in Ostasien. Zeitschrift der Deutschen Morgenländischen Gesellschaft, vol. 103 (New Series, 28), 1953.

Cohn, W., Buddha in der Kunst des Ostens. Leipzig, 1925.

Combaz, G., L'évolution du Stūpa en Asie. Mélanges chinois et bouddhiques, 2 (1932—3); 3 (1934—5); 4 (1935—6).

Conze, E., The Iconography of the Prajnāpāramitā. Oriental Art, II/2, Autumn 1949.

Coomaraswamy, A. K., Elements of Buddhist Iconography. Cambridge, Mass., 1935.

Getty, A., The Gods of Northern Buddhism. Oxford, 1914; 2nd ed., 1928.

Gulik, R. H. van, Siddham. An Essay on the History of Sanskrit Studies in China and Japan. Nagpur (India), 1956.

Kirfel, W., Symbolik des Buddhismus. Stuttgart, 1959.

Mallmann, M.-Th. de, Introduction à l'étude d'Avalokiteçvara. Paris, 1948.

Mus, P., Le Buddha paré. Bulletin de l'École Française d'Extrême-Orient, 28, 1928.

Mythologie Asiatique Illustrée, ed. by J. Hackin and others. (English translation: Asiatic Mythology, New York, 1932.)

Rousselle, E., [see under China.]

Saunders, D. A., Mudrā. A Study of Symbolic Gestures in Japanese Buddhist Sculpture. (Bollingen Series, 58.) New York, 1960.

Silva-Vigier, A. de, The Life of the Buddha ... Illustrated with ... Works of Asian Art. London, 1955.

Soper, A. C., The 'Dome of Heaven' in Asia. Art Bulletin, 29, 1947.

Le Symbolisme Cosmique des Monuments Religieux. (Serie Orientale Roma, 14.) Rome, 1957.

Tajima, R., [see under Japan.]

Tucci, G., Tibetan Painted Scrolls. Rome, 1949. [Important for Tantrism generally.]

Visser, M. W. de, [see under Eastern Asia.]

Ward, W. F., The Lotus Symbol: its Meaning in Buddhist Art and Philosophy. Journal of Aesthetics and Art Criticism, XI/2, December 1952.

Wegner, M., [see under China.]

INDIA AND CEYLON

Bachhofer, L., Die frühindische Plastik. 2 vols. Florence — Munich, 1929. (English translation: Early Indian Sculpture. New York, 1929.)

Bhattacaryya, B., The Indian Buddhist Iconography. London, 1924. [Tantrism.]

Cohn, W., Indische Plastik. Berlin, 1921.

Coomaraswamy, A. K., History of Indian and Indonesian Art. London, 1927. (B)

Coomaraswamy, A. K., The Invention of the Buddha Figure. Ostasiatische Zeitschrift, New Series, 1, 1924.

Coomaraswamy, A. K., The Indian Origin of the Buddha Image. Journal of the American Oriental Society, 46, 1926.

Coomaraswamy, A. K., The Origin of the Buddha Image. Art Bulletin, 9, 1926—7.

Fischer, K., Schöpfungen indischer Kunst. Cologne, 1959; 2nd ed., 1961. (B)

Foucher, A., La vie du Bouddha d'après les textes et les monuments de l'Inde. Paris, 1949.

Franz, H. G., Der indische Turmtempel und seine Vorstufen. Forschungen und Fortschritte, 32, 1958.

Franz, H. G., Die Entwicklung des indischen Turmtempels. Ibid.

Franz, H. G., Ein unbekannter Stūpa der Sammlung Gai und die Entwicklung des Stūpa im Gebiet des alten Gandhāra. Zeitschrift der Deutschen Morgenländischen Gesellschaft, 109 (New Series, 34), 1959.

Franz, H. G., Pagode, Stūpa, Turmtempel. Kunst des Orients, 3, 1959.

Govinda, A. B., Some Aspects of Stūpa Symbolism. Journal of the Indian Society of Oriental Art, 2, 1934; 4, 1936.

Grousset, R., De la Grèce à la Chine. Monaco, 1948.

Grousset, R., De l'Inde à l'Indo-Chine. Monaco, 1950.

Härtel, H., Indische und zentralasiatische Wandmalerei. In: Meisterwerke aussereuropäischer Malerei, ed. F. A. Dargel. Berlin, 1959. (B)

Kramrisch, S., The Art of India. London — New York, 1954.

Lohuizen de Leeuw, J. E. van, The 'Scythian' Period. Leyden, 1949. (B)

Myer, P. R., The Great Temple of Bodhgayā. Art Bulletin, 40, 1958.

Ramachandra Rao, P. R., The Art of Nāgārjunikonda. Madras, 1956.

Rau, H., Die Kunst Indiens bis zum Islam. Stuttgart, 1958.

Rowland, B., The Art and Architecture of India. (Pelican History of Art.) Rev. ed., Harmondsworth, etc., 1956. (B)

Rowland, B., The Wall-Paintings of Central Asia, India and Ceylon. Boston, 1938.

Waldschmidt, E., Grünwedels Buddhistische Kunst in Indien. Berlin-Lankwitz, 1932.

Yazdani, Gh., Ajantā. 4 vols. of text, 4 portfolios of plates. London, 1930—5.

Zimmer, H., The Art of Indian Asia. Ed. by Joseph Campbell. 2 vols. (Bollingen Series, 39.) New York, 1955. (B)

Zimmer, H., Kunstform und Yoga im indischen Kultbild. Berlin, 1926.

Gandhāra and Neighbouring Areas:

Ahrens, D., Die römischen Grundlagen der Gandhārakunst. (Orbis Antiquus, 20.) Münster, 1961.

Barthoux, J., Les Fouilles de Hadda. I: Paris, 1930; III: 1933.

Bernet Kempers, A. J., Die Begegnung der griechisch-römischen Kunst mit dem indischen Kulturkreis. Handbuch der Archäologie, vol. 2. Munich, 1954. (B)

Deydier, H., Contribution à l'étude de l'art du Gandhāra. Essai de bibliographie analytique et critique. Paris, 1950. (B)

Foucher, A., L'art gréco-bouddhique du Gandhāra. 4 vols. Paris, 1905, 1918, 1922, 1951.

Foucher, A., The Beginnings of Buddhist Art and other Essays in Indian and Central Asian Archaeology. London — Paris, 1917.

Ingholt, H., Gandhāran Art in Pakistan. New York, 1957.

Marshall, Sir John, Taxila. 3 vols. Cambridge, 1951.

Marshall, Sir John, The Buddhist Art of Gandhāra. Cambridge, 1960.

Rowland, B., Gandhāra and Late Antique Art. American Journal of Archaeology, 46, 1942.

Rowland, B., Gandhāra and Early Christian Art. Ibid., 49, 1945.

Rowland, B., A Note on the Invention of the Buddha Image. Harvard Journal of Asiatic Studies, 11, 1948. [Udayana legend.]

Rowland, B., The Hellenistic Tradition in Northwestern India. Art Bulletin, 31, 1949.

Soper, A. C., The Roman Style in Gandhāra. American Journal of Archaeology, 55, 1951.

Wheeler, R. E. M., Romano-Buddhist Art: an Old Problem Restated. Antiquity, 23 (no. 89), 1949.

INDONESIA

Bernet Kempers, A. J., Ancient Indonesian Art. Amsterdam, 1959. (B)

Krom, N. J., Barabudur. Archaeological Description. 2 vols. The Hague, 1927.

Krom, N. J., The Life of the Buddha on the Stūpa of Barabudur according to the Lalitavistara Text. The Hague, 1926.

Le May, R., The Cultures of South-east Asia. London, 1954; 2nd ed., 1956. (B)

Mus, P., Barabudur. 2 vols. Hanoi, 1935. (Also in Bulletin de l'École Française d'Extrême-Orient, 32, 1932; 33, 1933.)

INDOCHINA AND THAILAND

Bowie, Th. (ed.), The Arts of Thailand. Bloomington, 1960.

Döhring, K., Buddhistische Tempelanlagen in Siam. Berlin, 1916.

Dupont, P., La statuaire préangkorienne. (Artibus Asiae Supplementum, 15.) Ascona, 1955.

Dupont, P., L'archéologie Mōne de Dvāravatī. (Publications de l'École Française d'Extrême-Orient, 41.) Paris, 1959.

Griswold, A. B., Dated Buddha Images of Northern Siam. (Artibus Asiae Supplementum, 16.) Ascona, 1957.

Groslier, B. Ph., Angkor. Paris, 1956 — Cologne, n.d.

Heine-Geldern, R., Weltbild und Bauform in Südostasien. Wiener Beiträge zur Kunst- und Kulturgeschichte Asiens, 4, 1930.

Le May, R., A Concise History of Buddhist Art in Siam. Cambridge, 1938.

Le May, R., [see also under Indonesia].

Lippe, A., A Dvāravatī Bronze Buddha from Thailand. Metropolitan Museum of Art Bulletin, January 1961. [Cf. appendix of plates, 11.]

[Cf. bibliography in B. Ph. Groslier, Indochina (ART OF THE WORLD).]

CENTRAL ASIA (including Tun-huang)

Andrews, F. H., Wall-Paintings from Ancient Shrines in Central Asia. London, 1948.

Bachhofer, L., Die Raumdarstellung in der chinesischen Malerei des 1. Jahrtausends n. Chr. [mainly in Tun-huang]. Münchner Jahrb. der bildenden Kunst, New Series, 8, 1931.

Godard, A. and Y.; Hackin, J., Les Antiquités Bouddhiques de Bāmiyān. Paris — Brussels, 1928.

Gray, B., Buddhist Cave Paintings at Tun-huang. London, 1959. (B)

Grünwedel, A., Altbuddhistische Kultstätten in Chinesisch-Turkestan. Berlin, 1912.

Grünwedel, A., Alt-Kutscha. 2 vols. Berlin, 1920.

Hackin, J., Recherches archéologiques à Begram. Paris, 1939.

Hackin, J. (and others), Nouvelles recherches archéologiques à Begram. 2 vols. Paris, 1954.

Hackin, J., and Carl, J., Nouvelles recherches archéologiques à Bāmiyān. Paris, 1933.

Le Coq, A. von, Die buddhistische Spätantike in Mittelasien. 7 vols. Berlin, 1922-33.

Le Coq, A. von, Chotscho. Berlin, 1913.

Le Coq, A. von, Bilderatlas zur Kunst und Kulturgeschichte Mittelasiens. Berlin, 1925. (B)

Pelliot, P., Les grottes de Touen-Houang [Tun-huang]. 6 portfolios of plates, [text not published]. Paris, 1920, 1921, 1924.

Rowland, B., [see under India (Wall-Paintings ...).]

Stein, A., Serindia ... Explorations in Central Asia and Westernmost China ... 5 vols. Oxford, 1921.

Stein, A., The Thousand Buddhas. Ancient Buddhist Paintings from ... Tunhuang ... Vol. of text and portfolio. London, 1921.

Stein, A., Innnermost Asia. 4 vols. Oxford, 1926.

Stein, A., Ancient Khotan. 2 vols. Oxford, 1907.

Stein, A., Ruins of Desert Cathay. 2 vols. London, 1912.

Vincent, I. V., The Sacred Oasis. Caves of the Thousand Buddhas, Tunhuang. London — Chicago, 1953.

Waldschmidt, E., Gandhāra, Kutschā, Turfan. Leipzig, 1927.

Warner, L., Buddhist Wall-Paintings. A study of a Ninth-Century Grotto at Wan-Fo-Hsia [near Tun-huang]. Cambridge, Mass., 1938.

EASTERN ASIA (general)

Fischer, O., Die Kunst Indiens, Chinas und Japans. (Propyläen-Kunstgeschichte, 4.) Berlin, 1928.

Grosse, E., Die ostasiatische Tuschmalerei. Berlin, 1923.

Kümmel, O., Die Kunst Chinas, Japans und Koreas. (Handbuch der Kunstwissenschaft.) Wildpark — Potsdam, 1929. (B)

Seckel, D., Buddhistische Kunst Ostasiens. Stuttgart, 1957. (B)

Seckel, D., Einführung in die Kunst Ostasiens. Munich, 1960.

Speiser, W., Die Kunst Ostasiens. Berlin, 1946; reprinted 1956.

Visser, M. W. de, The Arhats in China and Japan. Berlin, 1923. (Also in Ostasiatische Zeitschrift, 7, 1918—9; 9, 1920—1; 10, 1922—3.)

Visser, M. W. de, The Bodhisattva Ti-tsang [Kshitigarbha; Jizō] in China and Japan. Ostasiatische Zeitschrift, 2, 1913—4; 3, 1914—5.

CHINA

Bachhofer, L., Die Anfänge der buddhistischen Plastik in China. Ostasiatische Zeitschrift, New Series, 10, 1934.

Bachhofer, L., Zur Geschichte der chinesischen Plastik vom 8. bis 14. Jhd. Ostasiatische Zeitschrift, New Series, 14, 1938.

Boerschmann, E., Chinesische Architektur. 2 vols. Berlin, 1925.

Boerschmann, E., Chinesische Pagoden. Berlin — Leipzig, 1931 [1 vol. only].

Chapin, H. B., A Long Roll of Buddhist Images. Journal of the Indian Society of Oriental Art, 4, 1936; 6, 1938. [See also Harvard Journal of Asiatic Studies, 8, 1944; cf. Plates on pp. 207, 249.]

Chavannes, E., Mission archéologique dans la Chine septentrionale. Paris, 1909—15.

Davidson, J. Leroy, The Lotus Sūtra in Chinese Art. (Yale Univ.) New Haven, Conn., 1954.

Fischer, O., Chinesische Plastik. Munich, 1948. (B)
Groot, J. J. M. de, Der Thūpa, das heiligste Heiligtum des Buddhismus in China. Abhandlungen der Preuss. Akad. d. Wiss., Jhg. 1919, Phil.-Hist. Klasse Nr. 11. Berlin, 1919.
Mizuno, S., Chinese Stone Sculpture. Tokyo, 1950.
Mizuno, S., Bronze and Stone Sculpture of China. Tokyo, 1960.
Mizuno, S. and Nagahiro, T., The Buddhist Cave-Temples of Hsiang-t'ang-ssu ... Kyōto, 1937.
Mizuno, S. and Nagahiro, T., A Study of the Buddhist Cave-Temples of Lung-men, Honan. Tokyo, 1943.
Mizuno, S. and Nagahiro, T., Yun-kang. The Buddhist Cave-Temples of the Fifth Century A.D. in North China. Detailed Report ... 16 double vols. Kyōto, 1952 —
Prip-Möller, J., Chinese Buddhist Monasteries. Copenhagen, 1937.
Reischauer, E. O., Ennin's Travels in T'ang China. New York, 1955. — Ennin's Diary (trans.). New York, 1955.
Rousselle, E., Vom Sinn der buddhistischen Bildwerke in China. Darmstadt, 1958. (Reprint of: Die typischen Bildwerke des buddhistischen Tempels in China. Sinica, 6—10, 1931—5.)
Rowland, B., Chinese Sculpture of the Pilgrimage Road. Bulletin of the Fogg Art Museum, IV/2, March 1935.
Rowland, B., Indian Images in Chinese Sculpture. Artibus Asiae, 10, 1947.
Sickman, L. and Soper, A., The Art and Architecture of China. (Pelican History of Art.) Harmondsworth, etc., 1956. (B)
Sirén, O., Chinese Sculpture. 4 vols. London, 1925.
Sirén, O., Kinas Konst under tre artusenden. 2 vols. Stockholm, 1942—3.
Sirén, O., Chinese Painting. 7 vols. London, 1956, 1958. (B)
Soper, A. C., Literary Evidence for Early Buddhist Art in China. (Artibus Asiae Supplementum, 19.) Ascona, 1959.
Soper, A. C., South Chinese Influence on the Buddhist Art of the Six Dynasties Period. Bulletin of the Museum of Far Eastern Antiquities (Stockholm), 32, 1960.
Speiser, W., Meisterwerke chinesischer Malerei aus der Sammlung der japanischen Reichsmarschälle Yoshimitsu und Yoshimasa. Berlin, 1947; new edition, Berlin, 1958.
Studies in Chinese Art and some Indian Influences. London, 1937.
Sullivan, M., An Introduction to Chinese Art. London, 1961. (B)

Tokiwa, D. and Sekino, T., Buddhist Monuments in China. 5 double vols. Tokyo, 1925—38.
Wegner, M., Ikonographie des chinesischen Maitreya. Ostasiatische Zeitschrift, New Series, 5, 1929.
Willetts, W., Chinese Art. (Pelican Books A 358—9.) 2 vols. Harmondsworth, etc., 1958. (B)
Wright, A. F., Buddhism in Chinese History. Stanford — London, 1959.
Zürcher, E., The Buddhist Conquest of China. The Spread and Adaptation of Buddhism in Early Medieval China. (Sinica Leidensia, 11.) Leyden, 1959.

KOREA

Chōsen Koseki Zufu. [Korean Monuments. Editor: Sekino Tadashi.] 15 vols. Tokyo, 1915—35.
Eckardt, A., Geschichte der koreanischen Kunst. Leipzig, 1929. [Ample illustrations; text now outdated.]
McCune, E., The Arts of Korea. Rutland, Vt. — Tokyo, 1962. (B)
Watson, W., The Earliest Buddhist Images of Korea. Transactions of the Oriental Ceramic Society (London), 31, 1957—9.

JAPAN

Anesaki, M., Buddhist Art in its Relation to Buddhist Ideals, with Sepcial Reference to Buddhism in Japan. Boston — New York, 1915.
Anesaki, M., History of Japanese Religion. London, 1930.
Auboyer, J., Les influences et les réminiscences étrangères au Kondō du Hōryūji. Paris, 1941.
Baltzer, F., Die Architektur der Kultbauten Japans. Berlin, 1907.
Bohner, H., Shōtoku Taishi. (Mitteilungen der Deutschen Gesellschaft für Natur- u. Völkerkunde Ostasiens, Suppl. Vol. 15.) Tokyo, 1940.
Buhot, J., Histoire des arts du Japon. Vol. 1 [no more published]. Paris, 1949.
Catalogue of Art Treasures of Ten Great Temples of Nara. 25 vols., 3 supplementary vols. Tokyo, 1932—4; 1934, 1935, 1940.
Drexler, A., The Architecture of Japan. New York, 1955.
Gundert, W., Japanische Religionsgeschichte. Tokyo — Stuttgart, 1935; 2nd ed., 1943. (B)
Hasé, A. and Seckel, D., Emaki. Die Kunst der klassischen japanischen Bilderrollen. Zurich (Munich), 1959.
Hasumi, T., Japanische Plastik. Fribourg, 1960. (B)

Henderson, G. and Hurvitz, L., The Buddha of Seiryōji. [Copy of Udayana Statue.] Artibus Asiae, 19, 1956.

Ishida, M. and Wada, G., The Shōsōin. An 8th-Century Treasure House. Tokyo, etc., 1954.

Moriya, K., Die japanische Malerei. Wiesbaden, 1953.

Naitō, T., The Wall-Paintings of Hōryuji. Translated and edited by W. R. B. Acker and Benjamin Rowland. 2 vols. Baltimore, 1943. (Contains: Rowland, B., The Frescoes of Hōryūji in their Relation to Indian and Central Asian Painting and Religion.)

Nihon Emakimono Zenshū (Japanese Scroll Paintings). 15 vols. to date. Tokyo, 1958—

Pageant of Japanese Art. Ed. by Tokyo National Museum. 6 vols. Tokyo, 1952—4.

Paine, R. T. and Soper, A., The Art and Architecture of Japan. (Pelican History of Art.) Harmondsworth, etc., 1955. (B)

Soper, A. C., The Evolution of Buddhist Architecture in Japan. Princeton, 1942. (B)

Swann, P. C., An Introduction to the Arts of Japan. Oxford, 1958. (B)

Tajima, R., Les deux grands Mandalas et la doctrine de l'ésotérisme Shingon. Tokyo — Paris, 1959.

Treasures of the Shōsōin (Shōsōin Hōmotsu). 3 vols. Tokyo, 1960—2.

Visser, M. W. de, Ancient Buddhism in Japan. Sūtras and Ceremonies in Use in the 7th and 8th Centuries ... 2 vols. Leyden, 1935.

The Wall-Paintings in the Kondō, Hōryūji Monastery. Portfolio and supplementary text (text by Ichimatsu Tanaka). Kyōto, 1951.

Warner, L., Japanese Sculpture of the Suiko Period. New Haven, 1923.

Warner, L., Japanese Sculpture of the Tempyō Period. Cambridge, Mass., 1959.

Warner, L., The Craft of the Japanese Sculptor. New York, 1936.

Yashiro, Y., Art Treasures of Japan. 2 vols. Tokyo, 1960.

Yashiro, Y. and Swann, P. C., 2000 Years of Japanese Art. London, 1958.

Yoshida, T., Japanische Architektur. Tübingen, 1952.

INDEX

The numerals in italics refer to the plates and figures.

abhaya-mudrā 35, 77, 95, 96, 133, *141, 142, 144,* 300

Acala Vidyārāja   *211,* 245, 278

acanthus   29

Achaemenids   25

Ādi-Buddha 88, 128, 130, *146, 198,* 203, *206, 211,* 225, 245, *280*

Afghanistan   28f., *35, 142,* 300

agriculture   66

Aizen-Myōō   *246*

Ajantā   43, 48, 49, 53, 70, *97, 117,* 137, *138, 147, 181,* 190, 204, 262, 285

Ajatashatru   265

Aka-Fudō   *211*

Akāshagarbha   243

Akshobhya   133

alamkāra   286

alchemy   92

Alexander the Great   25

Alexandria   32

altar   *212*

Amarāvatī 34ff., 43, 45f., 47f., 51, *54, 76,* 85, *95,* 108, *116,* 117f., 129, 171, 188, 189, 190, 217, 262

Amida: cf. Amitābha

Amida-Raigō   105, *178,* 229

Amitābha 87ff., 105f., 133, *139, 145,* 160, *164, 167, 178, 183, 186, 190, 194, 196,* 201, 220, *228,* 229, 240, 261, 270, *280,* 300

Amoghapāsha   150

Amoghasiddhi   133

Amoghavajra   88

Ānanda   46, 226, 250

ancestor worship 49f., 62, 82, 84, 94, 102, 104, 150

anda   114

andesite   *206*

Āndhra   39f., 42, 45f., 47f., *54,* 90, *95*

Angkor   50, 54ff., 201, 267; pre-Angkor 52

Angkor Thom   *37*

Angkor Vat   54, 59, 60

aniconic principle   27, *76,* 188, 204

animals   *57, 231, 255,* 262; cf. ape, bull, elephant, gazelle, horse, lion, stag, tiger

animism   49

anklets   237

An Lu-shan   90

Annam   42, 51f., 59, 61, 67, *95*

Antiquity 33f., 74, 178, 183f., 206, 250, 262, 282; Late Antiquity 31, 65, 69, 74, 117, 183, 205, 263

Anurādhapura   45, *119,* 188

ape   *181*

Apollo   184

apsaras   *57, 98, 167,* 266

Arabs   64, 90

Arhat 92, 154, *168, 215,* 219, 225, *231,* 236, 249, 250, 255ff., 259, *273,* 276

aristocracy, in Japan   102, 104f.

armlets   *197,* 237

arūpadhātu   246f.

āsana   184

Asanga   134f., 255f., 300

Ashikaga   106, 110, 221, 258, 276

Ashoka   15, 25, 26, 41, 45, 114

Asia, western 63, 66, 74, 89, 90, 107, 183, 225, 256, 282; cf. Central Asia and other regions

Asuka   218, 239

asura   241

atlantes   32

attributes   186, *197, 210,* 237, 240, 244, 280

Avadāna   134

Avalokiteshvara *37,* 87, 92, 105, *145,* 150, *167, 168, 178, 183, 190, 194,* 201, 239f., 242, 278, 300; thousand-armed 241; horse-headed 245, *210;* cf. Kuanyin, Kannon

Avatamsaka school   100, 103; *Sūtra* 134, 262

avatāra   45, 104, 249

a-vidyā   *211,* 245

axis: cf. cosmic axis

āyaka-stambha   41, *54*

Ayuthia   60ff., *120, 140, 141,* 201, 266f.

Bactria   30, 64

Bakheng   54

Bakong   54

Bali   50, 124

Balkh   117

Bāmiyān   64ff., 70, 72, *142, 151,* 151f., 175

Bangkok   62, *159, 161,* 299

Barābar   138

Batō-Kannon   *210*

Bayon   *37,* 59, 61, *190,* 201

beads   237

Bedsā   117, 147

Begram   32

bells   100, 125, *279,* 279

Benares   25, 26, 42, 67, *98, 183,* 186, *253*

Bengal   44, 149

Bezeklik   70. 71, *152,* 175

bhadrāsana 168
Bhājā *137*, 147, 247
Bhagavadgītā 177
Bhaishajyaguru 229, 248, 300
bhakti 28, 87, 172, 217, 236, 286
Bhamāla 117
Bhārhut 26ff., 39, 115, 171, 247f., 255f., 262, 299
bhūmi 131f.
bhūmisparsha-mudrā 36, 56, 133, *183*, 201, 299
Bihar 44, *56, 198*
bija 116, 279
Bīmarān 29, *35*
Bishamon: cf. Vaishravana
Blazing Pillar 76
Bodh Gayā 26, 44, 45, 67, 121, *124*, 149
Bodhi Tree 44, 45, 239
Bodhidharma 87, *250*, 257, 276, 300
Bodhisattva 20, 29f., 32, *39*, 43, *56, 57*, 80, 131, *142, 145*, 154, *167, 168, 170, 178*, 186, *193, 194*, 201, 203, 205f., *210, 213*, 219, 225, 226f., 236-46, 249, *253*, 257, 258ff., 267, 276, 277f., 299f.; cf. Amoghapāsha, Avalokiteshvara (Kannon, Kuanyin), Kshitigarbha, Lokeshvara, Padmapāni, Vajrapāni
Bombay 147
Borneo 42
Borobudur *36*, 48, 108, 118, 132ff., *134, 135, 139*, 190, 225, 230, *253*, 264f., 275, 299
bowl *130, 270;* begging-bowl 113, *273*
Brahmā 77, *178*, 238, 240, 247; Brahmanism 19, 52, 162, 300; Brahmins 15
brick *57*, 125, 158
bronze: bells 100f.; bowl *130;* finials 120, 126; head *140;* jar 116; mast 129; mirror 102, *215*, 216; statues 46, 49, 51ff., 62, 85, 90f., *94*, 94, 102f., *141, 144, 146*, 188, *192, 198*, 199, 201, 202, 205, 206, 219, 299, 300; *stūpa 56;* urn *130*
Buddha, the historical (Gautama Shākyamuni) 15, 26 (cf. also Shākyamuni); scenes from life of, in art 27 *54, 56*, 70f., 171, 247, 250, *252*, 261f., *263f.*, 264, *265*, 267f.; Enlightenment of 44, *54*, 171, 173; First Sermon of 42, *54, 98*, 134, 186, *253*, 263, 278;
Buddha, colossal 64f., 67, 103f., 109, 118, *142*, 153f., *164*, 205f; head-dress of *185;* head of 69, *140*, 178, 183, 299, 300; 'Buddha Light' *144*, 183; Buddha paré 60f., *141*, 203, 250;
Buddha of the Future: cf. Maitreya; of the Past 113, 239; cf. Ādi-Buddha, Amitābha, Dhyāni Buddhas, Prabhūtaratna, 'Pure Land', 'Thousand Buddhas'
Buddhism 15ff., 25, 43, 59, 62, 63, 68, 73, 91, 94, 103, 105, 110, 172; spread of 16ff., 40, 47, 63, 81ff., 89, 93f., 114, 216f., 258, 282; decline of 90ff., 101, 108, 149; Buddhist *oikoumene*

15, 18f., 102f., 123, 153, 187, 258, 277; Buddhist schools 16, 20, 255, 281
bull 25
burial 113
Burma 46, 47, 53, 60, 124, *125*, 149, 153
busshi 105f.
busts *213*
Byōdō-in Temple 300

caitya hall *137*, 138ff., *147, 148*, 160
cakravartin 183, 203, 238
Cambodia *37*, 46, 47, 52, 61, 118, *190*, 200f., 203, 238, 267; cf. Khmer
carving 105, 115; cf. rock carvings
caves 64, 72f., 87, 89, 108, 114f., *138, 143*, 147f., *152, 181, 193*, 206, *275;* cave-temples 85, 99, *117*, 117, 137, 147, 151f., *152*, 153, 227, 284; 'Caves of the Thousand Buddhas' 72; cf. Kirin Cave, Naksatra Cave, Sudāmā Cave
ceiling 73f., *142, 145*, 158, 224, *275*
Celebes 42
cell 70, *136*, 136, 137, *138;* cf. 'Thousand Cells'
cella 147f., *152, 299*
censer 120, *194, 215, 234*
centaur 32
Central Asia: architecture in 72, 118, 123, 151; art in 65, 68-80, 89f., 204, 284; history of 16, 28, 63f., 68, 71f., *233;* painting in 65, 70f., 72f., 74, 178, 221f., 226, 264, 267; printing in 79; religion in 64, 72; sculpture in 65, 69f., 71, 73, 174f., 205, 226;
—, Indian influence on 17f., 33, 44, 63f., 68f., 70f., 85, 151, 190, 204; links with China 64f., 66f., 68f., 71f., 73f., 81ff., 89f., 103; influence on China 67, 74, 88f., 123f., *193*, 206; influence on Japan 107; influence on Korea 94f.
ceramic ware 93, 100f., 116, *123*, 124, 216
Ceylon 40, 42, 44, 45f., 53, 60f., 67, *94*, 118, *119*, 153, 188, 204, 238, 250
Cham 59
Champa 51, 52, 59, 85
Ch'an 82, 87, 88ff.; school 91, 257, 275f.; sect 100, 257f.; art 92, 106, 110, 221f., 257, 281, 286, 300
Chang, family 73
Ch'ang-an 81, 83, 89, 103, *165*, 300
Chang Shêng-wên *168, 215*
chapels 49, 69f., 73f., *75*, 114, 121, 125, *131f.*, 138, *145*, 148, 150, *151, 152*, 152, 206, 267
Chapin, H. *215*
Charax 32
chatra *97*, 115, 120f., 131f.
Ch'eng-tu 83
Chen-la 52
Chên-yên 88, 104, 128
Ch'ên Yung-shih *165*
Chezarla 148

Ch'i Dynasty, Northern   85, *192*, 217, 300
Ch'ien-fo-tung   72
Chiengmai   60, 62, 201
Chih-i: cf. Chih-k'ai
Chih-k'ai   87
Chih-mêng   67
Chin Dynasty   82
China 17f., 65, 67, 81-92; Northern 16, 82ff.,
   92, 99, *122*, 122, *123*, *144*, *192*, 206, 216, *282*,
   300; Southern 60f., 83, 85, 87, 90, 160, *168*,
   206, 216;
—, architecture in *57*, 119, *120*, 121, *122*, *123*,
   123, 123f., *126*, 125f., 136, *145*, 152, 154,
   156f., *157*, 160f., 227f., 285f.; art in 30, 66f.,
   72f., 81, 85, 86f., 90, 94, 105, 108, 188, 260,
   281f.; history of 18, 64, 66; language of 18,
   82f.; paintings and scrolls in 72, 110, *165*,
   169, 218f., 267f., 269f., 275f.; religion and
   philosophy in 15, 17, 19, 81f., 88f., 105,
   120f.; sculpture in 174, 190, *192*, 205, *213*,
   215, 216f., *217*, 218f., 220, 226, 238, 239f.,
   242, 245, 247f., 250, *250*, 299, 300;
—, links with Central Asia 68, 81f., 88f., 103,
   104, 123f., 206; with India 33, 40, 72, 80f.,
   85, 88f., 109, *122*, 123f., 136f., *193*, 206; with
   Indochina 51, 54, 62; with Japan 102ff., 125,
   127, 156, 175, 216, 218f., 267f; with Korea
   93ff., 125, 126, 127, 156, 175; with Near East
   104
Ch'ing period   219
Chi-yeh   68
Chōnen   174
Chotscho: cf. Khocho
Chou Dynasty, Northern   217
Christianity   17, 63
chronicles 66; cf. temple chronicles
Chūgūji   299
Chu Hsi   91
Chunar   *98*
'Church Fathers'   40, 42, 67, 256
Chūson-ji Temple   *170*
cintāmani   *197*, *209*, 241, 244
Cintāmani-cakra-Avalokiteshvara   *197*, 241
circumambulation 73f., 114, 117, *119*, *125*, 125,
   132, *138*, 151, *152*, 154
clay *39*, 48, 70, 103, *142*, *143*, *145*, 203, 205,
   213, 300
coins   29, 91, *178*, 184
column   25f., *39*, 138
Confucianism 15, 19, 62, 83, 90, 91, 101, 106,
   110; Confucianists 82, 84
containers for relics   115, 116, 127, *130*
copper   189
corridor   125
cosmocrator   65, *142*, 153, 205, 240
cosmic axis *76*, 131f., 171; diagram 230; mountain *37*, 129, 132f., *145*, *163*, *166*, 185, *194*
cosmos 129, 131, 132f., 135, 152, 160, 171, 185,

   230, 286; cosmosophy 126
costume *35*, 68, 71, 77, 85f., *96*, *142*, *165*, *170*,
   175, 176, 177, 187, 188, 189, 199, 205, *213*,
   216, 217, 218, 220, 237, 240, 241, 242, 247f.,
   250, *251*, *253*, 278, 281
crafts   103f.
crown of *stūpa*   115, 118
crystal   184
cults 91; cult art 258; cult figures *37*, 49, 100,
   105, 121, *138*, 138, 147f., 150f., *152*, 154, *155*,
   158, 160, 173, 177, 202, *209*, 230, 235, 238,
   239, 240, 256, 261, 264, 266, 269, 286, 300;
   cult implement 279; cult symbols *198*, 204,
   280; cult temple 85; cf. ancestor worship,
   Shintō, sun cult; tea cult
cypress   75

Dainichi *211*; cf. Vairocana
Dai-Seishi   *178*
dancing   89, 107, 286
Darel   154, 205
Deccan   40
Dedes   *206*
Deer Park   25, *98*, 186, *253*
demon   *57*, 248
Dengyō Daishi: cf. Saichō
deva   246f.
devaloka   246
Devarāja   *37*, 203, 240, 248, 286
Dhamekh *stūpa*   117
dhāranī   114
Dhāranīndravarman II   59
dharmacakra 77, *278*; *dharmacakra-mudrā* 36,
   78, *98*, 133, *168*
Dharmakāya   172
Dharmaraksha   86
dhoti   *96*
dhyāna *164*, 172f., *186*, 187, 189, 200; *dhyāna-
   mudrā* 133, *139*, 300
Dhyāni Buddhas   150, 225
'diagram for meditation': cf. *mandala*
diamond *198*, 279 (cf. *vajra*); 'Diamond Vehicle' (*Vajrayāna*) 43; 'diamond seat' (*vajrāsana*) *183*; Diamond *Sūtra* 80; diamond world
   (*vajrādhātu*) 146, 230f.
Dieng plateau   49
Dīpamkara Jātaka   299
Docetism   172
dome of *stūpa*   55, *56*, 114, 117f., 120, 121,
   128f., 132; Dome of Heaven 275
Dong-duong   51, 59, *94*, 188
dragon *211*, *215*, *270*, 278; dragon king 249;
   dragon-tree *168*, 227
drawings   48, 73, 123, *129*, 171, *246*, *278*, *280*
dry lacquer   103, 219
Duksoo Palace   93
Dvārapāla   *57*, *169*, *212*, 226, 248
Dvāravatī 52f., 54, 60f., 108, 110, 119, 189, 199,
   200ff., 204, 299

ear-pendants 183
Egypt 32
Eisai 106
elephant 25, 244
Elūrā 42, 48, 49, 53, 147, *148*, 190, 204
emaki (emaki-mono) 269
engi-emaki 270
Enlightenment 26f., 92, 133, *165*, *169*, 172, 186,
   207, 221, 236, 237, 238, 249, 250, 257, 263,
   273, 278, 287
Ennin 91
Ephthalites: cf. White Huns
erotes 32
Europe 239, 284

Fa-hsien 67, 83, 243
Fa-hu: cf. Dharmaraksha
Fa-hua-ching: cf. *Saddharma-pundarīka-sūtra*
Fêng-hsien-see 300
feng-shui 126
fertility cult 49, 94
fish-basket 242
flask *130*
flowers *142*, *162*, *165*, *213*, *253*, 286; cf. acanthus, lotus, peony
fly-whisk *210*
Fo-kuáng-sse *157*
Fondukistan 65, 69, 203
footprints *76*, 171
fresco technique 70
frieze 30, 39, 54, 263, 267, 268, *278*
fruit 257
Fudō Myōō (Acala Vidyārāja) *211*
Fujii-Yūrinkan 300
Fujiwara period 104, 105, 109, *162*, *170*, 269
Fukūkensaku-Kannon 150
Funan 51, 52, 53, 85

gable 61; gable-roof 160
Gandhāra: architecture in 32, 53, *116*, 117,
   121, *122*, 123, 132, 137; art in 28ff., 32f., *35*,
   69f., 118, 177, 185, *213*, 237, 240, 248, 259,
   263, 264, *282;* history of 29; painting in 70;
   sculpture in 32, 34f., *78*, *143*, 172, 174f., 178,
   183, *187*, 187f., 189, 202, 205, 216, 223, 225,
   237f., 247, 250, 268, 275, *278*, 300;
—, links with Mathurā 39, 42, 63, *185*, *187*, 187;
   with Central Asia 33, 65, 69f., 72, 190, 204;
   with China 33, 72, 85, 87, 206; with Japan
   33; with Korea 33
Gandharvas *181*
Gandhavyūha 134
Ganges 26, 42, 67
garbha 114, 116; *garbhadhātu 146*, 224, 235
gateway 57, 154; cf. *torana*

gati 246
gazelle *98*, *143*, 186, 278
geomancy 126
Ghantashālā 115, *116*, 117
gilding 29f., 64, *76*, 77, *78*, 91, 123, *140*, *142*,
   144, *192*, *193*, *196*, *196*, *198*, 205, 300
Glasenapp, H. von 230
glass *130*
Gnostics 207, 243
gold *35*, *94*, 116, *130*, 148, *162*, *165*, *169*, *170*,
   178, *179*, *195*, *209*, *210*, *215*, 270, 273, 280,
   299; gold-leaf *163*, *196*, *209;* cf. gilding
Golden Hall 103, *156*, *194*, 219, 229, 300
Gopā 76
gorintō 129, *130*
'Great Gander Pagoda' 119
Greece 31, 33
Gridhrakūta 261
Grünwedel, Albert 65
Guardian of the Gate: cf. Dvārapāla
Guardian of the World: cf. Lokapāla
Gupta Empire 18, 34, 42f., 90; art of 31, 44f.,
   47f., 53, 65, 69, 72, 85, 108, 184, *185*, 202;
   architecture in 117, 121, 148, 218; painting
   in *181;* sculpture in 49, 52, 89, *96*, 188, 189,
   190, *193*, 199f., 204, 238, 268; Late Gupta
   42, 46, 108, 137, 149, 199, 200
gypsum 32

Hadda 32, 65
Hadrian 31
haiku 106
hairdress *143*, 199, *213*
Hakata 106
Hakuin 106, 276
Hakuhō 300
halls 90, 114, 137, *138*, 138, 152, 154, *155*, *156*,
   156, *157*, 158, *159*, 160, *164*, 226, 248; cf.
   caitya, Golden Hall, Meditation Hall,
   'Phoenix Hall'
hand-scrolls: cf. scrolls
Han Dynasty 72, 81, 93, *122*, 124, 156, 216
hanging scrolls: cf. scrolls
Hannya-haramitta-shin-gyō: cf. *Prajñāpāra-
   mitā-hridayasūtra*
Han-shan 257
Haripunjaya 53, 60; cf. Lamphūn
Hārītī 249
harmikā 56, 115, 120, 121
Harsha 42
Hatra 178
Hayagrīva *210*
head-dress *181*, *183*, *191*, *196*, 237, 241; cf.
   Buddha (head-dress of)

heads 32; of Asanga 300; of Brahman 300; of Bodhisattvas 241, 299, 300; of Buhhda 299, 300; of Lokeshvara *190, 201*

Heian period 104, 105
Heiji period 269
Hellenism 26, 30, 31f., 65
hermitage 70
Hiei-zan 104
Hīnayāna 20, 42, 45, 47, 53, 54, 60, 68, 71, 86, 110, 162, 183, 256; in architecture 26f., 132, 161; in art 41, 61, 69, 256, 281; in painting 267, 269; in sculpture 188, 190, 199, 201, 203, 204, 223, 235, 238, 255
Hinduism 15, 17, 40, 42, 43f., 47, 59f., 88, 110, 122, 149; Hindu architecture 147; Hindu art 49f., 61, *181,* 184, *198,* 204, *206,* 230, 243, 246, 267, 281, 285; Hindu mythology *210,* 238, 245
Hindu Kush 64
hinoki; cf. shingles
Hōkiji 123
Hokkedō 150
Hokke-kyō: cf. *Saddharma-pundarīka-sūtra*
Hōnen Shōnin 270
honorific umbrella: cf. *chatra*
Hōōdo: cf. 'Phoenix Hall'
Hopei *144*
horse 25
Hōryūji Temple 89, 102, 103, 123, 127, *128, 130, 157, 192, 194,* 219, 284, 285, 300
Hsiang-t'ang-shan 85, 152
Hsien-t'ung-sse *155*
Hsiung-nu 82, 83, 94
Hsüan-tsang 40, 65, 67, 121, *142,* 174, 205, 270
Hua-yen: cf. Avatamsaka school
Hui-k'o 276, 300
Hui-Yüan 87
Hwa-om: cf. Avatamsaka

Ichijō-ji *233*
I-ching 47, 67
I-hsien 152
implements 48, 113
India 25-45, 67f., 132, 183f; central 123; eastern 53, 123; northern 16, 28, 34, 40, 42, 122, 151; north-eastern 15, 44, 48, 88, 149; southern 39, 41f., 45, 54, 67, *116, 206;* western 117, 137; cf. Gandhāra and other kingdoms;
—, architecture in 25ff., 70, 114ff., 120, *136, 136f., 137, 138, 147, 148, 149,* 149, 151, 154, 160, 189f., 200; art in 31, 34, 42, 44, 65, 68, 89f., 108f., 121, 162, 188, 203, 225, 250, 268, 275, 282; history of 25, 42; painting in 137, 226; religion in 15, 17, 19, 33, 40, 61, 64, 80, 86, 90, 110, 249; sculpture in *97,* 153f., 174f.,

225f., 243, 246, 264, 285;
—, influence on Burma 149, 203; on Central Asia 17f., 69ff., 151; on Ceylon 40, 42, 44; on China 30, 40, 48, 51, 82f., 87, 89, *122,* 122, 124f., 137f., 282; on Indochina 40, 51f., 61f., 149; on Indonesia 40, 47, 149; on Japan 107, *129,* 137, *273;* on Korea 99; on Nepal 149, 203; on Tibet 203
Indochina 47, 51-62, 240; architecture in 45, 118, 160; art in 49, 62, 108, 186, 266; culture of 15; sculpture in 189, 190f., 202, 203, 204;
—, Chinese influence on 51; Indian influence on 40, 51, 137f.; affinity with Indonesia 50; influence on Korea 99
Indonesia 18, 47-50, 63, 68, 108, 109, 114, 188, 204, 250, 266 (cf. Java); Indian influence on 40, 44, 47, 190; affinity with Indochina 50
Indo-Sythian 86
Indra 59, 77, *178,* 238, 247, 248, 259
Indus 28, 154, 205; Indus valley culture *177*
ink: on paper *165, 169, 215, 234, 250,* 269, 300; on silk *167, 178, 194, 209, 210, 211, 212, 231, 232, 271, 273,* 300; ink-drawing *244;* ink-painting 88, 92, 106, 110, *234,* 257, 276; ink-painters 221
inscriptions 25, 69, *144,* 153, *178, 194,* 300; cf. votive inscriptions
Ippen Shōnin 275
Iran, Iranians 31, 63, 67ff., 69, 71f., 74, 85, 89f., 239, 240, 267; influence on China 87
irrigation 66
Ishiyama-dera *129*
Islam 17, 39, 42, 44, 46, 50, 61, 63f., 65, 162, 282
ivory 48

Jago, *tjandi* 150
Jain 147, 176
Jamālgarhī *136*
Japan 102-107; architecture in *75,* 102, 105f., 123, 131, 151, 154, *156, 157, 158,* 285; art in 47f., 79, 87, 94, 104f., 106, 108f., 237, *246,* 247, 249, 260, 282, 285; drawing in *244, 278, 280;* history of 269; literature in 106, 269; painting and scrolls in 89, 106f., *170, 178, 195, 210, 211,* 218, *231, 234,* 264, 267, 269, *273,* 276; religion in 17, 88, 91, 100, 103ff., 249, 270; sculpture in 150, 154, *187,* 190, 218f., 239, 245, 248f., 249, 250, 256, 260, 285, 299, 300;
—, influenced by Central Asia 107; by China 92, 101; by India 44, 107, 137, *273;* by Korea 93f., 101, 106f., 126, 175; by western Asia 107
jar 300
Jātaka 27, 30, 70, 74, 134, 171, 238, *255,* 262,

266, 266, 267f., 275; cf. Dīpamkara, Mriga Jātaka

Java 41, 44, 47f., 49f., 108, 118, 132f., *134, 135, 135f., 139,* 149f., 190, 202, *206,* 237, *252,* 266, 299

Jayavarman VII   *37, 59*

Jelālābad   *35*

jewellery *142, 198,* 203, 237, 238, 241, 247, 278, 286; cf. anklets, armlets, beads, *cintāmani,* ear-pendants, pectorals, pendants

Jīna   150, 176

Jingyoji   *162*

Jizo: cf. Kshitigarbha

Jōchō   105, 220, 300

Jōgan style   175, 220, 300

Jumna   28

Jung, C. G.   235

Jurchen   100

Kabul   29, 32

Kaesong   100

kaki   257

Kako-Genzai-Inga-Kyō: cf. *Sūtra of Cause and Fruit*

Kalasan, *tjandi*   150

kāmadhātu   133, 246

Kamakura 105f., 157; period 105, 109, *164,* 220f., 270

kami   249, 270

Kanishka, king   29, 31, 34, *178; stūpa* 123

Kannon 105, *178, 194,* 240; cf. Avalokiteshvara

Kanshin-ji   *197*

kanshitsu: cf. dry lacquer

Kansu   28, *39*

kapardin   *185*

Kapilavastu   26

Kara-Chodja: cf. Khocho

Karakorum   64

Karashahr   175

Kārlī   39f., 117, *147,* 147

karma   81, 134, 173, 229, *255,* 270, 286

karunā   236

Kashgar   68

Kashmir   83

Kāshyapa   226, 250

Kausambi: cf. Vatsa

Ke-gon: cf. Avatamsaka school

Keishū: cf. Kyongju

Kenninji   106

Khmer *37,* 50, 52f., 54ff., 108ff., 119, *190,* 199, 200f., 203, 217, 266

Khocho   70f., 205, 300

Khotan   28f., 67ff., 117, *165,* 205f., 299

Kiangsu   81

Kinnaras   *181*

kirikane: cf. gold-leaf

Kirin Cave   *143*

Kistna: cf. Krishna

Kitan   100

knights   105, 106

kō-an: cf. *kung-an*

Kōbō Daishi: cf. Kukai

Kōfukuji   219, 250, 300

Koguryo   93f.

Kokuri: cf. Koguryo

Koma: cf. Koguryo

Kondō   *156, 194*

Kōrai   100

Korea 93-101; architecture in *58,* 100, 102, 123, 126f., 151, *154,* 154; art in 16, 87, 90, 92, 93-101, 108f., 126, 156; ceramic ware in 93, 101; Ch'an school in 88; sculpture in 93, 100, *146,* 154, 190, *192, 193,* 218, 260;

—, influence on Japan 93f., 101f., 106f., 126; influenced by Central Asia 99; by China 93ff., 124, 156, 175; by India 99; by Indochina 99

Koryo period 93, 109; culture 100

Kōryūji   *192*

Kōya-san   104, *211*

Kozan-ji   *234*

Krishna, river   40

kroblylos   184

krodha   245

Kshitigarbha   *209,* 244, 259

Kuang-yüan   152

Kuan-shih-yin: cf. Kuanyin

Kuanyin 87, 92, *168, 194, 196,* 239, 241, 242, 249, 257, 300; cf. Avalokiteshvara

Kuchā   67, 68, 70f., 83, 151, 183, 205, 267

Kudara: cf. Paekche

'Kudara style'   94

Kūkai   104

Kumārajīva   67, 80, 86

Kumrahar   121f., 299

Kumsan-sa   *58*

Kumtura   70f.

kung-an   275

Kung-hsien   85, 152

K'un-lun range   66

Kushān, king   *178,* 184

Kushān Empire 16, 18f., 28f., 31, 34f., 44, 63, 69, 123

Kushinagara   26

K(w)anseum: cf. Kuanyin

K(w)an-ze-on: cf. Kuanyin

Kyongju   99, *146, 154*

Kyōto 104ff., 157, *163,* 174, *187, 233, 234,* 300

Kyūshū   106, 154

Kyzyl   70, 152, 171, *265, 266*

lacquer 219; cf. dry lacquer
lakshana 183, 277
Lakshmī 59, 248
Lakshmīndralokeshvara 59
Lalita Vistara 134, 172, *253*
Lamaism 42, 64, 92, 118, 219
Lamphūn 53, 60
landscape painting 201, *170, 178*, 257, 267, 270
languages 68, 79
Lannā 62
lantern roof 152
Laos 62
Le Coq, Albert von 65
legends 87, 92, 134f., *145*, 200 228, *250*, 261f., *265*, 268, 270f.; cf. Jātaka, Udayana, Ma-lang-fu
Li: cf. Yi
Li, family 73
Liang K'ai 221, 300
libraries 90, 156, 160
limestone *76*
lingam 50
Ling-yen-sse *126*
lion 25, *54, 57, 77*, 176, 184f., 226, *233*, 244
literature 18, 42; cf. legends, poetry, *sūtra, Tales of Prince Genji*
Lohan: cf. Arhat
Lokapāla *145, 168, 178*, 226, *233*, 248, 259
Lokeshvara *37*, 49, 59, 61, 150, 201, 238, 240, 243, **299**
Lo-lang 93, 94
Lopburi 53, 201
Lo Tsun 72
lotus flower *181, 194, 209, 212*, 229, 237, 240, 278, 300; ornament 25, *39, 56, 76*, 131, *275*; pond 226, *253*; throne *57, 78, 97, 98*, 160, *162, 183*, 184, 185, 194
'Lotus of the True Doctrine': cf. *Saddharma-pundarīka-sūtra*
Lotus Sūtra: cf. *Saddharma-pundarīka-sūtra*
Lo-yang 81, 83, 85, 152
Lumbinī Grove 26
Lungmên 85, 122, 124, 152, 205, 216, 299, 300

Mādhyamaka-darshanam 40
Mādhyamika 86, 134
Magadha 67, 261
magic 42, 43, 82, 88, 92, 174, *215*, 240, 255; spell 88; cf. *mantra*
Mahābodhi Temple 121, *124*
Mahācetiya *116*
Ma-hao *215*, 215
mahārāja-līlā *196*

Mahāsattva *255*
Mahāsthāmaprāpta *178*, 240
Mahāyāna: history and philosophy of 18, 20, 28, 41, 42f., 45, 47, 52f., 54, 60, 62, 68, 80, 86ff., 92, 103f., 114, 172, 175, 204, *206*, 230, 243, 249, 255, 256, 257, 263, 275; in architecture 114, 130f., 135; in art 39, 43, 52, 59f., 61f., 71, 74, 108, 172f., 223, 237f., 244, 247, 250, 259, 269, 277, 281, 286; in sculpture 46, 187, 204, 235f.; Late Mahāyāna 203
Mai-chi-shan 85, 153
Mainamati 149
Maitreya 87, *168*, 172, *192*, 205, 224, 227, *239*, 239, 261, 278, 299, 300
Ma-lang-fu 242; cf. Kuanyin
Malaya 47, 93
Manchuria 93
mandala 48, 64, 88 *129*, 131, 133, *146*, 149f., 160, 203, *224*, 225, 235, 243, 246, 249, 261, 280
Mandalay *125*
Manichaeism 63f., 79
Manjushrī *57*, 243, 244
mantra 88, *233*, 279
mappô 105
Māra *56, 265*
marble 300
Mathurā: architecture in *123*; art in 28, 31, 34f., 42, 69, 108, 171, 183, 225, 247; history of 34; sculpture in 39, *96*, 175, *176*, 183, *187*, 187, 189, 199, 204, 216, 223, 248;
—, links with Amarāvatī 41, 188; with Gandhāra 39, 42, 63, *185, 187*, 187; with Nāgārjunakonda 41
Maudgalyāyana 174
Maurya Dynasty 25, 138
Māyā *273*
medallion *76, 143*
medhi 114
meditation *183, 190, 192*, 201, 227, *234*, 238f., *250*, 261, 263, 276; Meditation Hall 156; cf. *dhyāna*
Menam, river 53
Mendut, *tjandi* 48, 49, 150, 299
meru 124, *125*
Mesopotamia 31, 32, 79, 118, *143*, 267, 284
metals 125; cf. bronze, copper, gold, silver
migrations 63, 66, 82
Mikkyō 104
Ming Dynasty 81, 101, *155*; period 92, *155*, 219
Ming Oï 70
minting 91
Mirān 69f., 72
Miroku: cf. Maitreya

mirror 102, *215*, 216
missionaries 15, 18, 40, 52, 67, 82, 123
mithuna 27
Mi-tsung 88, 104
Mohenjo-daro *177*
Mon 53, 60
monasteries 17f., 20, 25f., 29, 34, 40f., 43, 45f., 47f., 59f., 67f., 82f., 87, 90f., 104, 106, 113f., 121, *136*, 136—161, *233, 234*, 299; cf. monks
Mongols 63ff., 92, 99, 100, 269
monks 17f., 20, 25, 32, 46, 71f., 80, 81, 89f., 92, 100, 102f., 106, 114, 136, *145*, 154, 160, *167, 170*, 174, 187, 188, *209*, 223, 225, 226, 227, 238, 244, 249, *250*, 250, 256, 259, 267; monk-painters 106, *234*, 276; monks' cells 149, 154, 160; cf. monasteries
moon 247
mountain, sacred 91; cf. cosmic mountain, Potala
Mriga Jātaka 299
Muchaku: cf. Asanga
Mu-ch'i 257
Mucilinda 186, 200
mudrā 88, *146*, 187, 199, *210*, 225, 277, 278; cf. *abhaya-mudrā, bhūmisparsha-mudrā, dharmacakra-mudrā, varada-mudrā, vitarka-mudrā*
Murō-ji Temple *75*, 300
Muromachi 106
music 41, 107, 286
Myōe Shōnin *234*, 257
Myoo-in *211*
myths 91, *232*, 261; mythology 27, 173, *210, 231*, 238, 245, 247, 248, 259, 279

nāga 249, *253*
nāgarāja 227
Nāgārjuna 40, 86, 256
Nāgārjunakonda 41, *54, 116*, 117, 148, *149*
Naksatra Cave *213*
Nālandā 42, 44, 48, *56*, 121, *198*
Nang-nang: cf. Lo-lang
Nanking 81, 82
Nara *75*, 89, 100, 102f., 105f., 108f., 123, 150, *156, 157*, 157, *215*, 218, 219, *282, 284*, 299, 300
Near East, art of 31, 74f., 225, 229, 239, 282; influence on Central Asia 267; on China 87, 104; on India 33, 118
nectar 237
Neolithic 93, 102
Nepal 44, 48, 88, 124, 149
Nestorian Christianity 63
niche *39, 56*, 117, 118, 123, 125, 136, *139*, 150, 153f., *213*

Nirmānakāya 172
nirvāna 25ff., 33, 40, 43, 46, *55*, 92, 113, 133, 135, 162, 171ff., 177, 236, 249, 250, 264, 266, *273*
nomads 16, 28
North Vietnam: cf. Annam
nuns 90
Nyoi-rin Kannon *197*

oasis 66, 68
Oc-eo 52
offerings: cf. votive offerings
ornamentation 79, 89f., 92, 100, 107, 125, 127, 153, 158, 186, 277-287, *282, 283, 284*
Osaka *197*
Otto, Rudolf 245

Padmapāni *181, 183*, 285, 300
Paekche 93ff., 102
pagoda 29, *58*, 60, 90, 99, 113-135, *122, 123, 126, 128, 130;* cf. individual pagodas
'Pagoda of Many Treasures': cf. *tahōtō*
Pahārpur 149
painters 69, 102, *165, 169, 215*, 221, 257; cf. monk-painters, poet-painters
painting 72f., 74f., 89, 92, 127, 158, 255, 259, 262, 266f., 281, 284; cf. ink-painting, landscape painting, scrolls, wall-paintings
Pakistan 28, *78*
Pāla period 44, 48, *56*, 88, *183*, 203, 204; art in 48, 108, 190, 202, 204, 238
palaces 45, 156; cf. Duksoo Palace
Pāli Canon 18, 162
Pallava Empire 44, 46
palmette 282
Palmyra 30, 32, 178, *282*
Pamirs 17, 63
paribhogika 113
parivāra 226
Parthia, Parthians 30, 32, 118, 178
Pātaliputra 25, 42, 67, *176*, 299
patina *141*
Patna: cf. Pātaliputra
patriarchs *233, 250*, 256, 257, 259, 276f.
peacock *181*
pectorals 237
Peking *57*
Pelliot, Paul 65, 73
pendants 237
peony *215*
Persia 41, 52, 79, 83, *143*, 225
Peshāwar 29, 123
philosopher 250
'Phoenix Hall' 105, 300
pilgrims 17f., 26, 29, 39, 42, 45, 47f., 52, 59,

64ff., 68, 83, 89, 123, 133f., 138, *142*, 174, 205, 270f.

pillar 41, *55*, *97*, *119*, 125, 127, 129, 132, 151f., 158f., 171, 230; cf. Blazing Pillar

Ping-ling-ssu   153
pipal-tree   *278*
Plaosan, *tjandi*   48
plaque   121, 299
plaster   *37*, *38*, 70, 74, *75*, 115, 127, 129, *274*
poet-painters 106; poetry 106
points of the compass *56*, 115, 118, 121, 125, 128, 130, 132, 148, *198*, 229, 247

Polonnāruwa   46, *119*, 119
Potala   *196*, *197*
Prabhūtaratna   128, 225
pradakshinā 73f., 114; *pradakshinā-patha* 115, 132
Prajnāpāramitā 49f., 59, 80, 86, *207*, 243, 245
Prajñāpāramitā-hridaya-sūtra   *170*, 244
pranidhāna   71
Pranidhi scenes   70ff., 267, 299
pratītya-samutpāda   270
Praxiteles   32
Preah Khan   59
preta   241
priests, priesthood   102ff., *214*, 255, 257, 270
princes   68, 113, *170*, *233*, *254*, 268f.
printing   79
'psycho-cosmogram': cf. *mandala*
pūjā   114, 172, *213*, 266
Pulkuk-sa   *146*
'Pure Land' 87, 105, *194*, 229, 239, 261, 270, 280

Rāgarājā   *206*
Rāhula   *76*
Raigō   105, 240
railing   *76*, 114f., 248, 299
Rājagriha   261
Rakan: cf. Arhat
Raku-rō: cf. Lo-lang
Rāma Kamheng   60
Ratnasambhava   133
Rawak   69, 117, 205, 299
reeds   70
relics   115, 127, 147, 174
reliefs 25f., 27f., 29f., *35*, 41f., 48, 54, *55*, *57*, 69, *76*, 77, *78*, 85, 117, *122*, 122, *123*, 125, 132, 134f., 137, *139*, 148, 150, 153f., 172, *215*, 215, 223, 227, 247, 248, 250, *252*, 262, 263, 267, 275, 299, 300
reliquary   29, *35*, *122*, 129, *130*, *131*, 148
repoussé work   *35*
Ri: cf. Yi

rites 48, 88f., 100, 113f., 125, 132, 136, 138, *152*, 160, 171, 173, 256, 257; ritual implements 90, 123
rock carvings   43, 46, 53
rock crystal   116
Roman Empire 30, 31f., *35*, 40, 52, 63, 65, 79, 178, 250
roof *58*, 61, *75*, 124, 126, 129, 148, 158; roof-tiles *57*, *122*, 127; cf. gable-roof, lantern
rosary   *198*, *234*
ruby   *35*
rūpadhātu   246

sacral kingship 203, 240, 286; cf. Devarāja
Saddharma-pundarīka-sūtra   67, 86, 128
sādhana   *206*
Sādhanamālā   246
Saichō   104
saint   176
sāla   *273*
Samantabhadra   243f.
Samarkand   67
Sambhogakāya   172, 203
samsāra 33, 40, 43, 81, 134, 162, 172f., 177, *182*, 185, 236, 237, 249, 256, 258, 264, 278
samurai   105f.
Sānchī 26ff., 30, 39, 41, 114, 115, 118, *122*, 171, 224, 226, 262, 275
sandalwood   174
sandstone *37*, *96*, *98*, *142*, *182*, *191*, *193*, 299
sanghātī   *96*, 187
Sanskrit   18, 80, 82f., 243
San-tsang: cf. Hsüan-tsang
sarcophagus   30, *35*, 262
Sārnāth   26, 42, 117, *182*, 189, 190, 299
Sassanid Empire   29, 32, 63, 65, 74, *143*, 284
Sat Mahal Pāsāda   119
satori   275
schist   29f., *78*
scholar 68; schools 256
'School of the True Word'   88
Scopas   32
scripture   67, 80, 82
scrolls 73, *79*, 228, 237; hand-scroll *168*, *215*, 267, 268, 269; hanging scroll *162*, *165*, *167*, *178*, *194*, *209*, *210*, *211*, *212*, *231*, *233*, *234*, *250*, *270*, *273*; cf. *mandala*
sculpture 25f., 31f., *37*, *39*, 39, 41f., 44ff., 48, 49, 51f., 54f., *56*, *57*, 61f., 64f., 67f., 70f., *73*, 73, 85f., 89ff., 93ff., *96*, 102f., 106, 114f., 117f., 121, 124f., 125f., 127, 137, 138, *139*, *144*, *145*, 150, *151*, 153f., 158f., 174ff., 176, 178f., *181*, 184f., 188f., *192*, *193*, *197*, 203, 205f., *206*, *213*, 216f., 218f., 219f., 225f.,

241f., 247ff., 249f., 255f., 259f., 281, 284f., 299; cf. Buddhas (colossal), reliefs

seal 177

'seeds': cf. *bīja*

Seiryōji 174f., *187*

Seleucia 32

Sena Dynasty 44

Sengai 106, 276

Seoul 93

sepulchre 129, *131*

'Sermon of the Heart of Perfect Wisdom': cf. *Prajñāpāramitā-hridaya-sūtra*

Sesshū 106, 276, 300

Sewu, *tjandi* 48f., *150*, 150

Shailendra Dynasty 18, 47f., 52

Shaka: cf. Shākyamuni

shakti 50, *142*, *181*, *206*, 240; shaktism 88

Shākyamuni 15, 27, 44f., 70, 93, 113f., 132ff., 154, *162*, *165*, *168*, 171f., 178f., *183*, *192*, 204, 221f., 223ff., 226f., 235f., 243, *253*, 261f., *265*, 267, *270*, *273*, 300

shamanism 94

Shansi *155, 157, 193*

shānta 245

Shantung *126*

Shan-wu-wei: cf. Shubhākarasimha

sharīra 113

sharīraka 113

Shātavāhana Dynasty 39f.

Shigisan-Engi-Emaki 270

Shih-tê 257

shikhara 122

shingles *75*, 127

Shingon 48, 104, 128

Shintō, Shintoists 15, 17, 102, 104, 249, 270, 285

Shiragi: cf. Silla

Shi-Tennō (Lokapāla) *178*

Shiva 45, 49, 238, 240, 243, 245; Shivaism 42, 49, 52, 54, 203, *210*, 240, 245

shōgon 286

shōguns 106

Shōmu, emperor 103f.

Shorchuk 70, *143*, *213*

Shōsōin 103, 284

Shōtoku, crown prince 102

Shrī 247

shrine 118, 147, 150, *181*

Shrīvijaya kingdom 47f., 50, 52, 67, 238

Shubhākarasimha 88, *233*

shūnyatā: cf. Void

Siän-fu 119

siddham 88, *178*, 230, 279, *280*, 280

Siddhārta 263

silk *162, 167, 178, 210, 212, 231,* 300

'silk roads' 17f., 66

Silla 93ff., 100, 103, 108, 175, *192;* Greater Silla Empire 99; United Silla Empire 99, *146*

silver: container *130;* jar 116; on paper *170*

Simhala-dvīpa 45

Singhasāri *206*

Six Dynasties period 74, 86, 90, 108, 152, 239, 259, 260, 284

snake king 186, 200, 227

Sokkul-am 99, 108, 154

Son: cf. Ch'an

Sophia *206*, 243

spell 114

stag *143*, 186, 299

stairs 118, 125, 131

Stein, Aurel 65, 73

stele: cf. votive stele

stone 32; jar 116; in architecture *58, 76,* 99f., 114f., *122,* 124f., 125f., 148, 299; in sculpture 52f., 85, 90, 137, 199, 299, 300; cf. votive stele

Straits of Malacca 47

stucco 29, 32, 41, 53, *57,* 61, 65, 137, 266, 299, 300

stūpa 25ff., 29, 39, 41, 48, 53, 113-135, 136, *136,* 138ff., *139*, 150ff., *159*, 160, 230, 264, 266; cf. individual *stūpas*

Sudāmā Cave 138

Sudhāna 134, 262

Sui Dynasty 74, 85, 86, 90, *165*, 218

Sukhāvatī *39*, 87, 160, *167*, *194*, *195*, *228*, 229f., 240

Sukhothai 60f., 109, 201, 266

Sultanganj 189

Sumatra 41, 47, 67

Sumeru 129, 132, *163*, 185

sun cult 94, 247

Sung Dynasty 88, 91, 100; art of 74, 92, 100, 109, *196*, 219, 221, 242, 255, 258; Southern Sung Dynasty 276

Sung-shan 123

Sūryavarman I 54

Sūryavarman II 59

'Sūtra of Cause and Fruit in Past and Present' 268

sūtras 28, 83, 86, 114, 125, 134, 174, *207*, 226, 261, 266, 268, 270, 275; *sūtra* scroll *79*, *167*, *170*, 228f.; cf. *Avatamsaka Sutra, Diamond Sūtra, Vairocana Sūtra, Vimalakīrti Sūtra*

Sutta Nipāta 162

swastika 277

sword *211*, 237, 278

symbols, symbolism 50, *76*, *78*, 88f., 113, 131f., 133f., 135, *144*, 147, *162*, 162, *168*, 171f.,

184f., *186, 197, 198,* 204f., *210, 211, 215,* 244, 259, 262, 264, *275;* cf. elephant, lion, *stūpa, vajra,* Wheel of the Doctrine

Syria   30, 32, *282*
Szechuan   83, 152, *215,* 215

tahōtō   127, *129,* 129, 133, 156
Taima-dera   *228*
Taima Mandara *228; Taima-Mandara-Engi* 270
Taizōkai mandara: cf. *garbhātu mandala*
Takshasilā: cf. Taxila
Talas, river   64, 90
Tales of Prince Genji   104, 269
Tamils   46
T'ang Dynasty 18, 88ff., 99f., *165, 193,* 219, 300; architecture of *39,* 89; art of 71f., 74, 86, 90, 92, 108f., 219, 247, 260, 268, 282, 284; culture of 89; literature of *165;* painting of 219, *275;* scrolls of *167, 194, 212, 270;* sculpture of 100, 104, *146,* 218ff., 227, 238, 245, 259f.; T'ang period 34, 73, 86; Late T'ang 74, 152
Tantrism 61, 88, 92, 150, 184, *207,* 240f., 243, 244 245f., 248f., 281
Tao 82; Taoism 15, 17, 19, 62, 82, 83, 90, 92, 126, 242, 255

tapestry   *228, 270*
Ta Prohm   59
Tārā   242
Tarim basin   66
tathatā   135, 172
Ta-t'ung   206
Taxila   29, 32, 117, *136,* 136
tea cult 106; tea-shrub *251;* tea-ware 101
temenos   115
tempera technique *39,* 70, 74, *181, 194, 255, 275,* 299
temples 49, 52, 82f., 84f., 91f., 106, 113f., *136-161, 158, 159, 164, 212,* 224; temple chronicles 270; temple-mountain 59, 119; Temple of Enlightenment 121; cf. cave-temples, halls, pagodas, *stūpas, tjandis* and individual temples
Ten-dai   128
terracotta   29, 53, *57,* 121, *183*
terrace (of *stūpa*)   132ff., 135, *139*
textiles   281
Thailand 46, 52f., 60f., 110; architecture of 118, *120,* 149, *159,* 160; art of 53, 60ff., 266; sculpture of *140, 141,* 153, 184, 199, 201f., 203, 204, 238, 299;
—, Indian influence on   41, 44
Theravāda   45, 53, 60
'Thousand Buddhas' 71f., 74, 125f., *142,* 172, 224

'Thousand Cells'   70
Three Jewels   *76*
Three States, period of   99, 239
throne 76, 77, *98, 145, 162,* 171, 184, 186, 278, 281
'thunderbolt': cf. *vajra*
Thūpārāma   *119*
Tibet   44, 48, 64, 73, 88, 92, 118, 240
T'ien-lung-shan   89, 108, 152, *193,* 218
T'ien-ning-sse   *57*
Tien-shan range   66
T'ien-t'ai school 87, 105, 128, *233;* doctrine 104
T'ien-ti-shan   153
tiger   *255,* 267
tiles: cf. roof-tiles
Tita   69
Titus: cf. Tita
tjandis 149f.; cf. Jago, Kalasan, Mendut, Plaoson, Sewu
Tocharians   68, 79
Tōdaiji   100, 103, 219
Tokugawa period   106
Tongking   51f., 81, 85
T'o-pa Tartars   16, 83, 85
Top-i-Rustam   117
torana   26, 115, *123,* 130f., 172, 263
Tori   102, 300
T'o-shan   152
Tōshōdaiji   103, *156,* 219
towers *37,* 53, 118ff., 121f., *123,* 124f., 148f., 299
trade 39, 45, 51f., 63, 66, 68, 72, 81, 104; traders 39, 47, 68; trade-routes 17, 29, 47, 51, 64, 66, 81, 82; cf. 'silk roads'
translator, translation 67, 80, 82, 83, 86, 88, *233,* 270
treasury   103
trees 132, 138, *165,* 171, *192,* 227, *234, 273;* Tree of Enlightenment 132, 171, 172, 277, *278;* cf. Bodhi Tree, dragon-tree, pipal-tree
tribhanga   *181,* 237, 241
trikāya   172
triratna   *76*
Ts'ao, family   73
Tucci, G.   230
Tumshuk   69
T'ung-chiang   152
Tun-huang *39,* 64, 67f., 71ff., 73f., *79,* 79f., 81, 85ff., 89f., 105, *122, 145,* 151, 152, *167,* 175, *194,* 206, 219, 229, *255,* 268, 270, *275;* links with China 68
Turfan 64, 68, 70ff., 74, 79, 151, *152,* 175, 267, 299
Turkestan: eastern 28f., 64, *165;* western 90;

Chinese *143, 213*
Turkic peoples 16, 68, 83
Tushita heaven *55, 192,* 239

Udayana 173, *187*
uddesika 113
Uighur Empire 19, 64, 68, 71
Uji 105, 300
university 40, 42, 48, 148, *149*
Unkei 106, 256, 300
upāya 172, 236, 242
urn *130*
ūrnā 78, 178, 183, *196, 197, 206,* 244, 245, 277
ushnīsha 35, 77, 78, 94, 141, 165, 178, 184, 200f., 221, 263, 277
Usuki 154
U-Thong 62

Vairocana 103, 128f., *133, 146,* 150, *186,* 203, *211,* 225, 243, *244,* 244, 279, *280; Vairocana Sūtra* 233
Vaishravana *233*
vajra 48, *54,* 88, *168, 198, 210, 212,* 230, 248, 279; *vajra* bell 279
Vajrabodhi 88
vajradhātu; cf. diamond world
Vajrapāni 49, *54,* 150
vajrāsana; cf. 'diamond seat'
Vajrasattva 133, 203, 243, *244,* 244
Vajrayāna 43ff., 47f., 64, 88, 133, *146,* 150, 161, 184, *198,* 203, *210,* 225, 230, 240, 243, 245, *246,* 279, 281f., 286
varada-mudrā 97, 133, *142, 144, 183, 210,* 300
vase *215*
Vasubhandu 256
Vat Mongkut Krasat *161*
Vat Thephsirin *159*
Vatsa 173
Vedic religion 15, 162f., 247
vedika: cf. railing
vidyā 211, 245
Vidyārāja *210, 211,* 226, 245, 246, 261, 278f.
Vietnam 62; cf. Annam
vihārā 136f., *137,* 138, 148f., 151, 161
Vijnāna 134
Vimalakīrti Sūtra 227, 262
vine-scroll *282,* 282
Vishnu 45; Vishnuism 49, 52
vitarka-mudrā 94, 133, *143,* 162, *167,* 199
'Void', concept of 40f., 133ff., 287
votive inscriptions *54, 167,* 227; votive offerings 129, *170,* 174, 286; votive pillar *54;* votive stele 85, 226, 227, 299; votive *stūpa 56, 116,* 117, 136
Vulture Peak: cf. Gridhrakūta
Vyāghrī-Jātaka *255*
vyūha 286

wall-paintings *38,* 43, 65, 68, 69f., 73, 74, 90, *97,* 103, 105, *122,* 131, 137, *142,* 151f., 158f., 175, *181,* 183, *194,* 219, 229, *255, 265, 266,* 299; cf. *mandala*
wars 94, 99; warriors 105; warrior deities 218
Wata-da-ge *119*
Wat Kukut 53, 119
Wat Pencamapabitra 299
Wat Phra Pathom 119
weapons 245, 278, 279
Wei Dynasty 16, 93ff., 206; art of 70, 85, 87, 94, 102, 184, 216, 219; Eastern 84; Northern 74, 83, 84, 94; Western 74, 84
Wei-ch'ih I-sêng 90, *65,* 221
Wei-ch'ih Po-chiê-na *165*
Wên- jên 101
'Wheel of the Doctrine' 25, 27, *76, 77, 78, 98,* 184, 186, *197, 210,* 241, 277, *278,* 299
White Huns 29
'wish-granting jewel': cf. *cintāmani*
womb: cf. Akāshagarbha, *garbha, garbhadhātu*
wood: carving 300; carver 105; in architecture 72, *75,* 99, 120, *122,* 122ff., 126f., 129, 148, 157f., *164,* 227; in sculpture 48, 52, 70, 102f., *196, 197,* 205, 300; cf. sandalwood, wood-cut
wood-cut *79,* 80, *228*
Wu Dynasty 81
Wu-t'ai-shan *155, 157*
Wu Tao-tse 90
Wu-tsung, emperor 91

yaksha 27, 39, *57, 176,* 176, *212,* 225, 238, 248
yakshī 27, 39, 248
Yakushi 300
Yakushiji Temple 103, 219, *282,* 300
yantra 286
Yashodarā *76*
Yashovarman 54
'Yavadvīpa' 67
Yellow River 85
Yi 101
Yogācāra 134
Yogin 176f.
Yokohama 105
Yüan Dynasty 92
Yüeh-yao 216
Yünkang 85, 87, *122, 123,* 124, *152,* 152, 153, 205f., 216, 268, *282,* 284, 300
Yün-mên-shan 152

Zen Buddhism: cf. Ch'an Buddhism
Ze(n)-mu-i: cf. Shubhākarasimha
ziggurats 118
Zimmer, H. 162
Zoroastrianism 64, 239